CHINESE CHARACTERS

ACROSS ASIA

CHINESE CHARACTERS ACROSS ASIA

How the Chinese Script Came
to Write Japanese, Korean,
and Vietnamese

ZEV HANDEL

University of Washington Press   *Seattle*

Chinese Characters across Asia was published with the support
of a grant from the Joseph and Lauren Allen Fund for Books
on Asian Literature, Art, and Culture.

Additional support was provided by a generous gift from
Philip and Milagros Welt and by grants from the Chiang Ching-kuo
Foundation for International Scholarly Exchange and from
the China Studies Program, a division of the
Henry M. Jackson School of International Studies
at the University of Washington.

....

Design by Mindy Basinger Hill / Composed in Minion Pro

UNIVERSITY OF WASHINGTON PRESS / *uwapress.uw.edu*

Cataloging information is available from the Library of Congress
Library of Congress Control Number: 2025931556
ISBN 9780295753010 (hardcover)
ISBN 9780295753027 (paperback)
ISBN 9780295753034 (ebook)

♾ This paper meets the requirements
of ANSI/NISO Z39.48-1992 (Permanence of Paper).

Contents

MAP 0.1. The spread of Chinese characters across East Asia and part of Southeast Asia. Map by Ben Pease.

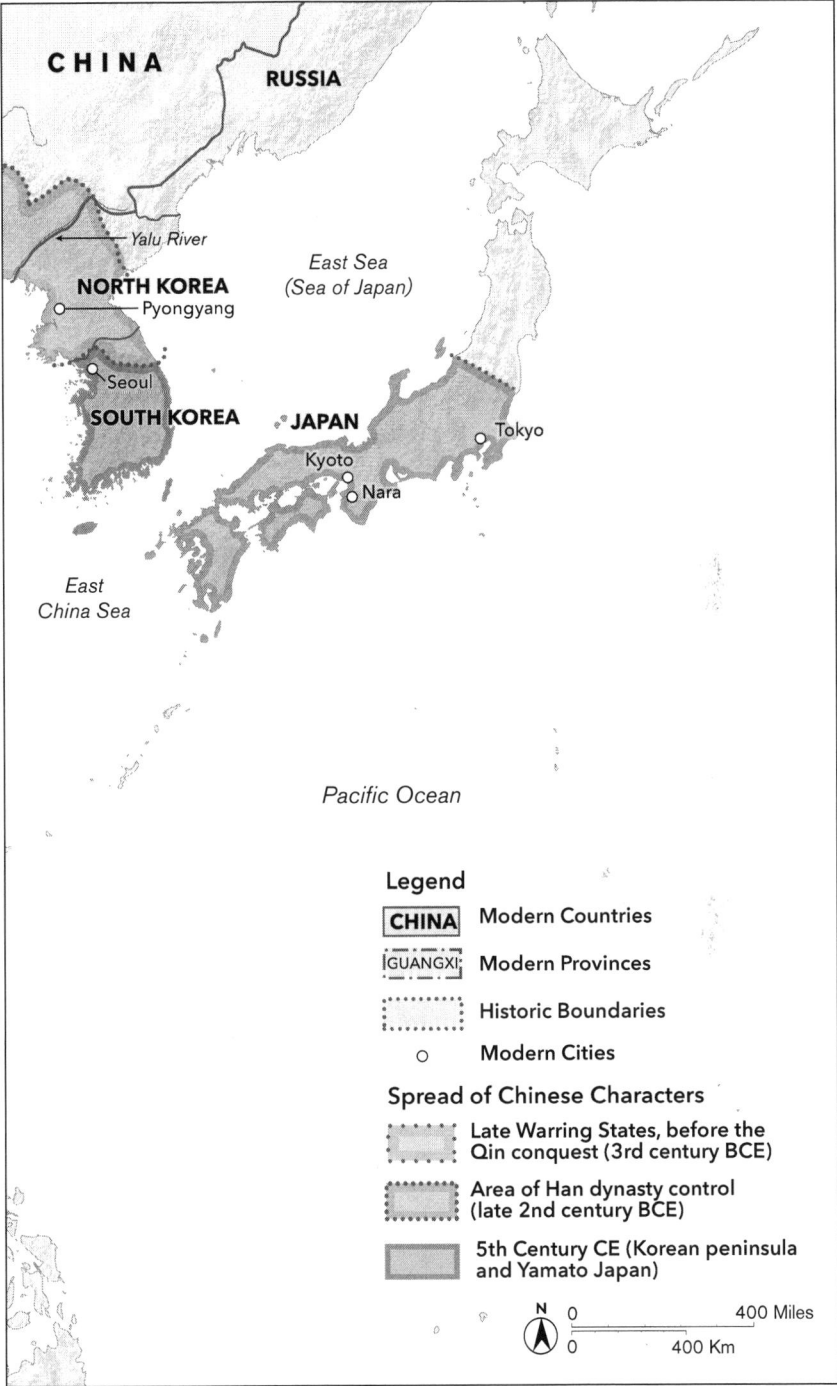

CHINA

RUSSIA

Yalu River

East Sea
(Sea of Japan)

NORTH KOREA

Pyongyang

Seoul

SOUTH KOREA   JAPAN

Tokyo

Kyoto

Nara

East
China Sea

Pacific Ocean

Legend

| CHINA | Modern Countries |

| GUANGXI | Modern Provinces |

Historic Boundaries

o   Modern Cities

Spread of Chinese Characters

Late Warring States, before the
Qin conquest (3rd century BCE)

Area of Han dynasty control
(late 2nd century BCE)

5th Century CE (Korean peninsula
and Yamato Japan)

N   0   400 Miles

0   400 Km

Preface

My personal relationship with Chinese characters began in 1985, my sophomore year of college, when I enrolled in a first-year Chinese language course. I already knew about their existence, of course, but had only the vaguest notions about them. They were something I saw on the signs for and menus of Chinese restaurants in the Boston suburb where I spent my childhood. I had a dim awareness that they represented entire words rather than functioning like letters of the alphabet.

We beginning students had to memorize characters, to learn to read and to write them. But we weren't given much direction on how to do so. As we learned elementary Standard Chinese (Mandarin) vocabulary and grammar, we also filled out character practice sheets. Over and over, we traced complex characters in square boxes, following the prescribed stroke order, trying to make them look elegant and balanced instead of like the awkward scrawls of small children.

As I learned more characters, I began to notice patterns: a part of one character would show up in another. Over time, more and more of the new characters I was assigned seemed to be made up of bits and pieces that I had already learned, assembled into new configurations. I was fascinated. But what did it all mean? Was there a method, a structure, a purpose?

This book is the product of a three-decade intellectual journey from that first exposure and those first searching questions. My interest in the history and structure of Chinese characters accompanied me through my graduate studies in ancient Chinese pronunciation and my teaching and research career at the University of Washington.

In graduate school in the 1990s, I started studying Japanese. Its use of kanji in writing opened up a new window on Chinese characters for me. Kanji clearly *were* Chinese characters, but their pronunciations and meanings—sometimes even their shapes—were not always the same or even similar across the two languages. After becoming a professor at the University of Washington in 1999, I started to learn more about the history of writing in Korea and Vietnam as well. The alphabets that are used to write both languages today have been around for about five hundred years. But, like Japanese, they were once written with Chinese characters, long before these alphabets were invented.

I began to think seriously about how all of this fit together. I read as much as I could about the history of writing in China, in Japan, in Korea, and in Vietnam. I offered a new course on the history of Chinese characters across these regions of Asia. Sometime around 2005 I decided to direct my research toward writing a book on the subject. Over the ensuing years, I continued to consult published scholarship and gained more familiarity with the languages and their histories.

The outcome of these efforts, my 2019 book *Sinography: The Borrowing and Adaptation of the Chinese Script*, attempted to describe and explain how and why Chinese characters were adapted to write different languages. It was an academic work, theoretical and technical in places. I never expected it to have much of a readership outside of a small circle of scholars.

But almost every time I described the topic of that book to a friend or acquaintance, I got the same response. People were fascinated by the topic. They wanted to know more.

So I decided to try to make this topic I loved accessible to a general readership. My goal in writing this book has been to tell the story of the global history of Chinese characters: to explain how they function and how they have been adapted, in a way that is approachable yet not overly simplified.

While this book will be of interest to readers who already know one or more of the languages discussed (Chinese, Japanese, Korean, Vietnamese, and Zhuang), I have strived to make it understandable and engaging for those who have no prior exposure to them at all or to Chinese writing. I have not presumed any knowledge of linguistics or of particular languages.

The three-thousand-year history of Chinese characters is but one instance of the incredible story of writing, perhaps the most transformative and powerful invention of our species. The creation, dissemination, and metamorphosis of writing systems has cut across cultural, linguistic, religious, and political lines over five millennia of human history, allowing us to record the fleeting ephemera of spoken utterances and convey detailed messages across vast distances and far into the future. I hope that in this book I manage to convey some of the enthusiasm and excitement that I feel when I think about this great story.

Acknowledgments

Writing a book on a complicated academic topic for a general readership has been an exciting and challenging endeavor. I have benefitted from the generous assistance, thoughtful advice, and scholarly expertise of many people.

This book discusses texts, graphs, and linguistic features of many different languages. Colleagues and friends have been gracious in reviewing these materials, making suggestions, and pointing out errors. I am grateful to Dominic Yu for assistance with Cantonese, Robert Hymes with Classical Chinese, Paul Atkins with ancient Japanese, Yen Kim Nguyen with Vietnamese, David Holm with Zhuang, James Clauss with Latin, and Talant Mawkanuli with Uyghur. In addition, Chan Lü provided me with helpful references related to Chinese literacy. Errors that may remain are of course my sole responsibility.

I wish to thank three librarians at the University of Washington for their assistance in finding Japanese, Korean, and Chinese language textual materials: Azusa Tanaka, Hyokyoung Yi, and Lucy Li.

Many friends inside and outside of academia kindly agreed to read early drafts and took time out of their busy lives to provide suggestions. Their feedback led to extensive changes, helping me to avoid excessive use of academic jargon, clarify confusing points, improve style and readability, and fill in lacunae. I owe thanks to Jonathan Hartmann, Josh Hou, Rafi Laufer, Seungmie Lee, Ichiro Matsumura, Ron Skoletsky, Sterling Swallow, and Kylie Wilson, and special gratitude to Mo Corston-Oliver, Liberty Lidz, Randall Lucas, Hilário de Sousa, and Jason Woolf. Without their feedback, the book would be much the worse.

Two anonymous readers, known to me only as A and B, provided valuable suggestions for improvements, which I have incorporated as best I could into the final version.

My editor at the University of Washington Press, Lorri Hagman, has been generous with her time, support, and expertise from the moment I first brought the book proposal to her in June of 2019. She has helped me navigate many challenges, and provided numerous substantive suggestions that have improved the structure and presentation of the material. Although she retired before the completion of the book, she kindly agreed to continue advising me to ensure that the project could be seen through to completion. I am also grateful to other current and former staff at UW Press for their help in putting the final book together. In addition, I owe thanks to Richard Isaac for his meticulous copyediting, which greatly improved the clarity of the writing and the consistency of the notation, and to Susan Stone for compiling an excellent index on short notice.

Teppei Fukuda was instrumental in helping me secure rights for images originally published in Japan. Liyao Chen provided invaluable assistance with proofreading, copyediting, tracking down bibliographic information, and helping with rights for images from China, Taiwan, and Hong Kong.

My wife, Ju Namkung, read multiple drafts and provided invaluable feedback. From the time I first conceived this book project, I have engaged in many conversations with her about these topics. I am deeply grateful to her, to my now twelve-year-old child, and to my mother Maryellen for their love and support over the years that I have been working on the book.

Many of the ideas reflected in this book were first developed in my 2019 monograph *Sinography*. The number of people who supported me in that work, and thereby indirectly influenced this current book, are too numerous to mention here. Their contributions are all recognized in the acknowledgments of *Sinography*.

Two major figures in my life passed away while I was working on this book. My father, Sidney Saul Handel (1937–2020), taught me how to navigate the world and inspired in me intellectual curiosity, a love of learning, and an appreciation for the humanities. My academic advisor, Professor Pang-Hsin Ting (1937–2023), was my first teacher in Chinese linguistics and remained a mentor throughout my career. A distinguished linguist, he not only taught me

Acknowledgments

how to be a scholar and teacher in my field but was also a model for treating people with respect and kindness in one's professional life.

My father died near the beginning of my work on this book, my teacher near the end. They were born within five days of each other, on opposite sides of the planet. This book is dedicated to their memory.

Conventions

Spelling

Most words and sounds presented for various languages are given in standard romanizations and spellings. The notes below explain sound values of letters that may be especially confusing for readers familiar with English orthography but omit many important details of pronunciation. More complete descriptions of these spelling systems are readily available on the internet. The name of the romanization system is given after the language name. Letters are presented in the following order: consonants, vowels, and (if applicable) tones.

Standard Chinese (aka Mandarin, Putonghua, or Guoyu):
Hanyu Pinyin

  c: like the *ts* sound in *hats*
  q: like the *ch* sound in *cheese*
  x: like the *sh* sound in *sheet*
  z: like the *ds* sound in *lids*
  zh: like the *j* sound in *journey*
  ü: like the French *u* or the German *ü* sound (not found in English)

The four tones of Mandarin are indicated by diacritic marks placed above vowel letters, illustrated here with the letter *a*:

  ā: first tone (high level)
  á: second tone (rising)
  ǎ: third tone (low dipping)
  à: fourth tone (falling)

Cantonese: Jyutping

    c: varies between the *ts* sound in *hats* and the *ch* sound in *chump*

    j: like the *y* sound in *year*

    z: varies between the *ds* sound in *lids* and the *j* sound in *jump*

    eo and *oe*: each represents a single vowel sound, both similar to the vowel in French *oeuf* 'egg' (not found in English)

    yu: like the French *u* or the German *ü* sound (not found in English)

The six tones of Cantonese are indicated by superscript numbers placed at the end of the written syllable:

    1: high level

    2: high rising

    3: mid level

    4: low falling

    5: low rising

    6: low level

Japanese: Modified Hepburn

All letters are pronounced similarly to their English sound values. A macron over a vowel indicates a long vowel sound: ō.

Korean: Revised Romanization

    s: like *sh* before *i* and *y*, like *s* otherwise

    pp, tt, kk, jj, ss: like *p, t, k, j*, and *s* but articulated with considerable muscular tension

    eu: a single vowel sound, like the *u* sound in *put*

    eo: a single vowel sound, like the *u* sound in *jump*

Vietnamese: Official Vietnamese Orthography (Quốc Ngữ)[1]

    c, k, q: like the *k* sound in *king*

    d: like the *z* sound in *zoo*

    đ: like the *d* sound in *do*

g: like Vietnamese *d* (the *z* sound in *zoo*) before *i*, otherwise
    same as Vietnamese *gh*

gh: like the *g* sound in *good*, but with friction

kh: similar to *h*, but with friction

nh: like the *ny* sound in *canyon* and the Spanish *ñ* sound

ph: like the *f* sound in *far*

r: like the *z* sound in *zoo*

th: like the *t* sound in *tea*

tr: like the *ch* sound in *chirp*

x: like the *s* sound in *see*

ơ: like the *u* sound in *jump*

ư: like the *u* sound in *put*

The six tones of Vietnamese are indicated by diacritic marks placed above or below vowel letters, illustrated here with the letter *a*:[2]

a (no diacritic): mid level

á: rising

à: low falling and breathy

ả: mid falling

ã: rising, with a "break" in the voice midway through

ạ: low falling and creaky

Zhuang: Standard Zhuang Orthography but with Superscript Tone Letters

c: like the *sh* sound in *sheet*

gv: like the *gu* sound in *guava*

s: like the *th* sound in *think*

w: like the *u* sound in *put*

Five tones of Zhuang are indicated by "silent" superscript consonants placed at the end of a syllable; another is indicated by no consonant:[3]

no consonant letter: rising

z: low falling

j: high level

x: falling

q: high rising

h: mid level

Two other tones are indicated by letters that are also pronounced:

p, t, k: high short

b, d, g: mid short

Other Notational Conventions

Italics are used for transcriptions of non-English terms, and to indicate words that are the object of analysis in their standard spelled forms:

banana: the English word *banana* (not specified as the spoken or written form)

Double quotation marks emphasize the pronunciation or sound value of words:

"banana": the pronunciation of the spoken English word *banana*

Single quotation marks give definitions and meanings:

'banana': the meaning of the word equivalent to *banana* in any language

Angle brackets indicate written symbols (when they are the object of analysis):

<b>: the symbol b

<banana>: the sequence of symbols used to write the word *banana*

Square brackets indicate phonetic symbols with specific sound values:

[b]: the sound b

Curly braces indicate the pronunciation and meaning of a morpheme:

Chinese {"shé," 'tongue'}: represents the sound and meaning parts of the Chinese morpheme *shé*, which has the pronunciation "shé" and the meaning 'tongue'

Note: The notations listed on the previous page are sometimes omitted for simplicity when no possible misunderstanding can occur.

Bold type indicates the first occurrence of a technical term that can be found in the glossary.

SMALL CAPITAL LETTERS indicate grammatical functions, as seen in the list of abbreviations below.

When giving sound values outside of the standard romanizations described above, I avoid specialized phonetic symbols wherever possible. For example, I use [ng] rather than [ŋ] for the sound written with *ng* in English. Old Chinese pronunciations are simplified from the system of Axel Schuessler.[4]

Abbreviations

ACC	accusative
BCE	"before the Common Era," a culturally neutral alternative to BC ("before Christ")
CE	"Common Era," a culturally neutral alternative to AD ("*Anno Domini*")
COM	comitative
EMPH	emphatic
HON	honorific
LOC	locative
MOD	modifier
MW	measure word, a part of speech in Modern Standard Chinese. When quantifying nouns, a measure word must be present between the quantifier (such as a number) and the noun. Where English has "five cars" or "three people," Chinese has *five* MW *car* and *three* MW *person*. Different measure words are used for different categories of nouns.
PAST	past tense
REQ	request
RESP	respect
TOP	topic

Script Direction

Some of the scripts discussed in this book are normally written vertically and/or from right to left. Examples in running English text are always given left-to-right horizontally. For example, Figures 7.3 and 7.4 show Japanese-language publications with the script running in vertical lines from right to left, but when excerpts from these publications are discussed as examples, they are written from left to right in the main text.

Chinese Dynasties and
Modern Historical Periods

People familiar with the history of China, including ordinary Chinese people, often refer to historical periods by dynasty name rather than specifying a range of years. This timeline lists the major dynasties, along with the post-imperial Chinese governments.

PERIOD	CAPITAL	DATES
Shāng 商	Ānyáng 安陽	sixteenth to eleventh c. BCE
Western Zhōu 周	Hào 鎬 (Xī'ān 西安)	1045 to 771 BCE
Eastern Zhōu 周	Luòyì 洛邑 (Luòyáng 洛陽)	770 to 256 BCE
Qín 秦	Xiányáng 咸陽	221 to 207 BCE
Western Hàn 漢	Cháng'ān 長安 (Xī'ān 西安)	202 BCE to 9 CE
Eastern Hàn 漢	Luòyáng 洛陽	25 to 220
Suí 隋	Cháng'ān 長安 (Xī'ān 西安)	581 to 618
Táng 唐	Cháng'ān 長安 (Xī'ān 西安)	618 to 907
Northern Sòng 宋	Biànjīng 汴京 (Kāifēng 開封)	960 to 1127
Southern Sòng 宋	Lín'ān 臨安 (Hángzhōu 杭州)	1127 to 1279
Yuán 元	Dàdū 大都 (Běijīng 北京)	1271 to 1368
Míng 明	Nánjīng 南京, Běijīng 北京	1368 to 1644
Qīng 清	Běijīng 北京	1644 to 1911
Republic of China	Nánjīng 南京	1912 to 1949 (to present on Taiwan)
People's Republic of China	Běijīng 北京	1949 to present (on mainland China)

CHINESE CHARACTERS
ACROSS ASIA

ONE
What Are Chinese Characters?

Chinese **characters** have long been an object of fascination and mythmaking in the West. Starkly different in function and appearance from the alphabetic writing used in Europe, Chinese writing has been perceived by outsiders as difficult and cumbersome, but also as mystically expressive. As far back as the sixteenth century, Western thinkers were grappling with the nature of Chinese writing and wondering if an understanding of it might somehow unlock deeper secrets about the nature of reality or of God.

Matteo Ricci (1552–1610) was an Italian Jesuit. The mission of the Jesuit Order was to spread the Catholic faith across the globe. Its members were expected to undertake long-term residency among the "unenlightened" in the most distant corners of the earth. Highly educated through years of training, they would learn the local cultures and languages and befriend societal elites, and in this way acquire the tools and access needed to persuade the local people to accept the Catholic faith. Ricci was a brilliant student of Chinese language and culture. He mastered both spoken Chinese and the classical written language. In 1601, nearly twenty years after arriving in China, Ricci was permitted to live in the capital city of Beijing and gained access to the imperial court. He developed close relationships with some of the highest ministers in government. Having gained unprecedented insight into the workings of Chinese elite society, Ricci wrote extensively about what he saw and experienced. After his death in 1610, his journals were edited and published, providing one of the earliest windows that European intellectuals had into a distant, ancient, and powerful realm that was still largely unknown and poorly understood in seventeenth-century Europe.[1]

Ricci was well positioned to explain Chinese writing to his fellow Europeans. A striking thing that he had observed was that Chinese texts were widely disseminated across East and Southeast Asia. They were read and understood by literate intellectuals who conversed in a wide variety of languages. Ricci explained the broad accessibility of Chinese writing this way in his journals:

> Any book written in Chinese . . . would also be understood by the Japanese, the Koreans, the inhabitants of Cochin China, the Leuchians and even by people of other countries, who would be able to read it as well as the Chinese. While the spoken languages of these different races are as unlike as can be imagined, they can understand written Chinese because each individual character in Chinese writing represents an individual thing.[2]

What Ricci had correctly observed was that a Classical Chinese book like the *Analects* of Confucius (figure 1.1) could be presented to well-educated people in Japan, Korea, or Vietnam, as well as any number of other places on the Chinese periphery, and they could all read and understand it perfectly well. Even so, they would have no hope of discussing its contents with each other, because they all spoke different languages. To Europeans, this was an astounding and marvelous phenomenon. It suggested that Chinese writing was achieving something very different from the alphabetic writing of the West, some rarefied way of transmitting ideas that transcended individual spoken tongues and the tedious details of their pronunciations, grammars, and vocabularies.

Ricci went on to speculate about the benefits that would ensue if Chinese characters were used more broadly throughout the world: "We would be able to transmit our ideas to people of other countries in writing, though we would not be able to speak to them."

Ricci was not the first Westerner to claim that Chinese characters directly represented "things" — not words or sounds, as the **letters** of Western alphabets do — and therefore had the capacity to serve as a universally understood written medium of communication. The English polymath Francis Bacon (1561–1626) described them as "characters real," by which he meant they were symbols that directly represented and reflected reality. He wrote this in 1605:

> It is the use of China and the kingdoms of the High Levant [i.e., East Asia] to write in characters real, which express neither letters nor words

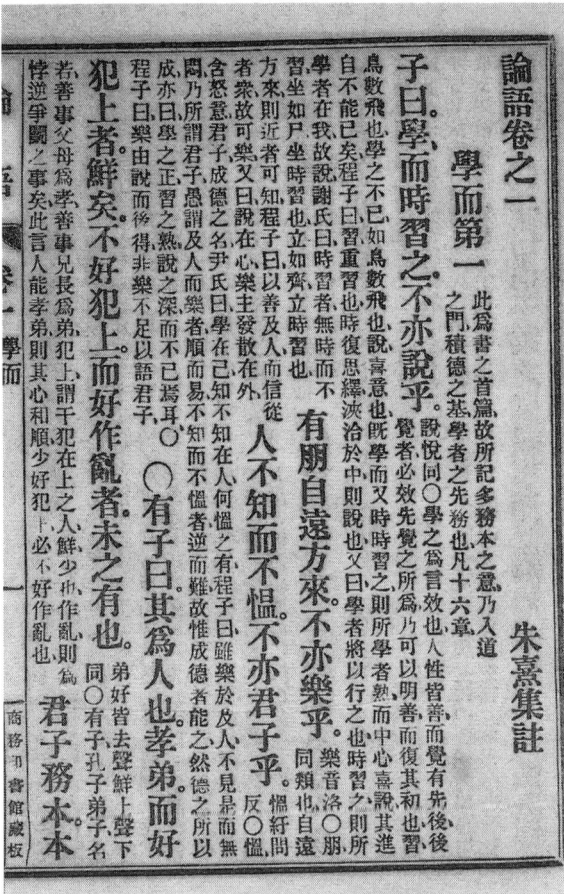

FIGURE 1.1. The first page of the *Analects* (Lunyu) of Confucius with commentary. Zhū, *Sì shū jí zhù* 四書集注.

in gross, but things or notions; insomuch as countries and provinces which understand not one another's language can nevertheless read one another's writings, because the characters are accepted more generally than the languages do extend.[3]

But Ricci and Bacon were wrong. Their observations about the widespread accessibility of Chinese writing in Asia were accurate, but the conclusions they drew from that fact were faulty. The misunderstandings about the nature of Chinese characters and writing that they communicated became widely believed and widely shared. These deeply influenced the way that Europeans thought about Chinese writing, and they persist today as myths about how the Chinese script functions.

It is not surprising that Western intellectuals who were used to the Greek and Latin alphabets found it hard to understand how Chinese characters could represent spoken words. Here, for example, is the Chinese character that writes the Mandarin word *lóng* 'dragon':

龍

How could a complex shape like this represent a word without spelling out its pronunciation?

In grappling with this question, European intellectuals developed and spread many inaccurate ideas about how Chinese characters originated and how they function. You have probably heard at least a few of them:

Chinese characters are the oldest writing on earth.
Chinese characters are pictures.
Chinese characters represent ideas.
Every word is written with a different Chinese character.
There are over fifty thousand (or eighty thousand or one hundred thousand) Chinese characters.
Chinese characters are understood by everyone in China no matter what dialect they speak.

Some of these ideas are half-true at best; others are completely false. What caused these myths to arise? And if they aren't true, then what are Chinese characters really?

Chinese characters don't directly represent ideas or objects. They aren't universal in their ability to convey meaning. They aren't even unique in the world as an alternative to alphabetic writing. But the real story of Chinese characters—how they were invented, how they developed and spread, and the role they played in the history of not just the Chinese language but also Japanese, Korean, Vietnamese, and other less well-known languages of East Asia—is even more fascinating and thought-provoking than the myths.

The true history of Chinese characters doesn't just elucidate the way they are used in modern Chinese and Japanese writing. It tells us something more fundamental about the way humans think, read, and write, and it sheds light on the early history of writing in other parts of the world far from China. It is, in other words, an important part of the history of our species, its cultures, and its civilizations.

The following chapters explore the origin, development, and spread of Chinese writing. By gaining a deeper understanding of how and why it functions, and what role individual Chinese characters play, we can learn how even a scholar as brilliant and culturally sophisticated as Ricci could get things so agonizingly wrong.

The Invention(s) of Writing

As far as we know, writing has been invented only four times in the history of our species. Just over five thousand years ago, around 3200 BCE, the Sumerians invented the precursor to the writing system we call cuneiform. Not long after, around 3100 BCE, the Egyptians created the writing system known as hieroglyphs. About two thousand years later, in the thirteenth century BCE, far from the Middle East, the Chinese invented their character-based writing system. Later still, about twenty-three hundred years ago in Central America, Mesoamerican peoples invented a writing system that we also call hieroglyphs.[4]

These four inventions—all most likely independent of one another—are each the product of a strikingly original and transformative idea: that the fleeting utterances of human speech can be accurately and permanently committed to visual form, thus enabling them to transcend the limitations of space and time that are inescapable aspects of human vocalization. It is an idea that seems obvious to us today—so obvious that you may find it difficult to conceive of writing as an invention. But it *was* invented, marking a great watershed in human civilization. For most of the tens of thousands of years that humans have been speaking to one another, writing did not exist, and the idea of writing was not dreamed of.

When we say that writing has been invented four times, we mean that this singularly powerful *idea* has been invented four times. To be sure, thousands of writing systems have been in use at one time or another over the last five thousand years. But nearly all of those were modified from earlier systems. And while history does give us examples of dozens of scripts that were invented from scratch, they were produced by people who already understood what writing was and deliberately set out to create a new incarnation of it.[5]

Of the four writing systems independently invented by people who lacked any prior knowledge of the concept of writing, only one has a continuous history of usage down to the present day. Sumerian cuneiform, Egyptian hieroglyphs, and Mayan hieroglyphs were each in use for millennia, but they all fell extinct long ago. Only Chinese characters are still in use. They are employed by approximately one billion people to write spoken languages that are directly descended from the ancient Chinese language that was first committed to written form over three thousand years ago. These characters are also used in the modern Japanese writing system, where they are called *kanji*. And they still play a role, although a diminishing one, in modern Korean writing. In their modern incarnation, Chinese characters look little different than they did 1,700 years ago at the conclusion of the great Chinese Hàn dynasty.

What about the familiar Latin alphabet? Its origins are believed to be indirectly connected to Egyptian hieroglyphs. The ancient Phoenicians, who were familiar with Egyptian writing and the Egyptian language, made use of just a few dozen hieroglyphs in a new way. They employed them to represent the starting sounds of Phoenician words that had similar meanings to the Egyptian words. For example, the hieroglyph 〰 originally wrote the ancient Egyptian word *nt* 'water'. The Phoenician word for water was *mem*. The Phoenicians used a modified form of the hieroglyph, ϓ, to represent the first sound of their word for water, [m]. Over the following centuries, the shape of the letter changed as the Phoenician way of writing was borrowed and modified, spreading across the ancient Mediterranean. Eventually, through the Greek, Etruscan, and Latin alphabets, it evolved into the <M> that we use today.

The influence of Chinese writing in Asia cannot be overstated. For approximately two millennia, Classical Chinese, written in Chinese characters, was the vehicle for the textual transmission of cultural knowledge throughout East Asia and adjacent areas.[6] Like Latin in medieval Europe, it was a living "dead" language. Although it had no native speakers, it was widely used in written form and played a vibrant role, knitting the region together in a common intellectual enterprise encompassing religion, philosophy, historiography, political theory, art, and literature.[7]

The widespread use of Classical Chinese as a transnational written language is the basis for Matteo Ricci's observation that any book written in Chinese could also be understood by educated speakers of Japanese, Korean, and Vietnamese. This state of affairs began over two thousand years ago and ended only in the twentieth century, when the modernizing nation-states of East Asia abandoned Classical Chinese as their standard **written language** in favor of **vernacular writing**, written versions of their local spoken languages: Modern Standard Chinese, Modern Standard Japanese, Modern Standard Korean, Modern Standard Vietnamese, and so on.

It is important that we carefully distinguish the written language of Classical Chinese from the script—Chinese characters—that was used to write it. Because even as Classical Chinese persisted as a widely used written language for over two thousand years, Chinese characters were spreading and changing, spinning away from the gravitational pull of the classical written language with which they were first associated. Although Classical Chinese texts were the medium by which Chinese characters became known beyond China, Chinese characters were not inevitably bound to this specific written language. As they spread throughout ancient East Asia, they underwent radical transformation and, in modified form, came to write many different languages, including regional varieties of spoken Chinese, which are commonly but misleadingly called "dialects," and many non-Chinese languages like Japanese.

These developments demonstrate that Chinese characters could in theory be used to write *any* language—even English. This is not because Chinese characters possess magical properties of disembodied meaning, as the myths would lead us to believe. On the contrary, it is because, like all other writing, including the alphabetic writing of Europe, Chinese characters are used to write specific words in specific languages. This imbues them with properties that make them adaptable. That adaptability has been exploited again and again over history to write different languages—in Japan, Korea, Vietnam, and elsewhere. In some ways, the story has been the same everywhere, because the basic mechanisms of adaptation are simple and recur through history. But in other ways, each instance of the adaptation of Chinese characters has been unique, in part because the spoken languages involved have different properties: different sounds, different grammars.

This capability for adaptation wasn't unique to Chinese writing; it was true of all four of the originally invented writing systems. Sumerian cuneiform originally wrote the Sumerian language. In the ensuing millennia, it was adapted to write many other ancient languages of the Middle East, including Babylonian and Hittite (as well as many lesser-known languages, such as Elamite and Luwian). Over thousands of years, Egyptian hieroglyphs were cursivized into the script known as Demotic. Six Demotic signs were adapted to write sounds in Coptic, a descendant of spoken ancient Egyptian. These supplemented the Greek-derived letters that formed the bulk of the Coptic alphabet.[8] The methods of adaptation seen in these transformations of cuneiform and hieroglyphs bear striking parallels to adaptations of Chinese characters. The history of the adaptation of the Chinese script is but one example of how writing spreads and changes. By studying the history of Chinese characters, we can gain insights into the history of writing itself.

What Is Writing?

The next chapter explores how Chinese writing functions today, and we travel back in time over three thousand years to observe how it came into existence. We will trace its development over those three millennia, and examine how the Chinese script continues to evolve today. But first, we need a clearer idea of what we mean by the slippery term *writing*, and for that we will need to understand some basic concepts about the structure of spoken language and its relationship to written representation.

It may come as a surprise that we need to clarify the concept of writing. After all, we are all familiar with writing. We live in a world where writing is commonplace and indispensable; it surrounds us, and we are immersed in it. Many of us interact with it every waking hour of every day. These interactions extend far beyond reading books like the one you now hold in your hands (or that is displayed on your screen). We encounter writing on signs, in advertisements, on clothing. We use it for text messaging on our phones, and to jot down notes on slips of paper. It is so ubiquitous that it is easy for us to overlook the fact that written representation of language is not the same thing as spoken language.[9] Even today, the majority of spoken languages used on our planet have no written form: they exist only as patterned vibrations of the air.[10]

For most of us, writing is our most salient and most commonly used means of nonspoken communication. If we think of it as a way of communicating information visually, we might imagine defining it something like this:

(1) Writing is the use of visual symbols to communicate information.

But on further reflection, this definition is far too broad to accord with our intuition about what writing is and isn't. There are many different forms of visual communication, some of which we would not feel comfortable calling "writing." Dance, for example, is a form of visual communication. So is visual art like painting and photography.

But why don't these forms of visual communication feel like they should count as writing? Perhaps it has to do with precision. You might feel that artistic expression in a visual medium shouldn't qualify as writing because the messages it communicates are vague, variable, or multifaceted. A piece of art can be interpreted in different ways by different people — or even by a single person. The well-known expression "a picture is worth a thousand words" recognizes that pictures have the capacity to depict what is sometimes difficult to express verbally. Yet ironically, it is because of the richness and complexity of pictures that they can be *less precise*, not more precise, than a spoken explanation.

For example, what message is communicated by the 1514 engraving *Melancolia I* by Albrecht Dürer (figure 1.2)? It seems advisable to modify our definition of writing to exclude this kind of complex artistic communication of ideas and feelings. So we can improve the definition by including the criteria of specificity and consistency. Consider this:

(2) Writing is the use of visual symbols to communicate specific ideas that are consistent for a community of people.

FIGURE 1.2. Albrecht Dürer's *Melancolia I*. Courtesy of the Metropolitan Museum of Art.

This definition would eliminate a dance performance or a work like *Melancolia I* from being considered writing, because the ideas they represent are too fluid. But the more specific visuals in figures 1.3a and 1.3b would still count as writing under definition (2). We would all agree that the one on the left (figure 1.3a) conveys the specific message "No Smoking" and the one on the right (figure 1.3b) conveys the specific idea of "Warning: Poison." While not everyone in the world will necessarily recognize these meanings, it's certainly true that the messages conveyed are "consistent for a community of people."

The sequence of diagrams in figure 1.4 would also fit our revised defini-

FIGURES 1.3A AND 1.3B.
No Smoking and Poison symbols.

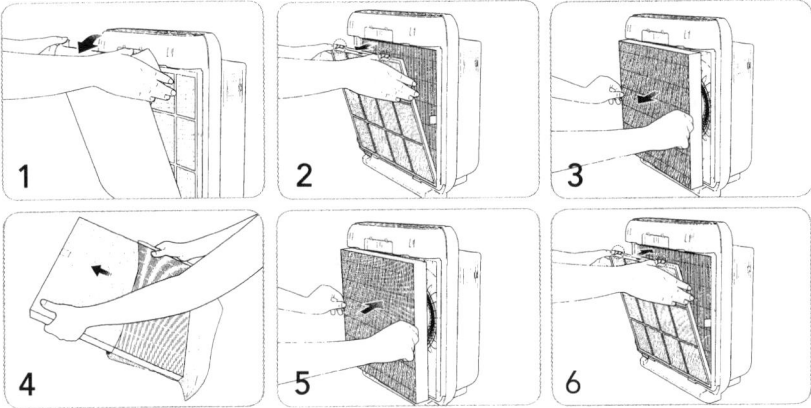

FIGURE 1.4. Instructions for replacing the filter of an air purifier.

tion of writing. After all, the communicated ideas in these images are quite specific. They can be expressed as follows:

1 Open the front panel.
2 Remove the outer screen.
3 Remove the old filter.
4 Take the new filter out of the bag.
5 Insert the new filter into the air purifier.
6 Replace the outer screen.

Is our revised definition of writing a good one? Should the images in figures 1.3 and 1.4, with their specific and consistent meanings, be considered writing?

Under our revised definition, the sequence of six sentences above would also count as writing because of its specificity and its consistency of meaning within a community of people.

But doesn't it seem like there's a crucial difference between the images in figures 1.3 and 1.4 on the one hand and those six numbered sentences on the other? The crux of that difference is this: There is only one way to read the sentences. Only one sequence of spoken words corresponds to the written form. It's not just that the communicated idea is specific. It is also the *linguistic form* in which that idea is expressed that is specific. An idea, even a very specific idea, can be expressed verbally in many ways within one language or across different languages, but the written sentences can be correctly read aloud in only one way and in only one language. (To be sure, the readings can vary in intonation, speed, accent, and many other factors. But the sequence of spoken words does not vary.) This one way of reading the graphic marks of the six sentences aloud into a sequence of words remains constant over spans of time, space, and personal identity. Two different literate English speakers, shown these written sentences at different times and in different places, will read them as the exact same sequence of spoken words.

But we cannot say the same of the image sequence in figure 1.4. Ask two English speakers to "read" the images at two different times, and you will surely hear different sequences of words. One speaker might read the fourth image as "Next, take out the new filter" and another as "Pull the filter out of the bag." Although the sequences of words are different, these would both be correct interpretations of the specific message that is visually conveyed.

With this in mind, consider the image ⊘ (figure 1.3a) and compare it with the written form NO SMOKING.

The image of the cigarette with a line through it can be verbalized in many different ways, including: "No smoking," "Smoking prohibited," "Do not smoke," "Don't smoke," "No cigarettes," "No smoking allowed," or any number of other formulations expressing the same idea. These are all correct ways of vocalizing the message conveyed by the image. And that's just in English. It can also be verbalized in any number of other languages: "Défense de fumer" in French, "No fumar" in Spanish, or "Qǐng wù xīyān" in Mandarin, for example, are perfectly legitimate ways to "read" the image.

But the written sentence NO SMOKING can only be read in English, and only as the two-word sequence "No smoking."

This distinction is a crucial one. The image of the cigarette with the line through it bears a very different relationship to spoken language than does the sequence of letters NO SMOKING. And this difference in turn affects the way that the visual forms are processed by our brains to convey information. It is not unreasonable to say that the image of the cigarette with the line through it represents an idea. That idea can in turn be expressed in many ways through spoken language. But NO SMOKING represents a specific, fixed sequence of words. And it is that sequence of words that in turn expresses an idea.

If we are going to analyze the way writing works—to really understand how it functions to communicate information—we need to distinguish these two methods of visual representation, because they do different things in different ways. For linguists, the researchers who study language, only the type of visual communication seen in NO SMOKING qualifies as writing.[11] We will follow their practice in this book.

Now we can again revise our definition of writing to capture this key conceptual difference:[12]

(3) Writing is the use of graphic marks to represent specific linguistic utterances.

Crucial to this understanding of writing is its direct connection to speech. Writing is a visual representation of *spoken language*.[13] Our definition of writing excludes other forms of visual communication like the No Smoking and Poison signs in figure 1.3 and the diagrammatic instructions for replacing an air filter in figure 1.4.

Now, what does this all mean for Chinese? If Ricci and Bacon were correct about Chinese when they said that each character represents a "thing" or an "idea," not a spoken word, then Chinese wouldn't count as writing by our definition. That would have dramatic consequences for our understanding of how Chinese characters communicate information. Their view was that because Chinese characters represent ideas, not words, they are not tied to specific sequences of spoken words in a particular spoken language. And for them, it is precisely this flexibility—the flexibility of the No Smoking sign—that gives Chinese characters their universal adaptability: the *ideas* represented by each character are constant but can be freely expressed in a variety of ways in many different languages. If Ricci and Bacon were right, then Chinese characters would be a transcendently powerful method of communication.

Let's illustrate their ideas with a concrete example. Consider the Chinese character 月, which is in origin a picture of the crescent moon. In its earliest form from three thousand years ago it looked something like this: 𝕯. According to Ricci and Bacon, this graph represents a "thing"—the moon—much like today's emoji 🌙.[14] And because this Chinese character is a visual representation of a thing, not a representation of any spoken word, speakers of different languages can "read" it aloud using whatever word or words express that thing in their own languages. In other words, it is more similar in function to 🚭 than to the written words NO SMOKING.

So as Ricci and Bacon conceptualize it, a Mandarin Chinese speaker would see the image of a moon, recognize it as a moon, and express the *idea* it represents in their language as "yuè." In the same way, a Cantonese Chinese speaker in Hong Kong would say "jyut⁶." A Hokkien Chinese speaker in Taiwan would say "goéh." A Japanese speaker would say "tsuki." A Korean speaker would say "dal." And, in theory, it could be used similarly by English speakers, who would see it and say "moon."

But is this a correct understanding of what the Chinese character 月 represents? Is this really the way Chinese characters function? Is there any test we can apply to determine if Chinese characters are, according to our technical definition, writing or not? This may appear to be a difficult question to answer, but the proposition is in fact easy to test. But before we do that, we need some vocabulary to help us talk precisely and accurately about writing. Taking our definition of writing as a basis, we will introduce a few key terms and provide examples, and then return to the question of whether Chinese characters represent things, ideas, or spoken words.

We have defined writing in such a way that it is inextricably tied to spoken language. This helps us to clearly distinguish it from forms of visual communication that are not connected to speech in the same direct way.

We are now in a position to analyze how writing works by focusing on the nature of its connection to speech. To do so, we will have to define some terms. A **graph** is a basic unit of writing. For example, in the type of writing in which this book appears, the graphs are the individual letters like p, x, and f. Note that a graph does not have a fixed shape but can be thought of as a collection or range of shapes that have equivalent function. So f, F, *f*, and **F** are not four different graphs but manifestations of one graph. We can indicate this abstract idea of a graph using angle brackets: <f> means "the graph F," whether realized as uppercase, lowercase, with or without serifs, in handwritten or typeset form, and so on.[15]

A graph can't function alone. A **script** is a set of graphs that share formal and functional features and are employed together in writing. What we casually call "the alphabet" is a script. More precisely, we should refer to it as "the Latin alphabet," to distinguish it from other ones, like Greek and Cyrillic.[16] The script used to write English contains the graphs <a>, <b>, <c>, and so on.

A **writing system** is a collection of one or more scripts together with the rules and conventions for applying them to the written representation of a particular spoken language. The English, Finnish, and Indonesian writing systems all use variants of the Latin alphabet script, but with different rules and conventions. The English writing system is not the same as the Indonesian writing system, which in turn is not the same as the Finnish writing system, even though they make use of the same set of graphs.

Most writing systems use just one script. English is such an example. A few of the world's writing systems regularly combine two or more scripts. As we will see, Japanese writing is such a **mixed-script writing system**.

Because writing represents speech, we can classify scripts according to the relationships between their graphs and elements of spoken language. Differences in the type of relationship are a basis for distinguishing types of writing. That is, we classify scripts according to how their graphs represent elements of spoken language.

We will consider three types of writing, based on three kinds of relationships between graphs and elements of spoken language. (There are others, but we won't need to address those for now.[17]) These are **alphabetic, syllabic,** and **morphographic**. The relationships are graph to sound, graph to syllable, and graph to morpheme, respectively.

The first kind is familiar to you. In this type, a single graph represents one consonant or vowel sound. In the Latin alphabet script as used in the English writing system, the graph <b> represents the sound [b]. (Symbols that represent sounds are placed between square brackets. For example, the symbol [b] represents the first sound in *ball*, a sound made by pressing both lips together to temporarily block the flow of air coming from the lungs.) Similarly, the graph <f> represents the sound [f], the graph <s> represents the sound [s], and so on. A script that embodies this kind of relationship between graphs and sounds is called by the familiar term *alphabet*.[18] Today, alphabets are the most common type of script that we find among the world's writing systems.

To be sure, the alphabetic ideal of one letter to write one sound is rarely realized in practice. Some writing systems get closer to this ideal than others. Finnish, for example, has a nearly perfect one-to-one relationship; English deviates quite a bit. Consider that some single sounds are written with two letters, like <sh> to write the sound at the start of the word *shirt*; conversely, a single letter can write a sequence of two sounds, like <x> for [ks] as in *box*; and some letters vary in the sounds they represent, like <c> writing either the sound [s] or the sound [k]. But even in English writing, with all its complications, it is clear that the basic graphs—the smallest indivisible units of the writing system—represent nothing more than sounds.

The second type of relationship is that of one graph representing an entire spoken syllable. If English were written syllabically, then the three syllables [ho], [mo], and [tel] would be written using three different graphs. Just for the sake of example, let's arbitrarily select some shapes to be those three different graphs:

<❀> represents [ho]
<↤> represents [mo]
<ᴛ> represents [tel]

If we were using this kind of syllabic writing system for written English, then the word *hotel* would be written ❀ᴛ, the word *motel* would be written ↤ᴛ, the word *tell* would be written ᴛ, and the name Moe would be written ↤. (The fact that standard English spelling uses a double *l* in *tell* and a silent *e* in *Moe* is irrelevant; the choice of syllabic graph is based on pronunciation alone.)

Chapter One

tell   ⊤
Moe   ↤
hotel   ✳⊤
motel   ↤⊤

A key difference between syllabic writing and alphabetic writing is that individual consonant and vowel sounds are not indicated by syllabic graphs. The syllables [ho] and [mo] share the sound [o], but the graphs <✳> and <↤> are indivisible, with no common component representing the [o] sound.

This kind of script is only practical for spoken languages that don't have too many distinct syllables. Syllabic writing would not be very practical for English, whose words contain thousands of distinct spoken syllables, requiring thousands of distinct graphs, one for each syllable. And we would have to memorize the representational values of all of them. Every single syllable, from simple common ones like *mo* and *in* to complex ones like *strict* and *slurp*, would each be written with a distinct graph.

Some spoken languages have many fewer syllables. Syllabic writing is practical for them. These are typically languages in which most or all syllables end with vowel sounds (like *mo*), and few if any end with consonant sounds (like *moat*). If most or all syllables consist of just one consonant followed by one vowel, there will be a limited number of possible combinations. Syllabic scripts typically have no more than a few hundred graphs. While this is more than the 20–40 found in most alphabets, it is a manageable number to memorize. As we will see later, two of the scripts used to write Japanese are syllabic.

Alphabetic and syllabic scripts share a fundamental property: the graphs represent sound alone. The alphabetic graph <b> represents the sound [b], which is itself meaningless. The [b] sound occurs in many different words, and no matter what those are or what they mean, the [b] sound in them is represented by the letter <b>.

Similarly, in our made-up example of syllabic spelling for English, the graph <⊤> represents the syllable [tel], which is itself meaningless. This syllable is just a sequence of sounds. The same graph is used to represent that syllable no matter what word it occurs in, whether *hotel*, *motel*, *tell*, *intel*, or anything else.

But there are also scripts in which each graph represents a *meaningful* unit of spoken language, and is only used to write a specific *combination of sound and meaning*. This third kind of relationship is dramatically different from the other two. Scripts with this property are called *morphographic*.

What would a morphographic writing system for English look like? It would use a distinct graph to represent each distinct *meaningful* element of the spoken language, whether pronounced the same or not. So we would need two different graphs for the two words *pit* (meaning 'a large seed') and *pit* (meaning 'a hole in the ground'), and two different graphs for the two words *trip* (meaning 'stumble') and *trip* (meaning 'a journey'). For example:

<△> for *pit* 'large seed'
<□> for *pit* 'hole in the ground'
<○> for *trip* 'stumble'
<◇> for *trip* 'journey'

At first glance, this may seem like far too complicated and burdensome a system to be practical. The vocabulary of spoken English contains tens of thousands of words, many more words than it has distinct syllables. If each word were to be written by a distinct graph, that would require memorizing the shapes of tens of thousands of graphs and also which spoken word is represented by each shape. It seems hopelessly impractical.

Yet scripts of the morphographic type are in common use today. There are several reasons that they are not just theoretically possible but also practical enough to exist in the real world. The first is that every spoken language contains far fewer meaningful elements than it does words. That may sound strange, because we are used to thinking of words as the basic unit of meaning in language. But in fact, many words are combinations of recurring mean-ingful parts. Consider these English words:

blueberry
bluebird
birdsong
bluer
heavier

Each one is made up of two meaningful parts:

blueberry is made up of *blue* and *berry*

bluebird is made up of *blue* and *bird*

birdsong is made up of *bird* and *song*

bluer is made up of *blue* and *-er*

heavier is made up of *heavy* and *-er*

Some of these meaningful parts are themselves words (like *heavy* and *bird*), but some meaningful parts are not words: *-er* is a suffix. The basic meaningful elements of a language are called **morphemes**. Morphemes are not the same as words. They are the building blocks out of which words are formed.

If each meaningful element were written with a distinct graph, then the ten words *blue, berry, bird, song, heavy, blueberry, bluebird, birdsong, bluer*, and *heavier* could be written with combinations of just six graphs: one for each of the morphemes *blue, berry, bird, song, heavy*, and *-er*.

It turns out that languages have considerably fewer meaningful units—fewer morphemes—than they do words. In fact, when we coin new words (like *laptop*), we typically do so by recombining morphemes that already exist in our language (in this case, *lap* and *top*). The number of commonly used morphemes in any given language is typically in the thousands, not the tens of thousands. Granted, that's still a lot of graphs to learn for a morphographic writing system. If all of the graphs were arbitrary shapes like <△> and <◇>, it would probably be nearly impossible to learn thousands of them and remember which spoken morpheme each one is associated with.[19]

This brings us to the second reason that real-world morphographic scripts are not just possible but also practical: their graphs are *not* completely arbitrary. Consider that the twenty-six letters of the Latin alphabet are arbitrary. We are so familiar with them that it is easy to forget that there is no obvious rhyme or reason to their shapes.[20] Why should the graph representing the sound [b] be shaped like the letter <b>, and why should the sound [t] be represented by a graph shaped like the letter <t>? As children, we must memorize the arbitrary associations between the graphic shapes and the sounds. With only twenty-six graphs to deal with, this is not particularly burdensome. You probably don't even remember doing it. But memorizing six or seven thousand arbitrary graphic shapes would indeed be a challenge for most people. So it is hardly surprising that in all known morphographic scripts, many of the graphs are structured in a way that is nonarbitrary. We will learn more about this in the next chapter.

You may have inferred by now that Chinese characters are a morphographic script. The spoken language is officially called Modern Standard Chinese (or Standard Chinese). It is also sometimes called Standard Mandarin (or just **Mandarin** for short). *Mandarin* is a term that linguists use to refer to the Chinese languages spoken in the north, west, and southwest of China. It is not a Chinese word. It comes into English from the Portuguese word *mandarim*, meaning 'a high government official in late imperial China'. By association, it came to refer to the spoken language employed by these officials, which was based on northern Chinese. The Portuguese word itself is believed to come from a Malay word that is ultimately derived from the Sanskrit word *mantrin* 'minister'. The official language of China is now referred to as Standard Chinese rather than Mandarin, but linguists still use the latter term to distinguish this standard variety of Chinese from others, such as Cantonese and Hokkien. This book sometimes uses *Standard Chinese* to refer to this official variety but also the term *Mandarin* when discussing and distinguishing different varieties of Chinese.

The written representation in Chinese characters of the spoken standard is called Standard Written Chinese. Below, six characters of Standard Written Chinese are listed along with the meaningful elements of spoken language (Standard Chinese morphemes) that they represent.[21]

人　*rén* 'person' (a word)
仁　*rén* 'compassionate' (not a word by itself)

糖　*táng* 'sugar, candy' (a word)
堂　*táng* 'hall' (not a word by itself)

十　*shí* 'ten' (a word)
食　*shí* 'eat' (not a word by itself)

Looking at each pair of characters, we can easily see that this script is neither alphabetic nor syllabic. As with our made-up example of English *pit* and *pit* written with △ and □, respectively, we can see here that distinct morphemes of spoken Standard Chinese are written with different graphs regardless of whether their pronunciations are the same or different: *táng* 'sugar' and *táng* 'hall' are pronounced the same but are written differently (糖 and 堂, respectively). The same is true of the pair of morphemes pronounced *rén* and the pair of morphemes pronounced *shí*.

Many English words are combinations of morphemes, and this is as true of Mandarin Chinese as it is of all other languages. Since each Chinese character writes a morpheme, and many Mandarin words are combinations of more than one morpheme, the result is that many Mandarin words are written with a sequence of two or more characters. Here are two examples of words made of morphemes from the list above, along with their written forms in Chinese characters.

食堂   *shítáng* 'dining hall'
食糖   *shítáng* '(edible) sugar'

You may be wondering how *shí*, written 食, could mean 'eat' but not be a word by itself. That seems strange. In fact, the ordinary spoken word meaning 'eat' in Modern Standard Chinese is something different: *chī*. *Shí* is a bit like *ed* in English. What is *ed*? I mean the *ed* that is part of the words *edible*, *inedible*, and the less commonly used word *edacious*. This English *ed* means 'eat', but it's not a word. It's a morpheme that is a part of words with meanings related to eating.

The three basic types of scripts are summarized in table 1.1. The first

TABLE 1.1. Three script types

SCRIPT TYPE	NAME OF GRAPH[1]	UNIT OF SPOKEN LANGUAGE REPRESENTED BY EACH GRAPH
alphabetic	**letter**	individual consonant or vowel sound, like [b]
syllabic	**syllabograph**	entire syllable, like [mo]
morphographic	**morphograph**	morpheme, like {"tang," 'sugar'}

1. Some scholars use the terms *syllabogram* and *morphogram* where I use *syllabograph* and *morphograph*. The *-gram* and *-graph* endings are completely interchangeable.

two types have graphs that represent meaningless sound units. The third type has graphs that reflect meaning differences. It's important to stress that these meanings aren't inherent in the graphs. The meaning differences are present in the words and morphemes of the spoken language that the graphs represent.

Alphabetic scripts typically have a few dozen graphs; syllabic scripts typically have a few hundred; morphographic scripts typically have thousands. We haven't seen any real-world examples of syllabic scripts yet. When we get to Japanese writing, we will. Besides Japanese, two other examples of syllabic scripts are Yi writing (a script of about eight hundred graphs that is used to write one of the major ethnic-minority languages of southwest China) and *nǚshū* ("women's writing," a script that was used to write a local Chinese language of Hunan).

The Structure of Spoken Chinese

Knowing about some of the features of the Standard Chinese spoken today is helpful for an understanding of how the Chinese script works to represent it.

One-Syllable Morphemes

Most morphemes of spoken Chinese are one syllable long. For example, *xiàng* 'elephant' is one syllable long. Chinese has very few morphemes that aren't one syllable long. English, in contrast, has many morphemes that are two or three syllables long, like the word *elephant*. Because Chinese writing is morphographic, each Chinese character represents a morpheme. And because almost every Chinese morpheme is one syllable long, almost every character represents a syllable-long element of spoken language.

No Consonant Clusters

Chinese lacks **consonant clusters**, two consonant sounds in a row within the same syllable. In the English word *splint*, there is a three-consonant cluster [spl] at the beginning and a two-consonant cluster [nt] at the end. These types of sound combinations do not occur in Chinese. (In a syllable like *xiàng*, which is the pronunciation of the word for 'elephant', it may look like there is a cluster at the end. But <ng> writes a single consonant sound, just as it does in English spelling. It does not write a sequence of an [n] sound followed by a [g] sound.)

Invariance of Word Forms

English words have different grammatical forms. To a linguist, *apple* and *apples* are not different words in any meaningful sense. Their difference is purely grammatical: one is a singular form of *apple*; the other is a plural form of *apple*. Similarly, *walks*, *walked*, and *walking* are just different forms of *walk*. You won't find *apples*, *walks*, *walked*, or *walking* as separate entries in most English dictionaries, because they are not distinct words requiring separate definitions.

The grammar of English requires that different forms of a word be used in different contexts. We do not say "I have two apple" but rather "I have two apples." But in Chinese, word forms are invariant. Nouns don't have plural forms, verbs don't have past-tense forms, and so on.

The Chinese word *píngguǒ* can be translated as the English 'apple' or 'apples'. The word *zǒu* can be translated as 'walk', 'walks', or 'walked'. The differences in meaning that are reflected in the English suffixes, like plurality and past time, can be expressed in Chinese, but it is not done through grammatical suffixation.

Tones

Chinese words are distinguished in pronunciation not just by having different combinations of consonants and vowels but also through their different syllabic pitch contours. In English, switching out a [p] sound for a [b] sound will change *pit* into *bit*, an audibly different word. The same is true for Standard Chinese: *pō* 坡 means 'slope' and *bō* 波 means 'wave'. But saying English *pit* with a rising intonation or a falling intonation won't result in a different word. In Chinese, however, switching out a level pitch for a falling pitch changes the word just like a change to a consonant sound does: *pò* 破 with a falling pitch means 'broken', and is audibly different from *pō* 'slope' with a level pitch.

Modern Mandarin has four distinct tones, which is to say, there are four different pitch contours that can occur on a syllable to distinguish meanings.

TABLE 1.2 The four tones of Modern Standard Chinese

1st tone *(high level)*	mā 'mom'	tāng 'soup'	shī 'apply'	yī 'one'
2nd tone *(rising)*	má 'hemp'	táng 'sugar'	shí 'ten'	yí 'move'
3rd tone *(dipping)*	mǎ 'horse'	tǎng 'lie down'	shǐ 'begin'	yǐ 'already'
4th tone *(falling)*	mà 'scold'	tàng 'burning hot'	shì 'is'	yì 'meaning'

These distinctions are illustrated in table 1.2 with four contrasting sets of Standard Chinese morphemes.

Tones have existed in Chinese for a long time. All modern spoken Chinese languages are tonal. But there was a time when Chinese did not have tones, which developed between fifteen hundred and two thousand years ago.

Grammatical Relations Are Expressed through Word Order

In some languages, the subject of a sentence is marked in a special way, and the object is marked in another way. If you have studied Latin, Russian, Korean, or Japanese, you are familiar with this kind of grammatical structure and the resulting flexibility in word order. For example, in Latin, the word for 'dog' is *canis* when it is the subject and *canem* when it is the object, regardless of whether it occurs at the beginning or the end of the sentence. In English, word order is more rigid, because the order itself expresses which part of a sentence is the subject and which is the object. "The dog chases the cat" has a different meaning from "The cat chases the dog."

Chinese is like English in this respect. Chinese word forms are invariant. They do not change form for singular or plural or for their roles as subject and object.[22] Those grammatical relations are expressed through word order, as in English, with the subject coming before the verb and the object coming after. In these two Mandarin sentences, the word for 'dog' is bolded:

Gǒu zhuī māo. '**Dogs** chase cats'.
Māo zhuī gǒu. 'Cats chase **dogs**'.

Chinese Characters: Words or Ideas?
Morphographs or Ideographs?

As seen in tables 1.1 and 1.2, Chinese characters appear to be morphographic, representing the specific elements of spoken language that we call morphemes. Yet seventeenth-century Europeans claimed that Chinese characters represent ideas. Which view is correct?

We have already encountered the Chinese character 食, which today writes the spoken Mandarin morpheme {"shí," 'eat'}. We have also seen that *shí* is not a word; it occurs only as a part of other words. Two earlier examples of such words are repeated here, along with three more:

食堂　*shítáng* 'dining hall'
食糖　*shítáng* '(edible) sugar'
食品　*shípǐn* 'food product'
飲食　*yǐnshí* 'food and drink; one's diet'
節食　*jiéshí* 'to diet, restrict one's food intake'

We have also seen that although *shí* clearly means 'eat', it is not the ordinary spoken Mandarin word meaning 'to eat'. You would not use it in the Mandarin sentence meaning 'I am eating lunch now'. So while *shí* is undoubtedly meaningful, it is no more an independent word than is the *gest* of *ingest* and *digest* or the *ed* of *edible*.

If the character 食 represented an idea—the idea of eating—and not the specific spoken morpheme *shí* 'eat', one would think that that idea might be expressed verbally in any number of ways. This is what we saw with 🚭 earlier, which represented an idea that could be expressed as "No smoking," "Do not smoke," "Smoking is prohibited," etc. Think about a visual representation of the idea of eating, such as a simple drawing of food going into somebody's mouth. A graph like that could be read aloud in English in many ways: as "eat," "ingest," "consume," "chow," "dine," "sup," "grab a bite," or any number of other ways of expressing the idea of eating through spoken utterances.

But the Chinese character 食 is *never* used to write the ordinary spoken Mandarin word *chī* 'eat'. A Mandarin speaker would never read the graph 食 aloud as *chī*, any more than an English speaker would read the sequence of letters <dine> aloud as "eat". It is also never used to write other words or phrases that convey the idea of eating. The graph 食 is associated with, and only with, one spoken morpheme: *shí* 'eat'. When Mandarin speakers want to write the spoken word *chī* 'to eat', they always and only use a completely different graph, 吃. In sum,

食 writes the morpheme *shí* 'eat' (which is not a word by itself)

吃 writes the morpheme *chī* 'eat' (which *is* a word by itself)

And this is by no means an isolated example. There are many Mandarin words that have meanings related to 'speak':

説 *shuō* 'say, speak'

講 *jiǎng* 'say, speak'

討論 *tǎolùn* 'discuss'

告訴 *gàosu* 'tell'

Although these words all convey the same basic idea, they are distinct words with different pronunciations and different morpheme compositions, and they are written with distinct characters.

As one more example, consider the character 走. In ancient times, it wrote a spoken Chinese word meaning 'to run'. Over time, that spoken word shifted in meaning. In Modern Standard Chinese, it is pronounced *zǒu* and means 'to walk', and is still written 走. In other words, the character 走 has conventionally represented this morpheme from ancient times to the present even as that morpheme has changed meaning over time. If the character intrinsically represented an idea—the idea of running—it would not be suitable for representing a word meaning 'to walk'.

The only way to make sense of these facts is to acknowledge that Chinese characters do not represent ideas. They represent specific morphemes, each one having its own pronunciation, its own meaning, and its own functional role as part of words in the language. In other words, these characters are morphographs, not **ideographs**. Like the English written forms *eat*, *consume*, *ingest*, and *dine*, they convey ideas only through the medium of the specific spoken language elements that they represent.[23]

This relationship between Chinese characters and particular spoken morphemes with specific pronunciations is not just a characteristic of modern Chinese writing. It has been true of Chinese writing since its invention over three thousand years ago. We will see more evidence for the inextricable connection between Chinese characters and specific pronunciations in subsequent chapters.

But if all this is true, then what about the facts that the brilliant Jesuit scholar Matteo Ricci observed and described to European readers—facts that led him to precisely the opposite conclusion about Chinese characters? How could it have been possible for people living in Japan, Korea, and Vietnam, people who could not speak a word of Chinese, to all read and understand Chinese writing? If the Chinese character 月 represents a specific Chinese morpheme, and not an idea, how is it that it can be read as *tsuki*, the Japanese word for 'moon'? Clearly there is something more complicated going on here than our brief foray into Chinese writing has so far revealed.

In the following chapters, we will trace the history of Chinese writing from its inception in the thirteenth century BCE to its modern incarnations in China. We will follow its export beyond the boundaries of Chinese-speaking areas, and discover how its graphs were changed and adapted for different purposes. And we will learn the amazing story of how characters can be simultaneously tied to specific utterances and infinitely adaptable to writing many different languages.

A final word of caution as we end this chapter. The journey we are about to embark on covers three thousand years of history and spans an enormous geographic area that has been home to hundreds of peoples with distinct cultures and languages. Over those three millennia, enormous changes have taken place. Kingdoms and empires have risen and fallen; wars, famine, and the quest for economic and agricultural opportunity have led to huge migrations across vast distances; entire ethnic groups and their spoken languages have been assimilated into dominant groups, sometimes leaving little or no historical trace; identities, languages, cultures, and political boundaries have shifted, dissolved, and reformed. The terms we use today to describe places, peoples, and languages of East Asia—such as *Chinese*, *Vietnamese*, *Japanese*, and *Korean*—are often inappropriate or misleading when applied to the past.

Even when describing the world today, they can be vague at best, contested at worst. Despite these problems, I will use these terms frequently throughout the book, because of their practicality and accessibility to the general reader, with only occasional reminders not to superimpose their meanings today on populations of the past.

TWO

Chinese Writing
From Antiquity to the Present

The origins of Chinese writing are not fully known to us, because the archeological record is incomplete. We know that Chinese writing was in existence by the middle of the thirteenth century BCE, but whether it was invented years, decades, or centuries before the earliest surviving records is impossible to determine with certainty. We do not know the who, when, where, or why of the invention of Chinese writing. Those details are probably forever lost to us. But we know a great deal about the how.

One reason we know how the writing system developed is that we can observe parallels in the early history of all four of the invented-from-scratch writing systems: Sumerian cuneiform, Egyptian hieroglyphs, Chinese characters, and Mayan hieroglyphs. These parallels show us that there are key concepts and practices that are integral to how humans create new writing systems that are capable of representing in written form anything that can be spoken. A firm grasp of those will allow us to trace and understand the early history and development of Chinese writing.

A Conceptual Breakthrough:
From Pictures to Pictographs

The earliest known Egyptian hieroglyphic writing dates back to between 3200 and 3100 BCE—just over five thousand years ago.[1] Figure 2.1 is a picture of an Egyptian text on a tomb stele dating to the mid-third millennium BCE, a few hundred years after Egyptian writing was invented:[2]

The carved images are beautifully rendered and well preserved. Look at the two horizontal lines of writing at the top. You should be able to make out

FIGURE 2.1. Limestone tomb wall panel known as the Panel of Iriy. © The Trustees of the British Museum. https://www.britishmuseum.org/collection/object /Y_EA1168. For more information on the panel, see Davies, *Reading the Past*, 74, 87.

wḏ ḥm.f ḥr wrryt.f nt ḏʿm ib.f ꜣw

'His Majesty departed upon his chariot of electrum, his heart joyful'

FIGURE 2.2. An illustration of Egyptian hieroglyphic writing (Davies, 107).

some representational figures: an owl, a snake, a jackal, a musical instrument, an old man leaning on a stick, and others. This raises an interesting question in light of the crucial distinction between writing and pictures that we worked so hard to incorporate into our definition of the former. How do we know this is writing—that it represents a fixed sequence of words that can be uttered aloud in only one way—and not a series of pictures conveying meaning through graphic representation? If you don't know how to read ancient Egyptian, it is not obvious how to answer this question. But Egyptian writing is well understood by experts, and there is no doubt that this is writing. We know the sequence of words represented.[3]

Figure 2.2 is another piece of Egyptian hieroglyphic writing that contains an image of an owl. Although it is not as detailed as the one carved in limestone in figure 2.1, it can be recognized and distinguished from other birdlike graphs by the unique combination of the tail shape and the orientation of the head toward the reader.

Investigation of these two examples of Egyptian hieroglyphic writing reveals something remarkable: The owl is not an owl. In fact, the owl represents nothing more than the consonant sound [m]. In the Panel of Iriy (figure 2.1), it writes the prefix *m-* meaning 'in'. In figure 2.2, it is writing part of the word *ḏʿm* meaning 'electrum' (an alloy of gold and silver, written 𓇋𓅓𓊪𓐙).

Let's think about this a bit more carefully. There is very clearly an image of an owl in both of these texts. It is detailed and precise enough that its pictorial value cannot be doubted. Yet the *function* of this image of an owl is not to represent an owl. The function is to represent the sound value [m], much like the function of the familiar letter <m> is to represent the sound value [m].

We are used to thinking of pictures and writing as quite different things. 𓅓 is a picture of an owl. In contrast, <owl> is a written representation of the spoken word "owl." But despite their different uses, pictures and writing don't always look different. The key to distinguishing them is function, not appearance. If an image represents a real-world object through similarity of appearance, it is a picture—and the representational value of that picture might be expressed verbally in several different ways. But if a graph represents a word or part of a word, then it is writing—and its verbal realization is fixed.

So how do we know when an owl is an owl and when it isn't an owl? How do we know when we are looking at a picture and when we are looking at written language?

The answer is: linguistic context. In the images above, the owl is embedded within a graphic context that permits only one interpretation of its function. To anyone who knows ancient Egyptian and how the writing system works, there is only one possible way to "read" the owl, and that is as a representation of the sound [m]. When a sequence of graphs must be interpreted as a fixed sequence of words, including grammatical elements, then we know we are looking at a written representation of language.

Let's consider this concept using examples from a more familiar language: English.

Here is a picture of a bee: 🐝. As a picture, it has no fixed linguistic value. In describing the representational value of the picture, you could say "bee" or "bumblebee" or "honeybee" or "flying insect," among other possibilities. You could insert this picture into a larger drawing of a lazy summer scene full of blooming meadow flowers, and there would be innumerable ways to describe the scene in words.

But look what happens when the picture of the bee is placed into a specific linguistic context:

(4) I've never seen anything like it 🐝fore in my life. What can it 🐝?

For someone who understands spoken English, there is no longer any ambiguity about the function of this picture: it has a precise linguistic value, namely to represent the first syllable of the word *before* and the syllable making up the word *be*. The sentence above simply cannot be interpreted as:

(5) I've never seen anything like it bumblebeefore in my life. What can it honeybee?

This bee image is like the Egyptian owl. Its function in writing is not the same as its representational value as a picture. Sentence (4) is not standard English writing, but it illustrates an important principle: the context in which a graph appears can determine whether or not it is functioning as writing, and if it is writing, exactly what linguistic unit it represents.

Even though the nonwriting function of 🐝 as a picture in a scene of meadow flowers and its function as a graph representing a syllable in the spoken words "bee" and "before" are distinct, the use of that particular picture to write that particular syllable is not random. There is clearly a relationship between the two uses. The nature of that relationship is profound but also trivially obvious: it has to do with the similarity between the pronunciation of the word *bee* and the pronunciation of the word *before*. You wouldn't write "before" as <🐜fore> with the image of an ant if you wanted anyone to read it successfully. What makes this trivial relationship profound? Because the use of an image that represents an object (such as a bee) to represent a word (such as the word *bee*) or a syllable (such as in the words *be* and *before*) is the key discovery that led to the development of true writing by humans five millennia ago.

In all four known instances of the invention of writing—Sumerian, Egyptian, Chinese, and Mesoamerican—the invention depended first on a crucial transformation of the function of pictures. That transformation is one of the most powerful ideas ever originated by our species: the use of a picture to represent a word. It is a transformation that is not visible in the historical record until long after it first took place, because it happened within the minds of a community of human beings.

We can illustrate this transformation with our honeybee example.

The earliest extant examples of representational art made by human beings date back nearly forty thousand years. So for tens of thousands of years before writing was invented, our species made use of two-dimensional images to represent real-world objects, such as a picture of a bee:

🐝

a bee

The leap—the crucial conceptual breakthrough that makes writing possible—is this one:

"bee"

What's the difference? The difference is in representational value. The first image is used to represent a real-world object, a bee. The second image is used to represent a spoken word: "bee." The graphic form is the same, only the usage is different.

a bee   "bee"

(picture) (pictograph)

We can use the terms picture and **pictograph** to capture the difference. A picture represents an object, while a pictograph is a picture used to represent *the word for the object depicted*. Pictographs are writing; pictures are not.

But they look identical! If I remove the labels, how can we know which is which? How can we pinpoint the origin of writing in the moment when a picture shifts to being a pictograph?

The answer is that we can't. Whether an isolated image of a bee—or a house, or an arm, or a river, or a tree—is a depiction of a bee—or a house, or an arm, or a river, or a tree—or is a representation of the spoken word "bee"—or "house," "arm," "river," or "tree"—cannot be determined in the absence of context. For an isolated image, it is a distinction that exists only in the minds of the human beings making and looking at the images. We who peer back from today through the misty obscurity of millennia are unable to see the precise moment when writing was invented. But we do know that this invention happened, and that it happened at least four times independently.[4]

The repurposing of pictures into pictographs is the key discovery that makes writing possible. It provides a mechanism for the representation of many words of spoken language. So to write the word "tree," one would draw a picture of a tree. To write the word "elephant," one would draw a picture of an elephant. Pictographs are the crucial starting point for writing. But they alone are not enough for a complete writing system.

Extension: How to Write What Pictures Can't

True writing, capable of representing any and all utterances in a given spoken language, requires a second conceptual breakthrough. This is because the set of words and morphemes that can be represented by pictographs is actually quite limited. If I want to write the words "tree," "water," and "dog," it's a fairly simple matter to draw objects, and then use the drawings as pictographs to represent the associated words. Most likely a reader would be able to decode my pictographs, figuring out on their own which words I intended to represent, even if I haven't had a chance to meet with them to go over my method in advance. For example, even if I don't explain to you what I intend by the pictograph 🐝, you'd probably guess that I mean the word "bee."

A word like "walk" is a bit more challenging. I might draw a pair of legs, but how to know that they write the word "walk" and not the word "legs"? In a case like this, some discussion of a convention among a group of people will do the trick. "I'm going to use this drawing of two legs to represent 'walk,'" I announce. "And I'll just draw one leg when I want to write 'leg.'" If it's a small group and everyone agrees to stick to the convention, we can avoid confusion.

But the unfortunate reality is that even with this kind of discussion to clarify the conventions of usage, pictographs aren't going to take us very far toward a full writing system. The reason for this is that so many of the words and morphemes we use in everyday speech are not amenable to representation by drawing.

It's not hard to see why. Consider sentence (6):

(6) I want to know if you are going there soon.

It has ten words made up of eleven morphemes (*going* contains the two morphemes *go* and -*ing*).[5] Are any of these words amenable to pictographic representation? Perhaps you can come up with a drawing to serve as a pictograph for *go*. But what about *I*? *want*? *if*? *there*? *soon*? *-ing*? English is full of grammatical words, prefixes, and suffixes that are not easy to represent pictographically, like *of*, *for*, and the past tense suffix *-ed*. Even many nouns are abstract in meaning and not easy to represent with drawings, like *justice*, *distraction*, and *legitimacy*. This isn't a peculiarity of English; it's true of every spoken language on Earth.

Now consider sentence (7):

> (7) My beagle is resting under an oak tree, and my terrier is relaxing under a beech tree.

Let's set aside for a moment the challenge of drawing representations of words like *is*, *an*, *my*, and *a* and focus on the words referring to concrete objects. The nouns here are not abstract. Sketching dogs and trees isn't that hard. But the words *beagle* and *terrier* for dog breeds and *oak* and *beech* for tree species are quite specific in reference. How can I consistently draw distinct pictographs for dozens of dog breeds and hundreds of tree species? Even if I were a very good and careful artist with a high degree of botanical knowledge, making detailed drawings of dozens of different types of trees would be tedious and time consuming, and the ability to read or write using them would not be easy to teach others.

Similarly, distinguishing near-synonyms like

rest, relax, chill
river, stream, creek
think, ponder, muse

pictographically would seem nearly impossible. If I draw a picture of running water, how can I possibly indicate if the word being represented is *river*, *stream*, or *creek*? Pure picture writing is simply impossible.

The problem of finding pictures to represent words that do not refer to easily drawable real-world objects would seem to be a huge impediment to developing a writing system with pictographic roots. But overcoming this problem is not as difficult as it might first appear. The solution came quickly and naturally to the first human scribes and led rapidly to full writing, capable of precisely recording any spoken utterance. This happened in essentially the same way in ancient Egypt, ancient Mesopotamia, ancient China, and ancient Mesoamerica. Historians of writing usually describe this breakthrough as the second stage in the development of writing, following the invention of pictographs themselves. But it's entirely possible that the first stage and the second stage happened very close together, if not at the same time.

The breakthrough solution is called **rebus** usage, or more technically, **phonetic extension**. It is a technique that is based on pronunciation. You are all familiar with it, even though you may never have thought of it as a foundational mechanism in the history of writing.

Consider this stylized drawing of an eye:

◉

As a drawing, it might communicate many different ideas. But suppose instead that we are using it as a pictograph to write the specific English word *eye*.

◉ writes *eye*

Remember, morphemes are indivisible meaningful units of spoken language. By definition, morphemes have both meaning and pronunciation. In the case of *eye*, the meaning is 'eye' (the body part) and the pronunciation is [ai]. We can use curly braces to show how these meaning and pronunciation components are combined in the morpheme: *eye* = {[ai], 'eye'}, meaning "the morpheme that has the pronunciation [ai] and the meaning 'eye.'" Now, that may seem like an unnecessarily roundabout way of representing the spoken word *eye*, but you will soon see the utility of separating out its sound and its meaning.

◉ writes {[ai], 'eye'}

After a period of time using this pictograph to write the word *eye*, our community of writers and readers become used to the conventional association of this particular image with the spoken word *eye*. The image and the word are tightly bound together. Something special happens then, naturally and without conscious effort: the image becomes strongly associated with a particular pronunciation. In fact, this association is so strong that we can take advantage of it to represent other words with the same or similar pronunciation to [ai], even though they have no connection to the meaning 'eye'. For example, we can use the image to write the word *I*, the first-person pronoun. Now our pictograph has two different functions, related by pronunciation:

First usage: ◉ writes {[ai], 'eye'}
Second usage: ◉ writes {[ai], 'I'}

This is rebus usage, and it is exactly what we saw earlier when we used a picture of a bee to write the first part of the word *before*. We also call this "phonetic extension," because it extends the use of the graph based on pronunciation. Words or morphemes that are identical in pronunciation are called **homophones**. So to be a bit more technical, we can say that phonetic extension allows a graph that is already conventionally used to write one morpheme to also be used to write a second morpheme that is homophonous.

This way of extending the function of graphs is incredibly powerful for two reasons. First, it allows all sorts of words or parts of words to be written, even if their meanings can't be easily depicted by a drawing.

Second, rebus usage is so natural and intuitive that a reader can decode it even without any instruction or training. You can do an experiment to show that this is true. Show sentence (8), without explanation, to anybody you know who speaks English, and they should have no difficulty reading and understanding it after only a slight hesitation:

(8) ◉'ve never seen anything like it 🐝fore in my life. What can it 🐝?

Pictographs are the foundation for the invention of writing. They are the conceptual breakthrough that makes written representation of some spoken words possible. Rebus usage is the conceptual breakthrough that ultimately makes written representation of all of spoken language possible. Phonetic extension builds the structure that rests on the foundation.

There are three points about rebus usage that are essential to the history of writing. It's worth our time to think about them carefully. The first is that

FIGURE 2.3. An English rebus. The images of an eye, can, knot, bee, leaf, and ewe (female sheep) write the sentence "I cannot believe you."

because it is tied to pronunciation, it is language-specific. You can't have rebus usage without spoken language, and a rebus usage that works for one spoken language is not going to work at all in others.

In English, the first-person pronoun *I* and the organ of sight *eye* are pronounced the same. This happy accident allows a pictograph writing *eye* to be repurposed to write the word *I*. But in Swahili, the word meaning 'eye' is *jicho* and the word meaning 'I' is *mimi*. A Swahili speaker can't use a picture of an eye to represent the word meaning 'I', and neither can a speaker of Spanish, or Mandarin, or Arabic, or French.

The second point is that rebus usage is intuitive. It doesn't need to be formally taught or learned. A writer can employ rebuses that nobody has ever used before, and can expect readers to decipher them fairly easily, without the need for instruction (figure 2.3). That's why rebus puzzles are so fun for five-year-old children—they don't take a lot of sophistication to work out.

And the third point is that rebus usage is more effective for writing some spoken languages than others. It's easy to give individual examples of how rebus usage of pictographs might represent English words, like ◉ to write *I* or 🥫 to write *can* (meaning 'able') or 🌊 to write *wave* (the hand motion). Even some multisyllable words aren't too challenging, if you use two rebuses in a row: 🐝≡ for *before*. But for many English words, it's not at all obvious that an appropriate rebus exists. What to do, for example, with the common words *if* and *soon*?

The problem is that the sound structure of English—what linguists call its **phonology**—permits many complex combinations of vowels and consonants to form syllables. As a result, English has thousands of distinct spoken syllables, from simple "oh" with one sound to complex "strength" with six sounds (<ng> and <th> each write one sound), with the result that many words and morphemes of English have no close homophones.

But English is a bit of an outlier in this regard. While languages with complex syllable structures like English aren't exactly rare, those with simple syllable structures are more common. Some languages have vocabularies built around only a few hundred distinct syllables.

Now that we've got some key concepts under our belt, let's move beyond thought experiments and hypothetical English examples to look at the early history of Chinese writing. We will examine real examples of pictographs and rebus usage during the time when true writing emerged in northern China in the late second millennium BCE. From there we will briefly trace the development of Chinese writing up to the modern era, tying that history together with some of the key concepts that were introduced in chapter 1.

The Origins of Chinese Writing

The earliest indisputable Chinese writing dates back to the mid-thirteenth century BCE, over three thousand years ago. To be sure, the archeological record contains man-made images that look like pictographs or resemble Chinese characters and are hundreds or even thousands of years older. But there is no way to prove that these images are writing, because they do not appear in a linguistic context that makes it indisputable that they are representations of spoken words.

For example, figure 2.4 is an image from a painted pottery piece dating to before 3000 BCE. It is over five thousand years old, and was produced by a culture that flourished in the Yellow River Valley of northern China.

The drawn elements are easy enough to identify: a stork, a fish, and an axe. But is it writing or drawing? What symbolic or representational value did it have? In theory, this could be a rebus writing of a word or phrase that sounds like, but has no meaning connection with, ancient Chinese words meaning 'stork', 'fish', and 'axe'. But this is highly unlikely, because from this era we have no examples of unmistakable written language, nothing that would suggest that writing had been invented and was being put to use to record spoken words and sentences.

Other pottery from this era displays painted decorative motifs like circles, crosses, and zigzags. Because some of these resemble the shapes of later Chinese characters, some people have claimed that the existence of these pictures

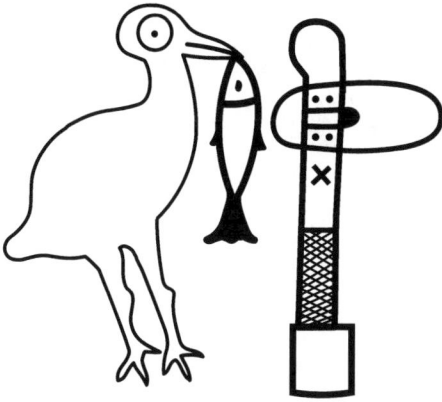

FIGURE 2.4 Image from painted pottery jar with stork, fish and stone axe design (Neolithic, Yangshao culture, ca. 5000–3000 BCE), excavated in Henan in 1978 and held at the National Museum of China, Beijing. Drawing by Natalie Warner, used by permission. A photo of the original artifact can be seen at https://en.chnmuseum.cn/collections_577/collection_highlights_608/archaeological_discoveries_609/201911/t20191121_172528.html, accessed September 21, 2023.

and character-like designs proves that Chinese writing is five thousand years old. But this is nothing more than wild speculation. There is no affirmative reason to think that any of these images are written representations of spoken utterances. If true writing had been invented by this time, we would expect to see written sentences, not just isolated graphs. The more plausible interpretation of the evidence is that these early drawings and abstract designs are just what they appear to be: drawings and abstract designs.

Starting from about 1250 BCE, however, we find unmistakable examples of written language in the archeological record. The **oracle bone inscriptions** of the Chinese Shāng dynasty (sixteenth to eleventh centuries BCE) were divinatory records made in the court of the Shāng king. The written records were inscribed on prepared cattle scapulae (shoulder bones) and turtle plastrons (belly shells) and were buried along with the king after he died. Lost to history for millennia, they were rediscovered at the end of the nineteenth century, when a combination of erosion and plowing in the area of the ancient Shāng capital brought them back up to the surface. These "dragon bones" were sold for medicinal powder in city markets until scholars in Beijing realized that the markings seen on some of them were an early form of Chinese writing. Although we don't know how many of these precious historical records were ground to powder and ingested for medicinal purposes, government-sponsored archeological expeditions in the early twentieth century recovered many thousands of inscribed oracle bones, and the process of deciphering the inscriptions began.

FIGURE 2.5. An inscribed turtle plastron from the Shāng dynasty. Courtesy of the Institute of History and Philology, Academia Sinica. See https://museum.sinica.edu.tw/en /collection/7/item/643/ for more details. A transcription and translation can be found in Keightley, *Sources of Shang History*, fig. 12.

It soon became apparent that the graphs on the oracle bones, though quite different in appearance from later known forms of Chinese writing, were directly ancestral to them. A subset could be readily identified with their later evolved forms. It was also apparent that the inscriptions were true writing. They represented all aspects of spoken language, including grammatical elements and abstract words. The inscriptions record ritual inquiries made by the Shāng kings of their deceased ancestors, usually in the form of divinations about the future.

The turtle plastron in figure 2.5 is one of the most arresting and best preserved of the surviving oracle bones. Its inscription, which runs in vertical columns from the outside edges toward the center, records a divination concerning the pregnant consort of the king, and a prediction about a favorable birth. It also records the disappointing result: a baby girl instead of the hoped-for male heir.[6]

Divinations were carried out by skilled specialists who applied heat to the prepared bones, causing them to crack. In some way that we do not understand, the cracks in the bone were interpreted as responses from the deceased ancestors. Sometimes it was the king himself who read the cracks and made an interpretation. After the divination ritual was finished, a record of the queries and responses was carved into the bone for posterity.[7]

This inscription is without doubt true writing, with the graphs representing a string of spoken words, including grammatical and abstract words like *if, perhaps, extremely,* and *not.*

But you may have noticed something puzzling as you look at this three-thousand-year-old object. Where are the pictographs? This does not look at all like Egyptian hieroglyphs, with its owls, snakes, and human figures. As it turns out, there are plenty of pictographs here: drawings of men, women, baskets, birds, and babies. But they are not easy to spot.

The reason it's not easy to recognize the pictographic quality of this writing is that the images, originally drawings, have become stylized and simplified. It's not really appropriate to call them drawings anymore. They are drawings in origin only. This is a natural development that is seen in the history of all early writing systems (including Egyptian, though we won't talk about that in any detail). Figure 2.6 shows examples of four oracle-bone characters (bottom row) and earlier drawings from the archeological record that are clearly ancestral to them. Consider the elephant. By the time this image came to be used as a pictograph to write the ancient Chinese word meaning 'elephant' on the oracle bones, it had lost much of its representational quality: it's been rotated ninety degrees, and the lines have been simplified. Even so, once you know its origin, it is easy to recognize that it was once a drawing of an elephant.

Why did this change happen? When newly invented writing is in its early stages, the pictorial quality of a pictograph is essential to its function. It is by recognizing the real-world object depicted by a graph that a reader is able to establish a connection to the word for that object. But once a graph

FIGURE 2.6. Four oracle-bone characters (bottom row) and the pictures of a fish, horse, elephant, and cow (top row) from which they derive. The modern character forms are 魚, 馬, 象, 牛. Based on Norman, *Chinese*, 59.

FIGURE 2.7. The development of the character 目, in origin a picture of an eye, from the earliest oracle-bone form to the Hàn dynasty form over a thousand years later. Based on Norman, *Chinese*, 66.

has been used for a period of time to represent a particular word, it is free to change form. The pictorial quality is no longer crucial to knowing what word it writes. The conventional association of the graph with the word is sufficient, and this conventional association is taught to new readers and writers and reinforced through exposure and practice. Many forces operate to reduce or eliminate the original pictorial quality of a graph: constraints imposed by the implements used to write and the medium of the writing; a natural inclination toward speed when writing; and the utility of having a simpler and therefore more consistent way of writing a word. You can observe many of these processes at work in figure 2.7 as the pictorial quality of the graph is reduced over time.

In the oracle bone texts, the representational quality of the pictographs is already significantly attenuated. This suggests that writing had been practiced for some time already before the date of the earliest surviving oracle bones, but whether that length of time was centuries or just a few years is impossible to know.

We observed earlier that the writing on the oracle bones was already a fully developed system. We can see that, despite a significant degree of stylization, many of the graphs are transparently derived from pictures of objects. Yet the writing system is also capable of representing words that have purely grammatical function or abstract meaning. A translation of part of the text in figure 2.5 shows many examples of such words: "'Fu Hao's childbearing will be good.' The king, reading the cracks, said: 'If it is a *ding*-day childbearing, it will be good. If it is a *geng*-day childbearing, it will be extremely auspicious.'"[8] So how are these grammatical and abstract words represented in the writing system?

The answer, of course, is rebus usage: phonetic extension. Consider the word *if* in the phrase "If it is a *ding*-day childbearing." You can imagine that whichever Chinese-speaking scribe first pondered how to represent this word in writing probably had difficulty thinking up a way to signify the word through a drawing of a real-world object or scene. Instead, that person wrote the word meaning 'if' by drawing a basket. You can see this drawing of a winnowing basket near the top right of the bone. The drawing has a cross in the bottom half to represent the woven pattern of the basket, and two gripping handles at the top. It looks like this: 𝕌.

Why a basket? Well, the ancient Chinese word for 'if' was pronounced [gə].[9] The ancient Chinese word for 'winnowing basket' was pronounced [kə].[10] The pronunciations are not identical, but they are very similar. (Try saying "kuh" and "guh" and focusing on where the back of your tongue touches the roof of your mouth on each consonant sound. Notice how similar the feeling in your mouth is when you pronounce these sounds: the same part of the tongue touches the same part of the roof of the mouth. Both the auditory impression and the feeling in your mouth of [k] and [g] sounds are much closer to each other than, say, [g] and [m] are.) The drawing of a basket is a pictograph that was used to write the word {[kə], 'winnowing basket'}. As a rebus, it was also used to write the similar-sounding (or, more technically, *near-homophonous*) word {[gə], 'if'}.

Perhaps you are wondering how confusion could be avoided if the exact same graph is used for two different words with identical or slightly different pronunciations. Rebus usage always creates this kind of ambiguity: Does 🐝 write *bee* or *be*? How does a reader know which word is intended? In the case of near-homophones, how does a reader know which pronunciation is appropriate? As it turns out, this is less difficult than you might suppose. In context, the word being represented is usually pretty obvious to someone who knows the spoken language well.

(9) I've never seen a 🐝 like that 🐝fore in my life. What type
of 🐝 can it 🐝?

Here the graph 🐝 is being used with three different representational functions: to write the word *bee*, the word *be*, and the first syllable of the word *before*. Yet as an accomplished speaker of English, you have no difficulty determining which usage is intended because of the grammatical and logical context provided by the surrounding words and phrases.

It even works with approximate pronunciations:

(10) That must 🐝 a very 🐝zy 🐝.

Were you able to read the second-to-last word in the sentence as *busy*? It's true that the first syllable of *busy* isn't pronounced exactly the same as "bee." But they are close enough that when you encounter the written form <🐝zy> and try saying "bee-zee" aloud, your knowledge of English and the context of the sentence helps you go from "bee-zee" to "busy" without much difficulty.

In this way, the graph derived from a picture of a winnowing basket could be used to write either the word meaning 'winnowing basket' or the word meaning 'if'. In the oracle bone text we were looking at, the meaning 'winnowing basket' wouldn't make sense or fit grammatically.

Many other words seen in the oracle bones are written with the rebus usage of a pictograph. Below are a few more examples.

ᘱ: Picture of a winnowing basket (modern character form: 其)
Pictographic use: represents {[kə], 'winnowing basket'}
Rebus use: represents {[gə], 'if'}

𒀭: Picture of an elephant (modern character form: 象)
Pictographic use: represents {[zang], 'elephant'}
Rebus use: represents {[zang], 'to resemble'}

𒀭: Picture of a cloud (modern character form: 云)
Pictographic use: represents {[wən], 'cloud'}
Rebus use: represents {[wən], 'to say'}

Notice again that these rebus usages are language-dependent. They rely on chance similarity in the pronunciation of pairs of words, which is something that varies from language to language. It wouldn't make sense to use a drawing of an elephant to write the English word *resemble*, or the drawing of a basket to write the English word *if*.[11] This is clear evidence, from the earliest known texts written in Chinese, that Chinese characters don't represent ideas divorced from specific utterances. Only by recognizing that Chinese characters write words with specific pronunciations can we explain how they were extended to write other words by means of rebus.

Compound Graphs for Disambiguation

There is a further development of the writing system, one that is essential to an understanding of the structure of Chinese characters today. It is the reason for some of the complexity of the characters used to write modern Mandarin that you saw in chapter 1, like 糖 (*táng* 'sugar') and 説 (*shuō* 'to speak').

Let's return to our now-familiar bee examples.

(11) 👁''ve never seen a 🐝 like that 🐝fore. What type of 🐝 🗄 it 🐝? It must 🐝 a very 🐝zy 🐝.

The graph 🐝 is ambiguous in its representational value. So far we have four different uses (representing *bee*, *before*, *be*, and *busy*), and there's nothing to stop us from coming up with more. While it's true that these many different uses of the 🐝 graph can all be disambiguated through context, as you read the sentence you may notice that it's starting to feel a bit complicated and burdensome to do so. Imagine if all the other words or syllables in the sentence were written not with ordinary English spelling as I've done here but with different pictographs that each have multiple rebus usages. The number of possible interpretations of each graph multiplies, and the number of permutations you have to sort through to determine the intended sequence of words becomes larger. This makes reading more cumbersome and time consuming.

What would be helpful here is some sort of disambiguating mechanism. Wouldn't it be great to have a clear indication as to when 🐝 writes *bee* and when it writes *be*? when 👁 writes *I* and when it writes *eye*? Or—to take the discussion back to the origins of the Chinese writing system—when 𑜀 writes {[kə], 'winnowing basket'} and when it writes {[gə], 'if'}?

You might be able to think up a number of different mechanisms for achieving this kind of **disambiguation**. For example, we could use an underline, so that 🐝 writes *bee* but 🐝̲ writes *be*. But keep in mind that a practical method needs not just to work for one or two graphs, like the bee and the eye, but to scale up to work with hundreds of graphs writing thousands of words, including graphs that might have three, four, five, or even more distinct rebus uses. And it has to be intuitive and nonarbitrary, so that readers who encounter it will be able to infer with reasonable accuracy which word the writer intended to represent. Underlining isn't going to cut it.

To illustrate what actually happened in the history of Chinese writing, let's go back to our inventory of English pictographs with rebus usage. We already have

🐝 writing both *bee* and *be*
👁 writing both *eye* and *I*
🥫 writing both *can* (the object) and *can* (meaning 'be able to')

To these we will add a fourth graph:

🌊 writing both *wave* (the object) and *wave* (the hand motion)

Finally, let's add two more usages of the graph 👁, one pictographic and one rebus:

👁 writing both *see* and *sea*, as well as *eye* and *I*

For each graph writing a pair of words, the first use listed is pictographic. The second use listed is a phonetic extension. Although the latter usages depend on the pictographic ones, after they have been in use for a while, they too become conventionalized. In other words, readers begin to strongly associate each graph with both of the two words it can represent, without considering one use more basic than the other.

We mentioned earlier the possibility of disambiguating by modifying the graph with an arbitrary mark, like an underline. But it would be more effective if we could do so with something that isn't arbitrary, something connected to the meaning of the word being written. After all, the multiple words written by a single graph share a pronunciation. What distinguishes the morphemes *eye* and *I* is meaning, not sound. So if we can give the reader a clue to the intended meaning, we can disambiguate the usage.

There are several different ways we might provide a meaning clue. Here are three of them:

1. Visually indicate the category to which the intended meaning belongs. For example, a bee is a type of insect and an eye is a body part.
2. Visually indicate the material out of which an object is made. For example, a can is made of metal and a wave is made of water.
3. Visually indicate a concrete object closely associated with the meaning of the word. For example, the meaning of the verb *to wave* is closely associated with the hand.

Notice that all three kinds of meaning clues are, to some degree, culturally dependent. Sure, an eye is a body part in all human societies. But is a spoon prototypically made of wood, bamboo, plastic, or metal? Does a bee belong to the category of flying animal or six-legged insect? The answers to these questions — and therefore the appropriateness of particular meaning clues — will vary from community to community across time and space.

Here are some ways we might use these three mechanisms to disambiguate the uses of our graphs:

Use butterfly wings to indicate the category of flying creature for *bee*:

🦋🐝 writes *bee*, contrast with 🐝 writing *be*

Use a person to indicate the category of body part for *eye*:

⚲ ◉ writes *eye*, contrast with ◉ writing *I*

Use a strong arm as an associated object for *can* ('be able to'):

🗄 writes *can* (the object), contrast with ✌ 🗄 writing *can* (meaning 'be able to')

Use water to indicate the material that a wave is made of, and use a hand as an associated object for the verb *wave*:

◊ 🌊 writes *wave* (the object) and ✋ 🌊 writes *wave* (the hand motion)

Use an eye as an associated object for the verb *see*, and use water to indicate the material that a sea is made of:

👁 ◉ writes *see* and ◊ ◉ writes *sea*

Granted, this seems a bit complex. But it's also fairly intuitive. And the trade-off we get for increasing the complexity of our graphs is a reduction in ambiguity. For a reader who is encountering one of these compound graphs for the first time, the graph contains clues that guide the reader toward the only possible interpretation.

⚲ ◉ indicates "I write a word that sounds like 'eye' and is part of the human body": *eye*.

✋ 🌊 indicates "I write a word that sounds like 'wave' (the object) and is associated with the hand": *to <u>wave</u>*.

Each of these compound graphs has a "sounds-like" part and an "associated-meaning" part, or what we can more technically call a **phonetic component** and a **semantic component**. We can refer to the graphic structure of one of these combination graphs as a **phonetic-semantic compound**. The phonetic component is fairly precise. The semantic component is more generic. But the two together leave no uncertainty about which word is being written.

And don't forget that the choice of phonetic component is language dependent, because the similarity in pronunciation of *eye* and *I*, of *can* and *can*, and of *bee* and *be* is specific to English. And the choice of semantic component is culture dependent, because the way we categorize and associate meanings varies from community to community. Because the writing system is developing among a small community of writers and readers who share a language and a culture, these dependencies present no impediments, and in fact are likely to go unnoticed by members of the community.

Here is another English sentence written using some of our newly formed compound graphs:

(12) 👁 🔺🥫 🔸👁 a ◊🌊 on the ◊👁.

Is this easier to parse for you as *I can see a wave on the sea* than

(13) 👁 🥫 👁 a 🌊 on the 👁 ?

Both present challenges to the reader. But there is a crucial difference. The ambiguous graphs in the second example need to be puzzled out *each time they are used*. Having figured out that the final 👁 in sentence (13) represents *sea* doesn't help you when you encounter 👁 again in a different sentence: you have to start over from scratch figuring out how to resolve the ambiguity.

It's true that the compound graphs in the first example have to be puzzled out the first time you encounter them. But over repeated exposure, the consistent use of 🔺👁 for *eye* contrasting with 👁 for *I* creates a strong association between the distinct graphs and the words they write. After a while, you don't need to keep resolving the ambiguity through inspection: you just read 🔺👁 as a single graph for *eye*. The ambiguity is permanently resolved.

Now we've got everything we need for a full writing system. With a few hundred pictographs representing basic words that have fairly concrete, drawable meanings (nouns, action verbs) and, by rebus extension, most of the syllables of the spoken language, along with a several dozen graphs representing semantic categories, it's possible to mix and match to represent thousands of words. Over time, the system becomes stable and conventionalized. And once that happens, new compound graphs can be quickly constructed — and decoded by readers — without the need to pass through the rebus stage. In this way, graphic representations of all the words in the spoken language can be created and put to use to represent any possible utterance.

What do I mean by bypassing the rebus stage? Well, suppose I am a scribe writing a text and I want to convert a spoken word into writing for the very first time. Maybe it's the word *palm*. I can invent the compound graph < 👌 𥄂 >, with phonetic component < 𥄂 > for "palm" and semantic component < 🖐 > for *hand,* and its representational value will be easily worked out by readers. There is no need for me to first use < 𥄂 > for *palm* (the tree), then use it for a while as a rebus < 𥄂 > for *palm* (of the hand), and only later disambiguate by adding < 🖐 >. I can just come up with < 👌 𥄂 > right from the start. All the phonetic-semantic compounds that are already in my script serve as existing models for this kind of one-step creation of new compounds. And in this way the writing system can move from partial writing to full writing very quickly, certainly within a single generation if not even faster.

This is exactly how the Chinese writing system developed. Let's return to the earlier examples of oracle-bone pictographs and their extended rebus usages, and see how they were disambiguated through the addition of semantic components.[12]

> �: Picture of awinnowing basket (modern character form: 其)
> Pictographic use: represents {[kə], 'winnowing basket'}
> Rebus use: represents {[gə], 'if'}

To write [kə] 'winnowing basket' distinctly, the semantic component 'bamboo' (for the material of which it is constructed) was added to the top of the graph, eventually yielding the modern compound character form 箕. (The bamboo component originally looked like ⋀⋀ and has modern form ⺮.)

> �象: Picture of an elephant (modern character form: 象)
> Pictographic use: represents {[zang], 'elephant'}
> Rebus use: represents {[zang], 'to resemble'}

To write [zang] 'to resemble' distinctly, the semantic component 'person' was added to the left of the graph, eventually yielding the modern compound character form 像. (The person component originally looked like ⟋ and has modern form 亻.)

⟋: Picture of a cloud (modern character form: 云)
Pictographic use: represents {[wən], 'cloud'}
Rebus use: represents {[wən], 'to say'}

To write [wən] 'cloud' distinctly, the semantic component 'rain' (for the category of meteorological phenomena) was added to the top of the graph, eventually yielding the modern compound character form 雲.[13] (The rain component originally looked like ⟋ and has modern form 雨.)

It's interesting to observe that in the first and third examples, it is the original pictographic usage that has been modified into a compound graph, while the extended rebus usage of the graph remained unmodified. This is not what always happens, but it is a notable tendency. It's not surprising if you think about it. The original pictographic usage is concrete, while the extended usage is more abstract. It's easier to identify an appropriate semantic component for a concrete meaning than an abstract one. Winnowing baskets are made of bamboo. But what category, material, or association can be given for a word meaning 'if'?

Over time, new compound characters were created from scratch, rather than going through a prior stage of rebus extension. For example, the character ⟋ (modern form: 方) is a pictograph representing the ancient Chinese word {[pang], 'square'}.[14] To write the homophonous word {[pang], 'fragrant'}, a compound graph was created using 方 as the phonetic component with 'grass' added to the top, yielding modern form 芳. There is no example of 方 ever being used by itself as a rebus to write the word meaning 'fragrant'.[15]

I don't want to give you the impression that the development of Chinese writing was orderly and precise, or that the processes I've described here are the only ones that were at play as it developed. There was a great deal of inconsistency in how words were written, with different scribes employing different mechanisms at different times and places, even for the same word. But fluidity and variation are typical of premodern scripts and writing systems, especially in the absence of strong centralized government regulation and standardized reference works like dictionaries. Early Chinese writing was not exceptional in this regard. It is only with the great imperial consolidation of the mighty Qín (221–206 BCE) and Hàn (202 BCE–220 CE) dynasties, a thousand years after the invention of Chinese writing, that we begin to see comprehensive attempts to codify and stabilize Chinese writing. And as we will see in later chapters, when we shift our focus to other languages, like Japanese and Korean, this codification and standardization played an important part in determining how the script was exported into areas outside of China. But for the rest of this chapter, we will stick with describing the Chinese script as used to write Chinese, and follow its development over three millennia to the present day.

From Oracle Bones to the Digital Information Age

For about a thousand years after the invention of Chinese writing, written forms were highly variable. Multiple ways of writing the same word coexisted, or fell in and out of use. But nearly all Chinese characters were based on the same simple and intuitive principles: pictographs, phonetic extension (rebus), disambiguation through semantic components, and the creation of new phonetic-semantic compound graphs from scratch. Over time, two clear trends are apparent in the historical record: (1) increasing stylization, reduction, and conventionalization of graphic forms, and (2) an increase in the percentage of phonetic-semantic compounds in the script. (By most estimates, phonetic-semantic compounds make up well over 80 percent of the Chinese characters in use today.)[16]

What we mean by **stylization** is a decrease in the pictorial aspect of pictographs. Instead of being little drawings that resemble the objects they depict, they became transformed such that their pictographic origins were no longer obvious. Instead of being so representational that any person looking at them for the first time could identify the real-world object depicted, like the owl in Egyptian hieroglyphic writing, they became less obviously pictographic, like the oracle-bone forms in the second row of figure 2.6. Finally, by the early third century, their forms were not obviously representations of anything. The modern forms of the four graphs in figure 2.6 are: 魚 馬 象 牛. Try showing these four graphs to a friend who has no experience with Chinese characters, and ask them to guess what real-world objects are depicted.

What we mean by **reduction** is a reduction in the complexity of the graphic form. For example, note that the modern character writing Chinese word meaning 'fish', 魚, has a simple cross shape + indicating the scales on the body instead of the larger number of lines on the original drawing.

And finally, what we mean by **conventionalization** is the form of the graph becoming fixed over time. Early forms of the graph writing the Chinese word meaning 'horse' varied in the number of lines representing hairs of the mane. This number not only decreased over time (reduction), but became fixed (conventionalization). The modern form 馬 is always printed with four horizontal lines and four dots — never more, never less.

Stylization, reduction, and conventionalization are interrelated developments. As these processes happen, the pictorial aspect of the script loses importance. It is simply not needed. The conventional associations of graphs with the words they represent can be taught and learned without reference to concrete pictorial representation, thanks in large part to the recurrence of components that represent sound and meaning. Put another way, if you are a student of written Chinese you can learn that 魚 writes the Mandarin word *yú* 'fish' without knowing or caring that it derives from a three-thou-sand-year-old drawing of a fish.

Reduction has its limits. The main check on reduction proceeding too far is the necessity of maintaining distinctions among several thousand different characters. If all characters were reduced to being written with just two or three strokes of the brush or pen, there would be no way to keep them all visually distinctive. By the late third century, the writing system had become stable. While new characters continued to be created and variations in character forms persisted, the overall look and feel of the characters became essentially unchanging right up to the early twentieth century. And the set of phonetic components and semantic components that were available to mix and match in the creation of new compound characters became largely fixed as well. Any literate person in China in the year 1900 would have no difficulty recognizing certain Chinese characters written down 1,600 years earlier.[17] A major reason for this stability was an increasing attention to the importance of written forms of Chinese characters among social elites, expressed through a proliferation of dictionaries and government standards.

These stable, long-lasting character forms have now been standardized in a new way in the modern information era: they are encoded in **Unicode** and represented in digital fonts whose appearance still reflects the visual features imparted by ancient brush writing.

Script Reform through the Twentieth Century

Spoken Chinese underwent great changes between the third century BCE and the twentieth century CE. Dialectal and linguistic diversity have always existed in China, but the first great imperial expansion created a major change in the linguistic landscape with long-ranging ramifications. Spoken Chinese was carried to distant corners of the expanding empire, first by soldiers who established military garrisons, and then by Chinese-speaking migrants, who intermixed with local populations of non-Chinese speakers. Because of the vast distances involved, and because of the influence of local languages, the Chinese spoken in different regions changed in different ways over time. These changes accumulated over centuries, until the spoken languages had become so widely divergent that their speakers could no longer easily understand each other. As linguists say, these language varieties became mutually unintelligible. Although today we casually refer to these varieties of speech as "Chinese dialects," the spoken languages of Beijing in the north, Shanghai on the central coast, and Hong Kong in the south are at least as different from each other as are spoken French, Italian, and Portuguese. That is why linguists often refer to them as "Chinese languages" rather than "Chinese dialects." Depending on how you measure and count, there are anywhere from a dozen to around a hundred of these distinct languages within the Chinese language family.

Most of these spoken languages have never been written down. Prior to the twentieth century, educated Chinese speakers learned to read and write in Classical Chinese, which allowed them to communicate with each other in written form. This doesn't mean that all spoken forms of Chinese are written the same way; rather, it means that speakers of all these languages learned the vocabulary and grammar of Classical Chinese, much in the way that early modern speakers of French, Italian, and Portuguese learned to read and write in Latin as part of their education, and could communicate effectively with each other in written Latin. (We'll learn more about Classical Chinese in the next chapter.)

That's not to say that local Chinese languages could not be written. Over the last thousand years or so, as Mandarin developed in the north of China and then increasingly became a common language of government administration throughout the empire, the Chinese script was adapted to write colloquial Mandarin. This adaptation consisted of creating new characters or adapting existing characters to represent the spoken morphemes that had no equivalent in the classical language. The great popular novels of the premodern period, like *Dream of the Red Chamber* (Hóng lóu mèng) were written in Mandarin.[18] In just the last two hundred years, a vibrant written form of Cantonese has developed in the south, and it is widely used today in Hong Kong as well as other Cantonese-speaking areas, primarily in nonformal situations. Other Chinese languages, like Taiwanese and Shanghainese, also have written and literary traditions that developed in recent centuries.

Classical Chinese ceased to be the standard written language in the early twentieth century. It was replaced by a written language based on spoken Mandarin. These were enormously transformative changes in China that echoed across Asia as modernizing nation-states implemented language reforms and established official spoken and written languages.

Alongside these changes, there was also a major shift in the form of the individual graphs making up the Chinese-character script itself. That script had been stable and successful for two thousand years, with essentially no change in outer form or inner function. But as China faced increasing military and economic challenges from aggressive and powerful Western nations, the script was increasingly viewed by intellectuals as a liability for China. Late nineteenth and early twentieth-century Chinese intellectual reformers viewed it as too cumbersome to support the mass education and literacy that a modern nation-state required to compete on the world stage. They considered reform of Chinese writing to be just as important as political, social, economic, military, and scientific reform.

There was a great deal of debate among Chinese intellectuals and government officials about how to make Chinese writing more modern and accessible. A number of proposals were made to eliminate Chinese characters altogether in favor of an alphabetic writing system for Mandarin. For example, these two sentences of Standard Chinese appeared in a 1950 Shanghai magazine whose purpose was to advocate for, and help readers to develop facility in, a new way of writing Chinese, called Latinxua Sin Wenz ("Latinized New Writing"): "Iou igo Meiguo de kuolao, dao go zhou ky lyxing. Zai Chigako ta gen rhen daagia, ba rhengia daasle. Zhe Meiguorhen mashang paile i fung dianbao gei ta New York de faly guwen."[19]

It was even suggested by some that China might adopt English or Esperanto as its official written language, rather than using any form of Chinese.[20] But other reformers did not feel that such drastic changes were necessary. They advocated that the Chinese-character script be retained but simplified, so that there would be fewer characters to learn and fewer strokes in each character to memorize.

Despite many proposals and many false starts over several decades, no meaningful change happened to the script until the Communist revolutionaries overthrew the Nationalist government and established the People's Republic of China (PRC) in 1949. The new government made the decision to postpone consideration of the abolition of Chinese characters. Instead they pursued two directions of language reform. The first was the development of a new romanized transcription of Standard Chinese pronunciation, Hanyu Pinyin (literally "Chinese spelling"), to serve as a supplement to the Chinese character script and a vehicle for teaching and recording standard pronunciation. The second was the simplification of individual Chinese characters.[21]

The government set up a committee that began work on simplification in 1950. In 1956, the Committee on Script Reform published a recommendation list of simplified versions of 515 characters, which were widely adopted on a preliminary basis. The committee continued working, and in 1964 released an updated list of 2,238 simplified characters that was officially adopted. With only minor revisions, this list is the basis of the "simplified character script" in use in China today. Although thousands of characters were simplified in this way, thousands more were left unchanged.

In Taiwan, Hong Kong, and Macau, which were not under the control of the government of the PRC, the "traditional" or "complex" script continued to be used. Both Singapore and Malaysia, where Chinese is one of several languages with official status, today use the same "simplified" script as in mainland China.[22]

Table 2.1 shows examples of traditional-simplified character pairs. Many different techniques were employed to reduce the overall number of strokes in each character. In some cases, simplification reverted the graph to an ancient form, as with the character for the Chinese word meaning 'cloud'. After simplification, *yún* 'cloud' and *yún* 'to say' are both written the same way (云), just as they were in ancient times—reducing the overall number of characters in the script and reintroducing a potential ambiguity into the system.

In other cases, simplification just took cursive or calligraphic forms that were common and familiar in handwriting and made them official printed forms. It's analogous to replacing the letter forms <g> and <a> with printed versions of the simpler handwritten forms <g> and <a>.

Sometimes simplification preserved the structure of a compound phonetic-semantic graph, but one or more components were modified or substituted to achieve a reduction. In the case of *rèn* 'recognize', the seven-stroke phonetic component 忍 (*rěn* 'tolerate') is replaced with a different component that has a similar pronunciation, the two-stroke component 人 (*rén* 'person'). The

TABLE 2.1 Examples of twentieth-century simplified characters

STANDARD CHINESE MORPHEME	TRADITIONAL CHARACTER	SIMPLIFIED CHARACTER	EXPLANATION
{"yún," 'cloud'}	雲	云	throw away top part; becomes the same as 云 (*yún* 'say')
{"mǎ," 'horse'}	馬	马	calligraphic/cursive abbreviation
{"rèn," 'recognize'}	認	认	calligraphic/cursive abbreviation of semantic component 言 (*yán* 'speech'); selection of new phonetic component 人 (*rén* 'person') with fewer lines than 忍 (*rěn* 'tolerate')

Chinese Writing　　59

seven-stroke semantic component 言 (*yán* 'speech') is reduced to a two-stroke cursivized form, 讠. In this way the entire character is reduced from fourteen to four strokes. (A stroke is a single continuous motion of the pen or brush. The box at the bottom of 言 is conventionally written with three movements of the pen, which is why it is counted as three strokes rather than four.)

There were other techniques used as well, but these examples are sufficient to give you a general feel for how it was done. The basic look, feel, and function of the script as a whole was not changed, even though the visual form of many of the individual characters was.

Although thousands of commonly used characters were simplified, many of the most frequently occurring one hundred characters were not. This means that the majority of characters occurring in a long text are likely to be no different in the two scripts. Consider this passage from the modern Chinese-language novella *The Chess Master* (Qí Wáng) by A Cheng, published in 1984, presented here in both traditional and simplified character scripts:[23]

Traditional:　我奇怪了, 可還是拈起炮, 往當頭上一移。我的棋還沒移到, 他的馬卻「啪」的一聲跳好, 比我還快。我就故意將炮移過當頭的地方停下。

Simplified:　　我奇怪了, 可还是拈起炮, 往当头上一移。我的棋还没移到, 他的马却「啪」的一声跳好, 比我还快。我就故意将炮移过当头的地方停下。

The passage contains fifty-two characters, of which eleven have different simplified forms, about 21 percent. Of these fifty-two characters, thirty-eight are unique; only seven of them have different simplified forms, about 18 percent. The overall look and feel of the two sentences are similar, because most of the simplified characters bear a resemblance to their traditional counterparts.

Whether the simplification achieved its principal aim of making it easier to acquire literacy is debatable. In Taiwan and Hong Kong, where the traditional character forms remained in use, literacy rates skyrocketed in the twentieth century. So although mass literacy improved dramatically in mainland China after the introduction of simplified characters, this was more likely the effect of increasing wealth and an improved educational system than anything attributable specifically to the character forms themselves.

For the foreseeable future, there will be two Chinese-character scripts in use. It's a bit more dramatic than the differences between British and American spelling, but the two scripts are similar enough that readers don't have too much trouble reading the one they aren't familiar with, as long as they have some linguistic context to help them figure out which words are intended.[24]

"I Can't Learn Eighty Thousand Characters!": How Many Chinese Characters Are There, Anyway?

Perhaps you have read somewhere that there are ten thousand Chinese characters. Or fifty thousand. Or eighty thousand. Perhaps you have thought about learning Chinese but been dissuaded by this enormous number. "I can't learn eighty thousand characters!" you say. Well, you're not alone. Nobody else can either. Like so much else about Chinese writing, the notion that the script contains eighty thousand (or even fifty thousand) characters is a myth. But like many myths, it contains a grain of truth. Let's get to the bottom of it.

We'll start with Standard Written Chinese, the official written language of today's People's Republic of China. It's not easy to get precise figures on the number of characters in use, because estimates vary according to which sample texts are the basis of analysis and which methods are used to extrapolate from them. But we can approximate. If we restrict our inquiry to printed texts in the modern era, we find that fewer than seven thousand distinct characters account for well over 99 percent of the total graphs in use.[25] As it happens, this is about the number of characters found in an ordinary dictionary of Modern Standard Chinese, although more comprehensive dictionaries have closer to ten thousand.[26] College-educated adults today seem to have command of 4,000–5,500 characters: this range is in line with the typical number of distinct morphemes in common use in all of the major languages of the world. Quite a few of those morphemes are rare, technical, or obscure. If you are a second-language learner of Modern Standard Chinese, you will find that once you learn three thousand characters, you are able to read almost any text of a general nature.

So where do those larger numbers in the tens of thousands come from? Well, there do exist multivolume character dictionaries containing tens of thousands of entries.[27] But these are not collections of characters that make up the modern writing system. Indeed, at no time in history did any literate community use a writing system containing that many characters in active use. These megadictionaries are so huge because they contain characters from many eras and places across three thousand years of history, including tens of thousands that are vanishingly rare or merely variant forms of common characters. These dictionaries don't reflect a living language; they are scholarly reference works intended for researchers.[28]

One reason the number of characters in some reference works is so large is that the Chinese-character script is an open set. This is in contrast to alphabetic scripts, which are, at least over relatively short time frames, closed sets. We think of the modern Latin alphabet, as used to write American English, as a fixed script with twenty-six letters. As obsolete words fall out of use and new words enter the spoken language, these same twenty-six letters continue to be employed, in new combinations, to represent all vocabulary words in written form.[29] Many new words in Chinese are coined using existing morphemes in new combinations. In such a case, the word is written with the existing characters for those morphemes.[30] But a morphographic script requires a new graph when a new morpheme comes along and enters the spoken language.

As an example, consider the periodic table of the chemical elements. In the course of the twentieth and twenty-first centuries, chemists and physicists have discovered and even created chemical elements that were unknown to previous generations. And they have invented new names for those elements. These new names are new morphemes of spoken Chinese, so new graphs are needed to represent them.

The most recently discovered chemical element as of the time of this writing is tennessine (Ts, atomic number 117), first synthesized in 2010 and officially named after the state of Tennessee in 2015. In Standard Chinese, the name chosen for this element was *tián*, based on the sound of the first syllable of *tennessine*. How was a new character created to write this element name? The same way new characters have been most commonly created throughout the history of Chinese writing: by combining an appropriate sound component and meaning component. In this case, the homophonous character 田 writing {"tián," 'field'} was selected as the sound component, and the character 石 writing {"shí," 'stone'} was selected as the meaning-category component. (This latter choice is in line with the convention of using this component for all names of new chemicals that are nonmetallic solids at room temperature.) This resulted in a brand-new character that was added to the Chinese script: 础.[31]

Because the script is open-ended and new characters can be easily created, the number of graphs that have ever been in use has increased steadily and substantially over time, and comprehensive character dictionaries have gotten bigger and bigger. But it's important to keep in mind that the number of Chinese characters that have ever existed is a very different matter from the number that are in common use in the writing system of Modern Standard Chinese.

Although learning even a few thousand Chinese characters seems daunting, it's not as difficult as it may first appear. As we've already seen, Chinese characters aren't arbitrary in their structure. Most are logically constructed from sound and meaning components, making them easy to learn. The more spoken words you know, and the more components from other characters you know, the easier it is to learn new ones. A Chinese chemist will find it trivial to remember that 础 represents *tián* 'tennessine': "I'm the nonmetallic solid chemical element (石) whose name sounds like *tián* (田)," the character whispers up from the page.

To be sure, not all characters are such neatly solved puzzles for the language learner. The semantic components give only a general idea of the meaning domain. And many sound components give only an approximate, rather than precise, indication of the pronunciation of the morpheme being written. Sometimes, the sound component is not helpful at all, because pronunciations have changed so much since the character was first created. What made sense to a Chinese speaker 2,500 years ago may seem baffling today. Table 2.2 provides examples of phonetic-semantic compound characters with phonetic elements that range from more to less transparent to a modern-day speaker of Mandarin. The first one will be familiar to you.

In the last example in the table, you could certainly be forgiven for not realizing that 各, pronounced "gè" today, was selected as phonetic component when the character 路 was first created to write the word *lù* 'road'. This choice made sense at the time, well over two thousand years ago, when the pronunciations were something like:

各 : {[kak], 'each'}
路 : {[graks], 'road'}

(Say these ancient Chinese pronunciations out loud, and you'll hear the similarity.) Over millennia, the similarity between [kak] and [graks] diverged into a stark difference between *gè* and *lù* as pronunciations of these words shifted with the passage of time.

Although today some phonetic components are only approximate or even of no help at all, the fact that nearly all characters are formed out of familiar, recurring components with recognizable sound or meaning values is a great help to the learner of the script. It makes new graphs easier to learn, easier to remember, and easier to recognize, until with repeated exposure they become so familiar that their use no longer requires conscious effort.

Over the last three thousand years, the percentage of characters in active use that are phonetic-semantic compounds has steadily increased. This suggests that there is an advantage to this kind of character over others. Perhaps the advantage applies to both creator and learner: it provides a simple recipe for creating a new character in a nonarbitrary way, and makes the character easy to learn, memorize, and remember.

TABLE 2.2 Phonetic-semantic compound characters

	MANDARIN MORPHEME	PHONETIC COMPONENT	DEGREE OF SIMILARITY
芳	{"fāng," 'fragrant'}	方 : {"fāng," 'square'}	exact match
訪	{"fǎng," 'to visit'}	方 : {"fāng," 'square'}	close match, differing only in tone
洞	{"dòng," 'cave'}	同 : {"tóng," 'same'}	approximate match, differing in tone and beginning consonant sound
路	{"lù," 'road'}	各 : {"gè," 'each'}	appears not to match at all

Now that we have become familiar with the outlines of the history of writing in China, and with the structure and function of Chinese characters and their components, we can begin to explore the ways that they spread to places where other languages were spoken—both inside and outside of modern-day China's borders—and eventually formed the basis of new writing systems for those languages. As we've seen in the first two chapters, if we closely examine the apparent randomness and complexity of these processes, we will discover surprisingly clear patterns and structures. Later on, we'll consider what those patterns and structures mean—what they can tell us about how humans create, use, and modify writing systems for the languages they speak. And that in turn will help us to think more deeply about whether it's possible to create a writing system that does what Matteo Ricci thought Chinese characters could do: represent ideas directly, and thus serve as a universal tool of communication among peoples who cannot talk to each other.

A few key points from this chapter are worth remembering as we proceed:

- The Chinese script is primarily morphographic. That is, nearly all Chinese characters represent morphemes of spoken language, which are elements that have both sound and meaning.
- The vast majority of spoken Chinese morphemes are one syllable long, and this has been true for about two millennia or more.
- Chinese characters, because they write one-syllable morphemes, have an associated one-syllable pronunciation and an associated meaning.
- While a few hundred common characters are pictographic in origin, the vast majority are compound phonetic-semantic graphs.

The features described above have not necessarily been true for all of the known history of written and spoken Chinese, but they have been true for the past two thousand years or so. And that's the period we are interested in, because it is within it that we can historically trace and analyze clear cases of the spread of Chinese characters into non-Chinese-speaking areas.

THREE

Classical Chinese
A Written Language for East Asia

Throughout their three-thousand-year history, Chinese characters have represented specific Chinese words and morphemes, with specific pronunciations, and not "ideas" or "things," as Matteo Ricci thought. But Ricci was no fool; he was a shrewd and intelligent observer who was proficient in spoken and written Chinese. He was correct in asserting that written Chinese texts were readable and understandable in many places where Chinese was not spoken. His mistake was only in attributing that remarkable fact to a misunderstanding of how individual Chinese characters function.

This raises an interesting question. If Chinese characters are not ideographic, and Chinese writing is a written representation of spoken Chinese, how were people in Japan, Korea, and Vietnam who didn't speak Chinese able to read it?

Classical Chinese

The claim that Ricci made about written Chinese over four hundred years ago is no longer true today. If you give a modern Chinese book written in Chinese characters to a typical literate Vietnamese, Korean, or Japanese speaker, they will *not* be able to read it. The Japanese speaker may well recognize and understand quite a few words, and therefore get a general sense of what different sections of the book are about, but would not be able to provide a precise understanding of the sentences.

What has happened between Ricci's time and ours that has so drastically changed the role of Chinese writing as a cross-cultural and cross-linguistic form of communication in East Asia?

The written version of Chinese that Ricci was talking about is most commonly called "Classical Chinese" in English (other names for this written language include "Literary Chinese" and "Literary Sinitic"). For approximately 2,500 years, from about the fifth century BCE until the early twentieth century, Classical Chinese was the formal way of writing used throughout the Chinese cultural area. In its earliest incarnation, it was, like most written languages we are familiar with today, such as formal written English, a stylized representation of the spoken language of its time. Classical Chinese vocabulary, grammar, and pronunciation mirrored the vocabulary, grammar, and pronunciation of fifth-century BCE elevated spoken Chinese, which we today call **Old Chinese**. Over succeeding centuries and millennia, the vocabulary, grammar, and pronunciation of spoken forms of Chinese shifted, with gradual changes accumulating from generation to generation, and diverging from each other in different regions of China. Those spoken forms eventually became drastically different from their fifth-century BCE ancestor. Over this same time frame, the classical written language didn't change nearly as much.

This is not so different from the continued use of Latin as a relatively stable written language across medieval Europe up until just a few hundred years ago, even as the spoken Latin on which the written language was originally based evolved over time, and eventually turned into the modern Romance languages: Italian, Spanish, Portuguese, French, Romanian, and so on. The vast differences we observe today between Latin vocabulary, grammar, and pronunciation on the one hand and French vocabulary, grammar, and pronunciation on the other are paralleled by equally vast differences between Old Chinese and modern Mandarin.

This is a case where the names we apply to these ancient and modern languages can give us a false impression of their degree of similarity. We speak of "Old Chinese" (and the written language based on it, "Classical Chinese") and "Modern Chinese," which can give the impression that we are talking about minor variants of the same language. Perhaps this puts us in mind of the difference between the English of Shakespeare's day and our own. But the gulf is in fact much wider. If speakers of Old Chinese were to magically appear in the present day (choose your scenario: time machine, wormhole in the space-time continuum, cryogenic preservation), they would be utterly unable to carry on a conversation with modern Chinese speakers.

Conversely, if we referred to Latin as "Classical Italian" or "Old French," it might mislead us into thinking it had a greater affinity to these modern languages.[1]

Let's make this a bit more concrete. Consider the following sentence in Latin about the king's success in hunting, and its translations into modern French, modern Italian, and modern Spanish.

Meaning: 'The king got ten birds in one day.'

Latin: *Rēx decem avēs in ūnō diē obtinuit.*
            king - ten - birds - in - one - day - got

French: *Le roi a obtenu dix oiseaux en une journée.*
            the - king - has - gotten - ten - birds - in - one - day

Italian: *Il re ha preso dieci uccelli in un giorno.*
            the - king - has - gotten - ten - birds - in - one - day

Spanish: *El rey consiguió diez pájaros en un día.*
            the - king - got - ten - birds - in - one - day

Notice that some of the words are clearly historically the same, such as the words for 'king' and 'ten'. Latin *rēx* has become *roi*, *re*, and *rey*, and Latin *decem* has become *dix*, *dieci*, and *diez*. The similarity due to their common origin is still recognizable across the three modern languages even though their pronunciations have diverged from the older Latin pronunciation. But some of the words are completely different in two or more of the languages. Spanish *pájaros* 'birds' is not related to Latin *avēs* or to its French and Italian counterparts.

The grammatical structures are quite different too. We don't have to go into all the details, but just for starters, notice that the Latin verb *obtinuit* 'got' is at the end of the sentence, while the French, Italian, and Spanish verbs immediately follow the subject, as in English. The Latin nouns *rēx*, *avēs*, and *diē* have suffixes on them indicating their role in the sentence (subject, object, etc.). The modern Romance languages lack these noun suffixes. Latin has no articles like *the* and *a*, while the Romance languages all have them (notice the words *le*, *il*, and *el* meaning 'the' in front of the word for 'king'). And so on.

While you can't necessarily tell from a single example sentence, the fact is that modern Italian is more different from Latin than it is from modern Spanish. Whether we call Latin "Latin" or "Classical Italian," there is no doubt that it is a different language from modern Italian.

The situation with Classical Chinese and the modern Chinese languages is strikingly parallel. In terms of grammar and vocabulary, Classical Chinese is as different from Mandarin and Cantonese as Latin is from modern Spanish and French:

Meaning: 'The king got ten birds in one day.'

Classical Chinese: *Wang it nit nə gwrak gip gəm.*[2]
                    king - one - day - and.so[3] - get - ten - bird

Mandarin: *Guówáng yī tiān dédào shí zhī niǎo.*
                    king - one - day - get - ten - mw - bird

Cantonese: *Go³ gwok³wong⁴ jat¹ jat⁶ noi⁶ zuk¹dou² sap⁶ zek³
                    zoek³zai².*
                    the - king - one - day - in - catch - ten - mw - bird

We've seen a lot of parallels between Latin and the modern Romance languages on the one hand, and between Classical Chinese and the modern Chinese languages on the other. But in one respect, they are most definitely not parallel: how they are written. True, the basic script has not changed in each case. Modern French, Spanish, and Italian all use the Latin alphabet.[4] Classical Chinese and modern Standard Written Chinese both use the Chinese-character script. But in the case of the Romance languages, as they developed out of and diverged from Latin—both in spoken and written form—the particular combinations of letters used to spell each word shifted to reflect changes in pronunciation. In Chinese, the morphographic script's representation of a single morpheme remained fixed, even as that morpheme's pronunciation changed over time. This was the case even though many of those characters contain phonetic components.

Take a look at those example sentences again, this time written in Chinese characters. While we can still see the differences in grammar and vocabulary, what we can't see are changes in pronunciation. Notice that the character 十 appears in all three sentences, writing the word for 'ten'.

Classical Chinese:	王一日而獲十禽。
Mandarin:	國王一天得到十隻鳥。
Cantonese:	個國王一日內捉到十隻雀仔。

Compare the Latin written word for 'ten' with the French, Italian, and Spanish words for 'ten'. The different spellings track the differences in pronunciation.

Latin: *decem*

Spanish: *diez*

Italian: *dieci*

French: *dix*

The pronunciations of the Chinese word for 'ten' have similarly shifted a great deal:

Old Chinese: "gip"

Mandarin: "shí"

Cantonese: "sap[6]"

Despite the pronunciations having shifted dramatically over time—especially Mandarin, which has completely lost the ending [p] sound—the written representation has been static:

Old Chinese "gip" was written 十

Mandarin "shí" is written 十

Cantonese "sap[6]" is written 十

This stability of written forms has had a remarkable effect on how Classical Chinese is pronounced. Let's go back to our Latin example. As an English speaker looking at a written Latin sentence, you have a range of options for how to pronounce it. If you haven't formally studied Latin and want to read the sentence out loud, one option is to pronounce the words as best you can by following the rules of English spelling. Or, if you've formally studied Latin, you would use the pronunciations you were taught, which are closer to the way the Romans spoke in ancient times. The same range of options is available to a modern French, Spanish, or Italian speaker.

But the latter option is not available to modern-day Chinese speakers who study Classical Chinese. The ancient pronunciations are invisible, hidden behind the unchanging Chinese characters. Only a very small number of specialists know their ancient pronunciations. What this means is that, for all intents and purposes, Classical Chinese has become a language with a grammar and a vocabulary but no pronunciation. Or rather, it has many pronunciations. Modern-day speakers of Mandarin read it aloud with modern Mandarin pronunciations. Modern-day speakers of Cantonese do likewise but with modern Cantonese pronunciations. And so on. And this has been true for over two thousand years, as each successive generation of educated literate Chinese speakers has learned to recite Classical Chinese texts in the pronunciations peculiar to their time and place.

Meaning: 'The king got ten birds in one day.'

Classical Chinese in written form:
  王一日而獲十禽。

Classical Chinese in Mandarin pronunciation:
  "Wáng yī rì ér huò shí qín."

Classical Chinese in Cantonese pronunciation:
  "Wong⁴ jat¹ jat⁶ ji⁴ wok⁶ sap⁶ kam⁴."

Classical Chinese was not the only written language used by Chinese speakers before the twentieth century. It was the written language used for anything formal or important. But as vocabulary and grammar in spoken Chinese shifted over time, its speakers also had various reasons for sometimes writing in ways closer to how they were speaking. How did they do this? In the many cases where words of their spoken language were obviously related to those of the Classical Chinese written tradition, the existing character could be used. The unchanging use of <十> to write the word for 'ten' even as its pronunciation shifted from Old Chinese "gip" to Modern Mandarin "shí" is an example. But for new words and morphemes that had entered the spoken language and were not part of the Classical Chinese written tradition, new Chinese characters were needed. These were created in much the same way that we saw described in the previous chapter. Sometimes existing characters were employed as rebuses to write colloquial words; more often, entirely new phonetic-semantic compounds were formed from the existing stock of characters and character components.

It was an early form of Mandarin, the northern Chinese ancestor of modern Mandarin, for which this "vernacular" or "colloquial" writing became the most developed, most widely known, and most widely used. Indeed, many of the great novels of the Míng and Qīng dynasties were written in Mandarin. Over time, Mandarin writing came to be seen as a part of the mainstream Chinese written tradition, largely because of the cultural and political importance of northern China. That recognition was formalized in the early twentieth century when, alongside many other cultural, political, social, and scientific reforms, spoken Mandarin and a written version of it became official standards, ending the long reign of Classical Chinese.[5]

The superficial mechanics of Chinese writing also changed in the twentieth century. Historically, Chinese was written in top-to-bottom columns read from right to left. While modern Chinese texts can still be written and read this way, it is now more common for the language to be written in left-to-right horizontal lines. (Printed newspapers sometimes take advantage of this variability to write some headlines and articles vertically and others horizontally, in order to suit the layout needs of each page.) Written Chinese also uses modern punctuation similar to that found in written European languages.[6] But there are no orthographic spaces between individual characters or between groups of characters that write multisyllabic words; readers must determine word boundaries based on context and their knowledge of the language. See the passage from *The Chess Master* for an example (page 60).

Today, Cantonese is the most widely developed and used written Chinese language after Mandarin. This is in part due to the cultural and economic strength of Hong Kong—as well as its political independence from mainland China—during the nineteenth and twentieth centuries.

What does the existence of a separate Cantonese writing system, distinct from today's Mandarin-based Standard Written Chinese, tell us about the relationship between Chinese spoken and written languages? The oft-cited contention that the "Chinese dialects" are all spoken differently but written the same implies that although a Mandarin speaker and a Cantonese speaker would not be able to converse, they could nevertheless communicate easily with each other in writing. The existence of a distinct written Cantonese shows that things are not quite so straightforward.

It's not hard to see how this view came about. In Matteo Ricci's time, anyone in China who had received enough education to be literate would have learned to read and write Classical Chinese, which meant learning the vocabulary and grammar rules, in addition to the shapes of the Chinese characters used to write those vocabulary words. Take a look again at the spoken Cantonese and Mandarin sentences meaning 'The king got ten birds in one day':

Mandarin sentence in romanization:
Guówáng yī tiān dédào shí zhī niǎo.

Cantonese sentence in romanization:
Go³ gwok³wong⁴ jat¹ jat⁶ noi⁶ zuk¹ dou² sap⁶ zek³ zoek³zai².

They have the same meaning but differ in vocabulary, grammar, and pronunciation. A Cantonese and Mandarin speaker could no more easily have a conversation than an English speaker and a German speaker. But before the twentieth century, the educated Cantonese speaker could translate what they wanted to say into written Classical Chinese: 王一日而獲十禽. Since both of them would have learned this written language through many years of schooling, the Mandarin speaker could read and understand it.

But this ability to communicate through writing doesn't imply that Mandarin and Cantonese are both "written the same." It means that both the Mandarin and Cantonese speaker have learned to read and write *a third language* that they can use to communicate with each other. This is analogous to a medieval English and German speaker communicating with each other in written Latin, a third language that they had both learned.

Today, in the twentieth century, the situation in China has changed. All college-educated literate Chinese speakers learn to read and write Standard Written Chinese, which is based on Mandarin vocabulary and grammar.

Cantonese speakers learn this written language in school, just as Mandarin speakers do. So once again, they share a common written language. But this is not because written Cantonese is the same as written Mandarin. It is because through many years of schooling, Cantonese speakers have learned the vocabulary, grammar, and individual Chinese characters needed to write Mandarin words and sentences.

Written Cantonese is quite a different thing. It is a written representation of spoken Cantonese, reflecting Cantonese vocabulary and grammar. And it uses many characters that are not part of mainstream written Chinese, because the character set of the standard writing system is inadequate for representing many of the words of spoken Cantonese. These "Cantonese characters" are not used in Classical Chinese or modern Standard Written Chinese. Generally speaking, Mandarin speakers will not recognize these characters or be able to guess the meaning of the words they write. Even when Mandarin speakers recognize familiar characters in Cantonese writing, they cannot fully understand written Cantonese, because they have not learned its vocabulary and grammatical structures.

Here is how the two Mandarin and Cantonese sentences meaning 'The king got ten birds in one day' given above in romanized form are written in Chinese characters.

Mandarin sentence in romanization:
  Guówáng yī tiān dédào shí zhī niǎo.

Mandarin sentence in characters:
  國王一天得到十隻鳥。

Cantonese sentence in romanization:
  Go³ gwok³wong⁴ jat¹ jat⁶ noi⁶ zuk¹ dou² sap⁶ zek³ zoek³zai².

Cantonese sentence in characters:
  個國王一日內捉到十隻雀仔。

In Hong Kong, Standard Written Chinese is used for formal writing: newspaper articles, scholarly essays, government documents, and so on. These texts can be read and understood by any educated literate Chinese speaker,

FIGURE 3.1. A panel from the cartoon *McDull* in written Cantonese. Tse and Mak, *Mak⁶Dau¹ Sampler hou²siu³ bou⁶wai⁶*. Courtesy of Bliss Concepts Limited.

regardless of what variety of Chinese they speak. Written Cantonese is used for casual, informal writing, or to represent spoken dialogue: advertisements, comics, television drama scripts, and so on. It is this writing that cannot be fully understood by non-Cantonese speakers, because they lack knowledge of Cantonese vocabulary and grammar, not to mention the specialized characters used to write some of that vocabulary.

For example, consider this panel from a popular Hong Kong comic, about two little pigs named McDull and McMug (figure 3.1). They converse in Cantonese. The written Cantonese contains many Chinese characters that either are not found in the standard script, or have a very different usage and meaning than in Standard Written Chinese.

Among the characters in this cartoon panel that are not part of the standard script, or are used in different ways, are 啲, 嘅, 喺, 度, 吓, 唔, 嗰, 乜, 咁, 點, 㗎, and 俾.[7] Mandarin speakers who have never studied spoken or written Cantonese would not be able to read and understand this cartoon with precision, although they might be able to get the general gist based on the other characters that they do recognize.

Today Classical Chinese is unequivocally a dead language. It is still studied and read by scholars, and students are still exposed to it in school, but there is no significant community of ordinary people who use it as a written form of communication in their daily lives.

But the deadness of this dead language was not so unequivocal prior to the 1920s. For two thousand years, educated Chinese speakers used Classical Chinese to read and write. Although the language wasn't spoken for daily communication, for these literate Chinese speakers, it was a part of everyday life. For example, friends wrote letters to each other in Classical Chinese. This was not considered challenging or difficult but entirely ordinary, in much the same way that the educated elites of medieval Europe communicated effortlessly with each other in written Latin.

So while Classical Chinese was dead in the sense that the spoken language it was based on had stopped existing in that form in the late first millennium BCE, it was very much alive in that its written form was woven through the fabric of ordinary life. It is the language of the bulk of the literary tradition of China, the language in which the great cultural inheritance in philosophy, religion, statecraft, medicine, and many other areas of thought and inquiry was expressed and consumed.

Classical Chinese served this unifying role of cultural communication not only for speakers of the various languages referred to as the Chinese "dialects" but also for large groups of people speaking very different non-Chinese languages, in areas well outside of what we consider to be China proper. It is an important part of the story of how Chinese characters spread beyond China, and of how they eventually were transformed into ways of writing those other languages.

Classical Chinese Texts in East Asia

The cultural influence of China on neighboring peoples and polities has been enormous. Influence of course flowed in both directions: China's cultures, languages, and peoples were immensely influenced by their neighbors and by the peoples they conquered and/or assimilated. But because China was the first place where writing was invented in East Asia, because it became so large and so powerful both culturally and militarily, and because it was the main conduit for religions imported from western regions (notably Buddhism), its influence on places like Korea, Japan, and Vietnam was extensive, dramatic, and long-lasting.[8] And in areas that fell under direct Chinese political control as imperial power grew from its central stronghold in North China and extended east, west, and south, that influence was even stronger.

The Hàn dynasty (202 BCE–220 CE) was the first great, long-lasting imperial dynasty in Chinese history, and it left an indelible mark on almost every aspect of Chinese civilization down to the present day. Thanks to the military might of its vast armies and the expansionist aims of its emperors, the territory it brought under direct Chinese control expanded enormously, extending into part of present-day Korea in the east, Vietnam in the south, and Central Asia in the west. The Hàn inherited and refined from its short-lived predecessor, the Qín dynasty (221–206 BCE), a model of centralized administrative control that included the establishment of a sizable government bureaucracy and the standardization of many aspects of public life. It was also characterized by a flourishing of intellectual activity. The foundational nature of the Hàn can be seen in the fact that its name has become synonymous with Chinese identity: the ethnic group, the Chinese languages, and the Chinese script are all referred to as Hàn in Chinese today. (Indeed, the Japanese word *kanji* means literally 'Hàn characters'. The first syllable, *kan*, has the same source as the Chinese syllable *hàn*.)

Chinese writing was the vehicle by which Chinese cultural practices and ideas spread into the Korean Peninsula, the Japanese archipelago, and parts of Southeast Asia. As far as we can determine from the archeological and historical record, for well over a thousand years after its invention, Chinese was the only script known or used in East Asia, and Chinese writing was the only written language. Writing had of course already been invented thousands of years earlier in Egypt and Mesopotamia. By the time of the Hàn dynasty, the Latin alphabet was also already in widespread use in Europe in a form quite recognizable to us today, and Buddhist texts written in various Indic scripts and languages began penetrating into the western reaches of the Chinese Empire. But in these early centuries CE, no indigenous languages of the areas of modern-day Korea, Japan, or Vietnam could be written. The ancestors of today's Korean, Japanese, and Vietnamese languages had a purely oral existence.

Try to imagine what it must have been like the first time people living in a completely nonliterate society saw writing in use. For the peoples of northern Korea and northern Vietnam, who first fell under Chinese rule during the Hàn dynasty around two thousand years ago, Chinese writing must have seemed a very powerful art indeed. Remember, these peoples not only had no written language, it is highly likely that they had never been exposed to the idea of writing or the possibility of its existence. What would it be like to observe people making complex markings, and then later relying on those same markings to vocalize long and detailed utterances? The value of such a communication tool for administrative and military organization, its transformative capabilities for society, would have seemed immeasurably vast.

From our perspective today, it is very difficult to imagine such an encounter. We live in a world thoroughly permeated by writing, in which a variety of written languages proliferate. You might well think that the first response of non-Chinese speakers upon grasping how Chinese speakers were using writing would be to say, "I want to do that for my language too." But this kind of response presumes an understanding of the mechanics of writing and a recognition that different languages can be written down. Without that, just seeing it in use — someone speaks; a scribe makes marks; days, months, or even years later, another scribe looks at the marks and says aloud exactly what the first speaker had said — would not provide any helpful clues about how to create a new writing system.

Instead, non-Chinese speakers learned to read and write by learning Chinese. In a world in which only one language existed in written form, there could be no conceptual difference between "learning to read" and "learning to read Chinese."

How did this play out in practice? The armies of the powerful Hàn dynasty conquered areas of what is now northern Korea in 108 BCE, and subsequently established a military outpost to govern the region. Given the relatively small numbers of Chinese speakers compared to the local population of Koreans, the Chinese commanders had to enlist or coerce the help of locals for administration and communication with the populace.[9] And because written Chinese was an essential part of the administrative apparatus of the empire, Chinese leaders had to train a group of local scribes to read and write in Chinese.

That meant teaching the characters of the script, their pronunciations and meanings, and also the vocabulary and grammar rules of the written language. In other words, Korean scribes had to learn a foreign language: written Chinese.

Whenever a scribe had to write down information conveyed orally in Korean, he would have to first mentally translate it from the spoken Korean utterance into Chinese, and then record the Chinese sentences using Chinese characters. Conveying written information to local people involved the opposite process: reading Chinese one sentence at a time, mentally translating it into Korean, and then speaking it aloud.

The techniques that were used by locals to learn and memorize Chinese characters, and to mediate between their spoken languages and written forms of Chinese when writing and reading, would eventually prove essential to the development of ways to write down their own languages instead of writing in Chinese.

Even after ways of writing local languages were invented and refined, the pattern laid down by the early cultural and political role of Chinese writing persisted. Written Chinese remained the primary written language of administration, record-keeping, and intellectual and diplomatic discourse well outside of areas of direct Chinese control. Indeed, in what is modern-day Korea and Japan, Chinese writing persisted in widespread use over centuries despite the near total lack of Chinese speakers. Written Chinese was taught, learned, and used across generations of people who could not speak Chinese.

This form of writing would not necessarily have been conceptualized as a foreign language. It was simply the language of writing, and its use in so many parts of the known world must have made it seem like an inevitable and unquestioned facet of literate life. You read and wrote in Classical Chinese because that's what everybody did, from Japan to Korea to northern China to southern China to the Southeast Asian peninsula. It functioned, as Ricci observed, as a kind of universal writing.

And it wasn't just that Chinese writing was convenient because it was widespread: it was the medium by which important and culturally valued ideas were disseminated. To be literate in Classical Chinese meant you had access to centuries of accumulated wisdom and information: Confucian philosophy, manuals on war and government administration, medical and agricultural treatises, religious doctrines, and more.

Learning to read and write Classical Chinese may have been commonplace for educated elites, but it wasn't easy. Even in China proper, it took many years of formal schooling to master it, because it was so different from spoken Chinese. The divergence between written and spoken language was of course much greater outside of China, in places where the spoken vernaculars never had any historical connection to spoken forms of Chinese.

But despite the difficulty of acquiring literacy in Chinese, more and more people did. Educational systems arose, mostly taken advantage of by elites who had the time and money to devote to study and training. In Korea and Vietnam, and to a somewhat lesser extent in Japan, Classical Chinese remained a deeply embedded official form of writing until a powerful wave of national political reform swept over East Asia in the early twentieth century.

Although in some respects the use of Classical Chinese as a "universal" written language in East Asia paralleled the use of Classical Latin as a "universal" written language in Europe, there were key differences. Medieval speakers of different European languages could also converse with each other in spoken Latin. They had learned the vocabulary and grammar of Latin through acquisition of literacy. In addition, through oral recitation of Latin texts, they had acquired a common set of pronunciations anchored by the sound values of the letters of the Latin alphabet.

But Classical Chinese had no fixed pronunciation, so the way the characters were read aloud changed and diverged within different parts of China. The pronunciations of Chinese characters learned in Korea, Japan, and Vietnam in imitation of Chinese models were re-formed by local accents, and then diverged still further from Chinese pronunciations as they were passed down through the generations. Because the script was morphographic and not alphabetic, sound values of individual letters could play no role in keeping pronunciations from drifting very far apart from each other in different regions. This is how the Old Chinese pronunciation for 'ten', "gip," ended up being pronounced so differently in modern Chinese languages and in modern

Korean, Japanese, and Vietnamese, even though it was always written with the same character: 十.

Old Chinese: "gip"

Mandarin: "shí"

Cantonese: "sap^6"

Vietnamese: "thập"

Korean: "sip"

Japanese: "jū"

Because of this variation in the pronunciation associated with each Chinese character, literate users of Classical Chinese across East Asia would not have been able to communicate orally, even if they had been in the habit of learning to speak this language that they could read and write. The same vocabulary words uttered in the same grammatical order by a Korean speaker would not be comprehensible to a Vietnamese speaker. So, unlike Latin, Classical Chinese remained a purely written form of communication.

Comparison of different pronunciations of the same Classical Chinese sentence illustrates the great disparity among the modern systems of character pronunciation.

Meaning:	'The king got ten birds in one day'.
Classical Chinese written form:	王一日而獲十禽。
Cantonese pronunciation:	"wong^4 jat^1 jat^6 ji^4 wok^6 sap^6 kam^4"
Mandarin pronunciation:	"wáng yī rì ér huò shí qín"
Vietnamese pronunciation:	"vương nhất nhật nhi hoạch thập cầm"
Korean pronunciation:	"wang il il i hoek sip geum"
Japanese pronunciation:	"ō ichi nichi ni waku jū gon"[10]

All of the examples above, even those from modern Korean, Vietnamese, and Japanese, are "Chinese pronunciations" in that, as different as they sound,

TABLE 3.1 Words for numbers in Latin and three modern Romance languages

Latin	*trēs* 'three'	*sex* 'six'	*octō* 'eight'	*decem* 'ten'
French	*trois*	*six*	*huit*	*dix*
Italian	*tre*	*sei*	*otto*	*dieci*
Spanish	*tres*	*seis*	*ocho*	*diez*

they all derive historically from the same ancient Chinese pronunciations that spread across space and transformed over time, just as the pronunciations in modern Romance languages have diverged from Latin (table 3.1).

But while these pronunciation differences are reflected in the development of distinct spellings in the corresponding written words, in the case of Classical Chinese the written forms of the characters have remained unchanged, disguising the vast gulf in pronunciation across the reading traditions.

FOUR

Sound and Meaning
Adapting Characters to Write
Other Languages

As every student of Chinese as a foreign language quickly learns, Chinese characters have both sound and meaning. When I was a college student beginning my study of Mandarin, I had to learn a lot of characters. The list of new vocabulary for each lesson in our textbook included the word's pronunciation in Pinyin, its meaning in English, and the character or characters used to write the word. (Just about everything related to language study was on paper in those days: paper textbooks, paper dictionaries, paper notebooks.) Each character appeared to me to be nothing more than an arbitrary and dense collection of pen strokes bristling with sharp angles and conveying vaguely pictorial impressions. How would I manage to learn how to read and write these characters, and correctly remember which spoken vocabulary words they were connected to?

I copied all the vocabulary information onto flash cards. In the era before smartphones and tablets, the easiest way to study on the go was to carry around a pile of paper flashcards. (I liked to make them from three-by-five-inch index cards, cut in half to roughly a square). I bundled them with a rubber band, or punched a hole in one corner and put them on a big key ring. Then when I had a free moment waiting for the bus or sitting with a cup of coffee, I could pull the cards out of my backpack and study.

On one side of each card, I copied out a Chinese character. On the other side, I wrote its pronunciation and meaning (figure 4.1). To test my recognition of characters, I'd look at the first side, try to say the pronunciation and meaning aloud, then flip the card over to check my accuracy. To develop my writing ability, I'd start with the pronunciation and meaning, write the character on scrap paper, and then flip over the card to verify that I'd written it correctly.

It's an old technology, but it's simple and effective. Little did I imagine that

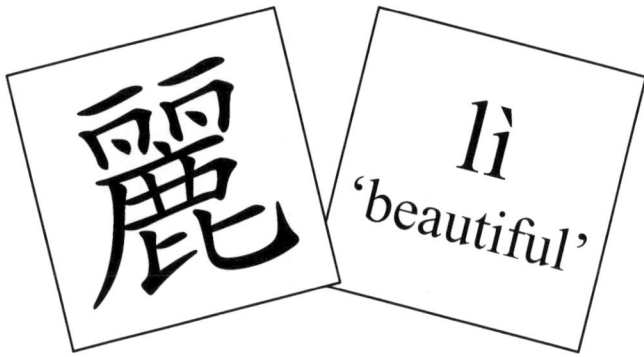

FIGURE 4.1. The two sides of a flash card for the Chinese character 麗 (*lì* 'beautiful').

the way I was associating each character with a pronunciation and an English meaning in the 1980s was a recapitulation of the very same techniques that had been used for centuries, even millennia, by second-language learners of written Chinese. And that those sound and meaning "tags" (notations like *lì* and 'beautiful') that I applied to each character were the very same building blocks on which entire writing systems were built in Japan, Korea, and Vietnam.

Could such associations also conceivably be a foundation for creating a new writing system for English, using Chinese characters?

English Written in Chinese Characters

Could English be written with Chinese characters? Stated more precisely: Could English utterances be represented directly in written form using the Chinese character script instead of the Latin alphabet? The test of whether this kind of true writing had been achieved would be that an English speaker could look at a sequence of Chinese characters and read it aloud as exactly the same sequence of spoken English words. But because this would be a written form of English, Chinese speakers who had not learned English would be unable to read and understand the writing, even though the individual Chinese characters would be familiar to them.

To think about this question accurately, we must be careful to distinguish script from spoken language. In modern life, we often encounter and interact with other languages in their written form, so it is natural for us to conflate script and language. Our perception is: Greek is written in the Greek alphabet, Russian in the Russian alphabet, Chinese with Chinese characters, Arabic in the Arabic script, Hebrew in the Hebrew script, and so on. But historical developments and current practice around the world show that scripts are *not* fixed to languages. Some languages have been written in completely different scripts at different points in time. A single script can be borrowed and modified to write many different languages. The connection between script and spoken language that appears so tightly bound is in fact easily broken.

We often think of the script used to write English as "the English alphabet." But in fact, this alphabet, descended from the one used to write Latin over two thousand years ago, is now widely used in slightly different forms to write languages all over the world: English, Spanish, Polish, Indonesian, and Swahili, to name just a few out of hundreds.

And while some scripts are used only for a single language, this is actually a rarity. Most scripts have spread and are used to write more than one language. The Arabic script is used to write Persian and Urdu, among others. The Cyrillic script is used to write Ukrainian, Bulgarian, Chechen, and Dungan, among others. Examples like this abound. So it shouldn't come as a surprise that Chinese characters have been used to write languages other than Chinese.

During the twentieth century, the Uyghur language (today spoken primarily in northwestern China) has been written in many different scripts. An excerpt from Abdurehim Ötkür's novel *Iz* (Trace) is transcribed below to illustrate four of the scripts, three of which are still in regular use.[1] Although visually quite different, the passage is linguistically identical in each script, meaning that it is the same sequence of Uyghur words and will sound the same when read aloud.

ARABIC-SCRIPT UYGHUR

ياش ئىدۇق ئۆزۈن سەپەركە ئاتلىنىپ ماڭغاندا بىز، ئەمدى ئاتقا
مىنگۈدەك بويىقالدى ئەنە نەۋرىمىز.
ئاز ئىدۇق مۇشكۈل سەپەرگە ئاتلىنىپ چىققاندا بىز، ئەمدى چوڭ كارۋان
ئاتالدۇق، قالدۇرۇپ چۆللەردە ئىز.

CYRILLIC-ALPHABET UYGHUR

Яш идуқ узун сәпәргә атлинип маңғанда биз, әмди атқа мингүдәк
бопқалди әнә нәвримиз.

Аз идуқ мүшкүл сәпәргә атлинип чиққанда биз, әмди чоң карван
аталдуқ, қалдуруп чөлләрдә из.

CYRILLIC-INFLUENCED LATIN-ALPHABET UYGHUR

Yax iduқ uzun səpərgə atlinip mangoɹanda biz, əmdi atқa mingüdək
bopқaldi ənə nəwrimiz.

Az iduқ müxkül səpərgə atlinip qiққanda biz, əmdi qong karwan
atalduқ, қaldurup qөllərdə iz.

LATIN-ALPHABET UYGHUR

Yash iduq uzun seperge atlinip mangghanda biz, emdi atqa mingüdek
bopqaldi ene newrimiz.

Az iduq müshkül seperge atlinip chiqqanda biz, emdi chong karwan
atalduq, qaldurup chöllerde iz.

TRANSLATION:

We were young when we rode off on the long journey. Now, look: it
seems our grandchildren are old enough to ride horses. We were few
when we rode off on the hard journey. Now we are known as a great
caravan. We left our tracks in the desert.[2]

(I called both Latin and Cyrillic "alphabets" but labeled the first passage "Arabic script" instead of "Arabic alphabet," because the Arabic script
(and also the Hebrew script) is not quite alphabetic: it has letters only for
consonants, not vowels. The vowel sounds are supplied by the reader, who
recognizes the words from the consonants and from context. It would be a
bit like if Nglsh ws wrttn ths wy wtht vwl lttrs. The technical terms for this
kind of script are **abjad** and **consonantary**.)

If we wished to write English in Chinese characters, there are a number
of approaches we might take. One is the arbitrary approach: Assemble a list

of English morphemes, assemble a list of Chinese characters, and randomly assign one character to each morpheme. Sadly, the result would be a morphographic script that would be impossible to learn and to use. Nobody would be able to memorize all the written forms and which morphemes they represent. At best, it could serve as a kind of code or encryption scheme. The only way to write and read it would be to use a look-up tool to convert each English morpheme to its corresponding Chinese character (for writing) and vice versa (for reading). That might be a great writing system for covert communication by spies, but it is far too impractical for everyday uses of written language.

A different, more practical approach would be sound-based. We could create an equivalent of the Latin alphabet by assigning a sound value to each of a small set of Chinese characters. For example, table 4.1 lists some Chinese characters we have encountered in earlier chapters, with some sound values I've assigned to them, ones that English speakers who know how to read modern Standard Written Chinese might choose, based on the characters' Mandarin pronunciations. Note that this method completely ignores the meanings that the characters have when writing Chinese. Since only a few dozen characters and sounds are needed, instead of thousands, it wouldn't take long for any English speaker to learn the script, even if they don't know Mandarin. It just requires a bit of memorization.

Now consider the sequence of three Chinese characters <十人堂>. You can sound out the new values I've assigned to them and discover that they are writing the word *shirt*. We could add <四> at the end to write *shirts*.

TABLE 4.1 Four Chinese characters and their sound values for writing English

CHARACTER	CHINESE MORPHEME	NEW SOUND VALUE FOR WRITING ENGLISH
十	{"shí," 'ten'}	sh
人	{"rén," 'person'}	r
堂	{"táng," 'hall'}	t
四	{"sì," 'four'}	s

TABLE 4.2 Four Chinese characters and their morphographic values for writing English

CHARACTER	CHINESE MORPHEME	NEW MORPHOGRAPHIC VALUE FOR WRITING ENGLISH
十	{"shí," 'ten'}	ten
人	{"rén," 'person'}	person
堂	{"táng," 'hall'}	hall
四	{"sì," 'four'}	four

What we have done here—in mere minutes—is modify a subset of Chinese characters into an alphabet.[3]

A different approach we might take is to consider the meanings of the Chinese morphemes that the characters represent, and use the characters to write English words that have the same meaning (table 4.2). In this way, I could represent the underlined words in the spoken sentence "There are <u>ten</u> <u>people</u> in the <u>hall</u>" with the characters <十>, <人>, and <堂> respectively.

In the first approach, we ignored the Chinese meanings of the characters, and used them just for their sound values. In the second, we ignored the Chinese pronunciations of the characters, and used them just for their meaning values. The second approach looks workable for English speakers who are fully literate in Chinese and know the meanings of thousands of characters. But as you dig into the details of how to implement it fully, significant challenges emerge. For example, Chinese lacks a distinction between singular and plural nouns. The Chinese word *rén* can be translated as 'person' or 'people' depending on context. How do we clarify when <人> writes *person* and when it writes *people*? How can we write grammatical words like *the* that have no equivalent in spoken Mandarin, and therefore for which no character exists that is suitable?[4] And what about other English words that have no precise meaning equivalent in Mandarin, like *mauve*? How should we distinctly write two words in English that both translate to the same word in Mandarin, like *rock* and *stone*—we can't use 石 {"shí," 'rock, stone'} to write both, because it will be impossible to know from context which English word the writer intended.

In addition to the alphabetic and morphographic methods just described, a third approach could be syllable-based. Nearly all Chinese characters write a single syllable. So we could try to turn the characters into a syllabary for English based on their Mandarin sound values. For example, we could use 堂 {"táng," 'hall'} to write *tongue*, which sounds quite close to the pronunciation of Mandarin *táng*.

Still another possibility is to combine the meaning-based and sound-based methods, so that English words that are hard to write with one method could instead be written with the other. A word like *tongue* would in theory have two possible written forms: 堂 {"táng," 'hall'} based on sound or 舌 {"shé," 'tongue'} based on meaning.

Maybe this is all getting too complicated. Perhaps it seems pointless, or simply too unwieldy to be practical. But there is a reason we are exploring it. We will soon see that all of these made-up approaches to writing English have at some point in the past been employed to write non-Chinese languages using Chinese characters. The motivation was much stronger than it is in our little thought experiment about English, because the speakers of those languages had no other writing systems available to them. They could either figure out how to adapt Chinese characters, directly or indirectly, to represent the sounds and morphemes of their spoken languages, or resign themselves to reading and writing only in Classical Chinese.

These methods of repurposing Chinese characters profoundly influenced the development of writing in Korea, Japan, Vietnam, and other locations in and near the territory of modern-day China.

Script Adaptation and Script Types

When a new script is invented from scratch for a language, it can be tailored to represent that language in a precise and rational way.[5] But this is not the way most writing systems come into existence. The vast majority of those that have been used, and of those that are in use today, were adapted. A script already in use to write one language was borrowed and modified to represent another language. When this happens, the script's fit to the new spoken language is usually imperfect despite the modifications, but native speakers are very good at working around imprecision and turning imperfect scripts into functional writing systems.

Consider the Latin alphabet. It works quite well for Latin. But English has more consonant sounds and more vowel sounds than Latin. Spoken Latin had five vowel sounds, represented by the five letters <A>, <E>, <I>, <O>, <U>. Spoken English has . . . well, more than ten; the exact number depends on your dialect of English. In the variety of English that I speak, there are fourteen distinct vowel sounds. They are illustrated by the following one-syllable words:

> *heat, hit, hate, head, hat, hoot, hood, hoed, hawed, hot, hut, hoist, height, how'd*

In my speech, no two of these words have the same vowel sound between the [h] sound at the beginning and the [t], [d], or [st] sound at the end. (Your mileage may vary depending on your dialect. For example, you might pronounce *hawed* and *hot* with the same vowel sound).

How do English speakers manage to represent a dozen or more vowel sounds with just five letters of the Latin alphabet? One way is by using different combinations of vowel letters, as you can see in the spellings of these words. But even so, some ambiguity is inevitable. The combination <ea> represents two different sounds in *heat* and *head*, and <oo> represents two different sounds in *hoot* and *hood*. Fortunately, native speakers can almost always use their knowledge and intuition to figure out which spoken words were intended by the person who wrote them down. That's why written words like *windy* and *lead* don't usually create problems for readers: "It was very *windy* along the *windy* path to the beach." "Growing food plants in soil adjacent to an old house can *lead* to *lead* poisoning."

Spoken Latin lacked several consonant sounds that occur in spoken English, among them the "ch," "sh," "th," and "ng" sounds. To represent each of these sounds in English, two Latin letters were combined. But this wasn't enough to eliminate all ambiguity. There are two different consonant sounds in English that are both written with <th>. Compare the pronunciations of *thigh* and *thy*, or of *teeth* and *teethe*, and you will hear the difference. The sound at the beginning of *thigh* and end of *teeth* is the same as that in *think*, *throw*, and *Thor*. The sound at the beginning of *thy* and end of *teethe* is the same as in *this*, *then*, and *the*. Both sounds are represented by one spelling.

The long history of script borrowing is full of adjustments, compromises, and imprecisions like this. Combining letters in new ways, adding or modifying letters, and adjusting the sound value of letters are three of the ways that adaptations can happen.

When the Latin script was adapted to write English, the script type didn't change. Latin writing was alphabetic, and after the script was adapted to write English, English writing was also alphabetic. The details of how the individual graphs of the script (letters) represent the individual elements of the spoken languages (consonant and vowel sounds) shifted, but the basic script type did not. Sometimes, however, borrowing of a script can lead to a more radical shift.

Consider the different ways we imagined adapting Chinese characters to write spoken English at the beginning of the chapter. The first resulted in an alphabet, where each Chinese character represents an individual sound, so that *shirts* is written as <十人堂四>. That would be a type shift from Chinese characters used as a morphographic script to their use as an alphabetic script. We also imagined an adaptation in which Chinese characters remained morphographic, representing specific morphemes of spoken English (such that *ten* would be written <十>), and another in which Chinese characters became syllabic, representing syllables (such that *tongue* would be written <堂>).

There is also the possibility of combining adaptation types, so that each English word or morpheme would be written with the method or combination of methods that best suits it. For example, the syllabic graph <堂> (representing the syllable sound of *tongue*) could be combined with the alphabetic graph <四> (representing the sound [s]) so that <四堂> together would write the English word *stung* and <堂四> would write the English word *tongues*.

Remember, the visual form of a graph does not determine its usage. Depending on the particular writing system, a graph that looks identical in appearance might have an alphabetic, syllabic, or morphographic function. The shape I is an alphabetic letter in English writing, a morphographic character in Chinese writing (representing Mandarin {"gōng," 'work'}), a syllabic sign in Japanese writing (representing the syllable "e"), and a syllabic sign in Cherokee writing (representing the syllable "qua").

Semantic Adaptation vs. Phonetic Adaptation: Pros and Cons

It may seem that reducing a morphographic script to a simple alphabet or syllabary is the most natural way to adapt it into a practical writing system for a second spoken language. For many of us who grew up with alphabetically written languages like English or Spanish, it feels intuitively obvious that using about thirty letters to spell words according to their pronunciation is preferable to memorizing thousands of forbiddingly complex Chinese characters. But this intuition may not be correct. There are other considerations that provide a different perspective.

To return to our thought experiment, imagine again that you are part of an English-speaking community that has never experienced any written language other than Chinese. The ability to read and write means the ability to read and write *in Chinese*. For many societal needs involving written language, this doesn't create difficulties. If someone requires a written record of some important information, or wishes to send a written message to someone, they can hire a scribe, speak the message in English, and have the scribe translate it into written Chinese. When that Chinese text is read by another scribe later, they can translate it back into spoken English. The result won't be the same exact sequence of English words, but for many purposes, that doesn't matter, because the overall meaning will be accurately conveyed.

But there will be some situations in which an exact written record of a sequence of English spoken words is desirable, situations in which a translation just won't do. Preserving oral poetry is a good example. Poetry depends not on meaning alone but on sound, rhythm, rhyme, and other devices that are impossible to fully preserve in translation. The desire to record English poems and songs would be a strong motivation for adapting Chinese characters into a script that writes English words, and thereby create a precise written representation of the English language.

As we saw in the previous section, one way to do this would be to use Chinese characters to represent syllables or individual sounds of English. If you were an English-speaking scribe literate in written Chinese, you would have long ago memorized the pronunciations of thousands of Chinese characters. Based on those familiar pronunciations, you could convert morphographs writing Chinese morphemes into letters or **syllabographs** writing English consonants, vowels, or syllables.

But there are good reasons you might prefer not to do so—or at least not for every English word. The representation of English sounds as strings of Chinese characters would seem unnecessarily and annoyingly lengthy and tedious to someone used to reading and writing in Chinese. For example, suppose you want to write the English word *elephant*. You could approximate the pronunciation using four Chinese characters, based on their Mandarin pronunciations:

餓 {"è," 'hungry'}
樂 {"lè," 'joy'}
凡 {"fán," 'all'}
特 {"tè," 'special'}

These four characters in sequence, <餓樂凡特>, would be read aloud as "èlèfántè," close enough to get an English-speaking reader to figure out that the intended word is *elephant*. But puzzling out the pronunciation is time consuming. Writing out all four of those complex characters to represent a single word is a hassle. And—because you are already a fluent Chinese reader—as you read, the meanings 'hungry', 'joy', 'all', and 'special' will surface in your mind because of your familiarity with the characters, interfering with your processing of the intended meaning. (And that's for a syllabic usage. If you wanted to do it alphabetically, you'd need seven instead of four characters, one for each of the sounds in *elephant*.)

For all these reasons, you—a scribe who lives and breathes Chinese writing—would probably find it easier to write the word *elephant* with just a single familiar character: 象. When you were first learning Chinese characters as a child, you memorized this one by associating it with the English translation 'elephant'. So what could feel more natural than using the meaning value of the character to represent the equivalent English word?

While both <象> and <餓樂凡特> can be used to represent *elephant*, the former is simpler, easier, and more natural. It's true that, collectively, thousands of Chinese characters used as morphographs to represent English words is a more complicated script than a few dozen used to represent individual sounds or a few hundred used to represent individual syllables—but remember that, in this scenario, *you've already learned all of the characters*. You know them inside and out. You're not creating a new script for English; you are rather adapting a familiar script to write English. In such a scenario, <象> wins out over <餓樂凡特> hands down.

This works great for words like *elephant* that have clear translation equivalents between Chinese and English and for which it is obvious which Chinese character to match up with the English word. But there are plenty of words for which this kind of **semantic adaptation** won't work at all. For example, some words in English are culturally specific and don't have an equivalent in Chinese, like *toast* or *raccoon*. Even more challenging are grammatical words in English that have no equivalent in Chinese. There is nothing like English *the* or plural *-s* in Chinese. In fact, Chinese has no singular and plural forms of nouns: The Mandarin word *xiàng* can refer to one elephant or many, equivalent to both *elephant* and *elephants* in English. And it can refer to an unspecified elephant or a specific elephant: *an elephant, the elephant* (or the plurals *elephants, the elephants*).

If we are limited to semantic adaptation, we would have to write all four of these English expressions (*an elephant, the elephant, elephants, the elephants*) with <象> and trust that readers will supply the correct word or sequence of words based on context and their native-speaker knowledge. But if we want or need more precision, **phonetic adaptation** might be the only option available for the English morphemes that don't translate easily to or from Chinese.

These were the kinds of choices and conundrums facing speakers of Korean, Japanese, and Vietnamese in ancient times. We have no direct evidence that these issues were grappled with in a conscious, deliberate way. But that wouldn't have been necessary. Intuition, combined with trial and error, would be enough for all these peoples to arrive at a workable combination of semantic and phonetic adaptation of Chinese characters to write their languages.

How might such a combination work? We could write *elephants* as <象 四>, a sequence of a semantic adaptation for *elephant* and a phonetic adaptation for plural *-s*. This mixture of methods may seem complicated, but it's actually a natural and sensible development given the starting conditions handed to us by history.

Sound and Meaning

Here is the key concept that will take us into the next two chapters: Phonetic and semantic adaptations are the two basic methods of adaptation of morphographic scripts like Chinese characters. A special kind of bilingualism developed in East Asia with the spread of Classical Chinese as a written language. Scribes in places like Vietnam, Korea, and Japan were native speakers of their local language. They also had command of written Chinese. The degree to which they could speak and understand any kind of spoken Chinese isn't clear, but it would not be necessary for a scribe to have such an ability. Instead, they had a command of the pronunciation of Chinese characters: the ability to recite a written text aloud, perhaps with a strong local accent, using the character readings taught to them by their own (also non-Chinese) teachers.

For these speakers, Chinese characters had a *sound* (the Chinese-based pronunciation used to read them aloud) and a *meaning* (expressed as a translated word in their native language). The sounds were a basis for phonetic adaptation; the meanings were a basis for semantic adaptation. These types of adaptation are made possible by two natural human abilities: the ability to translate words from one language to another, and the ability to apply the rebus principle. We've already seen that a purely semantic adaptation of a morphographic script for one language into a fully morphographic script for another language is probably impossible. English could not be written entirely by using Chinese characters for their meaning values, because there are so many morphemes in English that have no meaning equivalent in Chinese. In contrast, a purely phonetic adaptation of a morphographic script into an alphabetic or syllabic script is possible. But for various reasons—linguistic, sociological, cultural—the most successful adaptations of Chinese characters in East Asia combined both methods. While the details varied from place to place and language to language, the broad patterns were strikingly similar, reflecting the natural tendencies of humans to interact with morphographic scripts in certain ways.

Now that we have laid the groundwork to understand these processes, it is time to turn our attention in detail to how it happened for four languages.

Three of them are probably familiar to you, at least in name, while one may not be: Japanese, Korean, Vietnamese, and Zhuang.

Today, Chinese characters are no longer used to write Vietnamese. They are used only marginally in South Korean writing (and not at all in North Korea), and may soon disappear entirely from the Korean writing system. In Zhuang, they are still used by a trained minority of the population in certain ritualized cultural contexts. Only for Japanese, as *kanji*, do they remain firmly embedded in the modern writing system.

But Chinese characters were once the only way that existed to write all four languages. Indeed, it is not hard to imagine some plausible alternative historical events that would have resulted in Chinese-character-based scripts being the norm today for all four. Nor is it difficult to imagine the opposite scenario, in which they would have been abandoned entirely, even in Japanese and Chinese writing. In the next few chapters we will see how semantic adaptation, phonetic adaptation, and disambiguation played out in the development of new writing systems out of Chinese characters, and the fate of those ancient systems as Vietnam, Korea, and Japan developed into modern nation-states in the early twentieth century.

FIVE

Linear Adaptation
Korean and Japanese

How did people living in what is today Korea and Japan first become exposed to Chinese writing? How did they learn Chinese characters, and how did they leverage that knowledge into inventing mechanisms for writing their own spoken languages, which were the ancient predecessors of modern Korean and modern Japanese? The concepts and insights presented in previous chapters will allow us to understand the historical developments behind the Chinese-character-based writing systems that arose to represent spoken Korean, Japanese, Vietnamese, and Zhuang.

Transmission of Chinese Writing to Korea and Japan

The spread of Chinese writing beyond the area inhabited by Chinese-speaking people is connected to the first great Chinese empire and its powerful, conquering armies. The state of Qín defeated all the other warring kingdoms of China in 221 BCE, establishing the first Chinese empire and unifying a vast geographic area under a single ruler. In fact, it is from the name of this empire that our word *China* ultimately derives. The Qín dynasty was short-lived, however, collapsing after just fifteen years. But the imperial dynasty that followed it, the Hàn, lasted four centuries and established China as a dominant, expansive world power. During the Hàn era, Chinese soldiers conquered vast amounts of territory and imposed imperial rule over many peoples speaking a multitude of languages. This established a pattern of imperial expansion that continued, in fits and starts, through later eras. It propelled Chinese people, culture, and language out across an enormous geographical area.

Chinese expansion and domination has continued into the modern era.

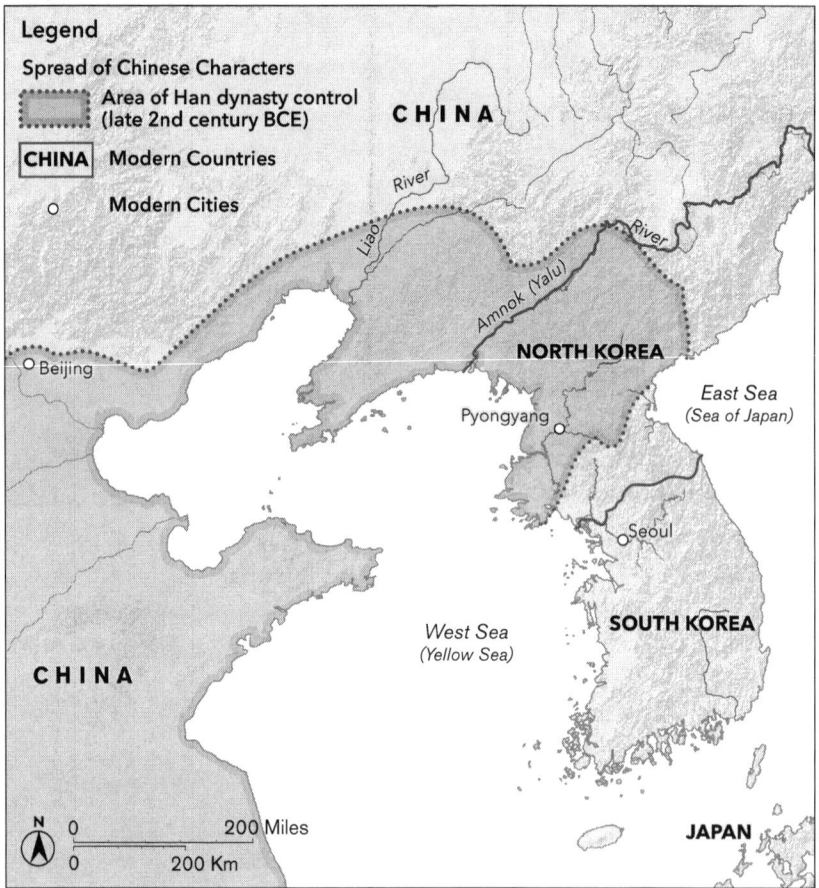

MAP 5.1 The Hàn empire's areas of control around the Korean Peninsula in the late second century BCE. Map by Ben Pease.

Today, forced and voluntary assimilation on the frontiers of the Chinese state continues, leading to the extermination of many languages and cultures as ever more ethnically non-Hàn peoples continue to be absorbed into the Chinese polity.[1]

Korea

The transmission of writing—by which we mean Chinese writing—into modern-day Korea began during the Hàn dynasty. In 108 BCE, Hàn troops conquered what is now the northern part of the Korean Peninsula, the area straddling the current border between North Korea and China (map 5.1). The Hàn established four military governorships to rule and administer the area. The largest of these was located near present-day Pyongyang, the North Korean capital. The military presence there lasted four centuries until the Goguryeo state, expanding from the south, finally wrested control from the Chinese in the early fourth century CE.

Chinese-speaking immigrants followed the Chinese-speaking soldiers. A bureaucracy was established to govern the area, which relied on written Chinese documents for political administration. Local inhabitants of non-Chinese ethnicity were recruited into the governing administration. Presumably, a fair number of these locals became bilingual, and could communicate orally with the Chinese speakers. Some of them would have served as translators. Still others would have learned to read and write Classical Chinese — already by this time notably different from the spoken Chinese language — and to serve as scribes in the administration.[2]

After Chinese control ended in the fourth century, the Chinese-speaking community seems to have disappeared, its members either migrating out to Chinese-controlled areas or assimilating into the local language and culture. The number of people speaking Chinese quickly dwindled away. But the written Classical Chinese language persisted. After all, it was the only kind of writing known, and it was essential to the apparatus of state administration. Goguryeo, the state that had reconquered the area, built an administrative system on the Chinese model. Local scribes used Classical Chinese to produce the written documents needed to support government administration. Knowledge and use of Chinese writing spread rapidly into the southern parts of the peninsula, beyond the areas under Goguryeo control. There must have been a sizable group of Koreans, literate in Classical Chinese, who acted as a conduit for Chinese cultural, religious, and political ideas that were transmitted in writing from China. By the end of the fourth century, Goguryeo had adopted Buddhism, established an academy to provide traditional Chinese-style education for government officials, and promulgated a law code.[3]

Goguryeo was one of three powerful states on the Korean Peninsula. The other two were called Baekje (in the southwest) and Silla (in the southeast). In the seventh century, Silla conquered both Goguryeo and Baekje, seizing control of the entire peninsula and establishing the kingdom called Unified Silla—the first Korean dynasty. The peninsula remained unified, under a succession of dynasties, until the middle of the twentieth century.

By the end of the eighth century, Classical Chinese as a written language was deeply embedded in the culture and society of Silla elites. It remained an essential part of elite Korean education until the early twentieth century. It is within this historical context that the Chinese script used to write Classical Chinese was adapted for writing spoken Korean.

Japan

Unlike in Korea, the initial transmission of Chinese writing to Japan took place in the absence of a Chinese-speaking community. Thanks to the protection offered by the water barrier between Japan and the mainland, the islands were never seriously threatened by Chinese imperial expansion.

Chinese writing reached Japan later than it reached Korea. It seems that the ability to read and write Classical Chinese was not present in Japan until about the fifth century. Accounts in two eighth-century Japanese histories describe the arrival of Korean scribes from Baekje around the beginning of the fifth century. These scribes were said to have taught the Japanese how to read and write. But it was not until two centuries later that literacy in Classical Chinese became widespread and deeply embedded in all aspects of Japanese society.[4] Beginning in the seventh century, we see the centralization of a bureaucratic state government; the production of legal codes, histories, and literary works; the circulation of Buddhist texts; and the formalized training of literate scribes and scholars. Individual Japanese began making trips to China to acquire language skills and bring back Chinese texts. As in Korea, the widespread use of Chinese writing and the existence of a sizable group of local people able to read and write Classical Chinese enabled the development of ways of writing the local language through adaptation of the Chinese script.

Reading Classical Chinese in Japan and Korea

The grammatical structures of both the Japanese and Korean languages are very different from Chinese. Systematic, intricate methods were devised to help readers smoothly transform written Classical Chinese texts into a styl-

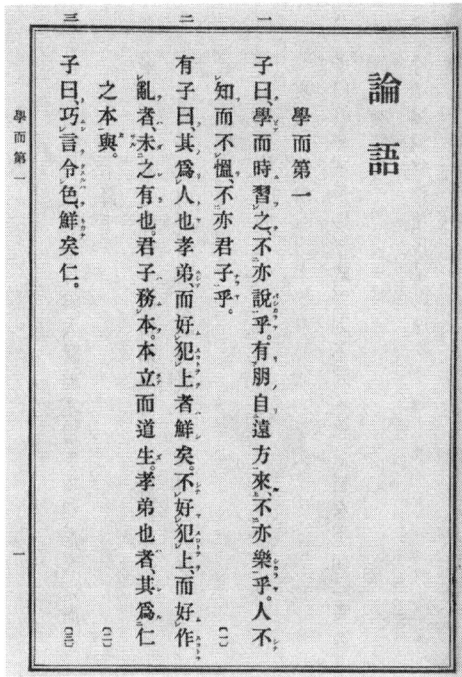

FIGURE 5.1 The first few lines of the *Analects* (Chinese: *Lunyu*, Japanese: *Rongo*) of Confucius, in Classical Chinese with Japanese *kanbun kundoku* markings. From Confucius, *Rongo*, 1. The small graphs to the right of the Chinese characters represent grammatical elements appended to the pronunciations of the characters, while the marks on the left indicate how to rearrange words and phrases to convert the Chinese word order into Japanese word order. (For an explanation of how this text would be read aloud in Japanese, see Kin, *Literary Sinitic and East Asia*, 8.)

ized version of the local spoken language. These methods involved making small marginal notations on a Classical Chinese text to guide the reader through the transformation (figure 5.1). (In Japan, this way of reading, called *kanbun kundoku*, is still taught today though no longer widely used.) Some marks specified how to reorder parts of the sentence, for example moving the main verb from its midsentence location in Chinese to the end of the sentence in Japanese or Korean. Other marks specified the grammatical bits that had to be added to the ends of nouns and verbs in order to translate the written Chinese text into spoken Japanese or Korean. These notations employed Chinese characters, sometimes in abbreviated form so that they would fit easily into the narrow marginal spaces between columns of Chinese characters. A small number of characters, adapted phonetically to represent consonants or syllables of Korean and Japanese, were sufficient to represent the pronunciation of the most common grammatical endings.

While these marked-up Classical Chinese texts are not written representations of spoken Korean and Japanese, the techniques that scribes developed for making and using these annotations would prove important for the development of true writing systems for the local spoken languages.

Structural Mismatch

As discussed earlier, phonetic adaptation, semantic adaptation, and disambiguation are the three key processes behind the borrowing of Chinese characters to write non-Chinese languages. They recur again and again throughout the history of the Chinese script. But the way these processes actually played out was not the same each time the script was borrowed. The differences seen in early Korean, Japanese, Vietnamese, and Zhuang writing practices are just as fascinating as the commonalities that link them.

One of the major factors that affect how scripts are changed as they are borrowed to write other spoken languages is **structural mismatch**. If the sound systems or the grammars of two languages are very different, it can present difficulties for the adaptation of the first language's script to the writing of the second. These incompatibilities between the script and the second language's structure steer the adaptation techniques in certain directions. For example, English has some sounds that do not occur in Chinese, such as "th," and English has some grammatical structures that have no equivalent in Chinese, such as the plural suffix -s and the article the. These mismatches would present challenges were we to adapt Chinese characters into a writing system for English. Structural mismatches like this are an important part of the story of how Chinese characters were adapted to write Korean and Japanese.

Speakers of different languages have been interacting with each other in East and Southeast Asia throughout recorded history. These interactions have caused significant changes in the languages, ranging from the borrowing of vocabulary words from one language to another, to the complete extinction of some languages. This kind of historical interaction is distinct from the kind of relationship that groups languages into what we call *language families*. Language families are made up of languages that descend from a single common ancestor. Modern Portuguese, Spanish, Italian, and French all descend from spoken Latin. Linguists say they belong to a single language family, called Romance. This terminology is analogous to a human family tree, in which people who are descended from a common ancestor are said to be in the same family.

As it happens, all five of the major languages discussed in this book belong to different language families. This is one reason that they are structurally different from each other. Just as the Romance languages descend from Latin, the Chinese languages descend from Old Chinese. Old Chinese in turn is part of a larger language family called Sino-Tibetan, which includes Tibetan and Burmese and has an even more ancient common ancestor. Vietnamese belongs to the Mon-Khmer family (which includes Khmer); Zhuang belongs to the Tai-Kadai family (which includes Thai and Lao); Japanese belongs to a small family called Japonic that includes Okinawan; Korean does not have any other family members.[5]

Spoken Chinese, Korean, and Japanese have changed in many ways over the last 1,500 years. The Chinese, Korean, and Japanese of those early times are called **Middle Chinese**, Old Korean, and Old Japanese, respectively.[6] But despite many changes in vocabulary and grammar and many shifts in pronunciation, a lot of the basic features of the languages have persisted over time. For example, Chinese then and now places the verb in the middle of the sentence, while Japanese and Korean then and now place it at the end. Because of these similarities, we can understand many of the features of those ancient languages using examples from modern ones.[7]

The features of today's Standard Chinese that were described in chapter 1 have also been true of spoken Chinese for most of the last two thousand years. As a reminder, these include the following:

- One-syllable morphemes
- No consonant clusters
- Invariance of word forms
- Tones
- Grammatical relations expressed through word order

The Structure of Spoken Korean and Japanese

Although their vocabulary and sound systems are quite different, Korean and Japanese share remarkably similar grammatical structures.[8]

Grammar and Vocabulary

Let's take a look at two sentences, one in modern Japanese and one in modern Korean, to illustrate their common grammatical features. These sentences are presented in the way that linguists use to show the grammatical structure of words, phrases, and sentences: Extra spacing is added between words so that there is room to align translations. Suffixes are separated by a hyphen <-> from the words they are attached to. A literal English translation is given word by word or morpheme by morpheme. Grammatical elements that don't have concrete meanings are explained with **abbreviations** that specify their function. Finally, a smooth English translation of the whole sentence is given.

JAPANESE:

Sachi-wa	*shinshitsu-de*	*ongaku-o*	*kii-te*
Sachi-TOP	bedroom-LOC	music-ACC	listen-and

musuko-to	*shinbun-o*	*yon-da*
son-COM	newspaper-ACC	read-PAST

'Sachi listened to music in the bedroom and then read a newspaper with her son.'

KOREAN:[9]

Jihye-neun	*chimsil-eseo*	*eumak-eul*	*deut-go*
Jihye-TOP	bedroom-LOC	music-ACC	listen-and

adeul-gwa	*sinmun-eul*	*ilk-eotda*
son-COM	newspaper-ACC	read-PAST

'Jihye listened to music in the bedroom and then read a newspaper with her son.'

Table 5.1 lists the meanings of the grammatical suffixes in these sentences.

In Korean and Japanese, the verb normally comes at the end of the sentence, with suffixes indicating tense and other grammatical features like politeness and intention. The various noun phrases come before the verb.

TABLE 5.1 Grammatical functions of Korean and Japanese particles and suffixes

TOP	topic	indicates what the sentence is about; 'as for'
LOC	locative	indicates the location where the action takes place; 'at; in'
ACC	accusative	indicates the direct object of the action
COM	comitative	indicates the person the action is performed with; 'with'
PAST	past tense	indicates the past tense of the verb

TABLE 5.2 Examples of Sino-Japanese and Sino-Korean vocabulary

	'bedroom'	'music'	'newspaper'
Middle Chinese[1]	*tsim sheet*	*im ngawk*	*seen myun*
Mandarin	*qǐn-shì*	*yīn-yuè*	*xīn-wén*
Japanese	*shin-shitsu*	*on-gaku*	*shin-bun*
Korean	*chim-sil*	*eum-ak*	*sin-mun*

1. The Middle Chinese pronunciations are given in an approximate form using English spelling conventions, to make them easier to compare with the modern languages. These Middle Chinese pronunciations are, roughly, the source of the Mandarin, Japanese, and Korean pronunciations through various transformations over time.

Appended to each noun phrase is a **case-marking particle** that indicates the role it is playing in relationship to the verb. In English (as in Chinese), these roles are instead indicated either through word order (subject before the verb, object after the verb) or with prepositions (*with, in, for, from, at*, etc.).

The Japanese and Korean sentences are remarkably similar in their structure. In this particular example, the word order and the function of the suffixes are identical. Although the grammatical structures are identical, many of the morphemes are completely different. For example, Japanese marks the direct object with *-o* and Korean marks it with *-eul*. The Japanese word for 'son' is *musuko*; the Korean word is *adeul*.

There is another similarity that may not be immediately obvious in these sentences, one that is related to vocabulary, not grammar. Several of the nouns in these sentences are words made up of borrowed Chinese morphemes. Although the pronunciations in Korean and Japanese are not identical, they are similar because they ultimately come from the same Middle Chinese pronunciations. These words are shown in table 5.2, where hyphens indicate the dividing point of the compound words.

How did these Chinese words get into Japanese and Korean? This is a result of the strong influence of the use of Classical Chinese over many centuries. Many of its words, pronounced in the Korean or Japanese manner, began to be sprinkled into the speech of literate elites. Eventually these borrowed words spread through the entire population. Today, there are enormous numbers of vocabulary words in both languages that are ultimately of Chinese origin. These sets of vocabulary words are called **Sino-Japanese** and **Sino-Korean** vocabulary (the prefix *sino-* means 'China'). In some ways they can be compared to the large number of vocabulary words in English that are built of Latin roots and are mostly due to the influence of French rule over England in the centuries after the Norman invasion of 1066.[10]

The verbs in these two example sentences are quite simple in structure. Japanese *yonda* 'read' consists of just a root and one suffix, indicating past tense. But verbs in Japanese and Korean can get quite complicated. It is not unusual for two, three, or even more suffixes to be attached to a verb root. For example, the Korean verb root *ilk-* 'to read' can be suffixed as *ilk-eusy-eo-ss-seumnida*, which is the formal polite honorific past tense form. A Korean speaker would use this verb form when talking in a formal setting (formal) to an audience deserving of respect (polite) about a person of high social status (honorific) who was reading in the past.

Another point worth noting about Japanese and Korean is that, unlike Chinese, these languages contain plenty of morphemes that are longer than one syllable. The Japanese word for 'car' is *kuruma* (three syllables); it does not break down into meaningful parts. The Korean word for 'sky' is *haneul* (two syllables); it also does not break down into meaningful parts.

Chapter Five

Pronunciation

It is in their sound systems that Japanese and Korean most noticeably differ from each other. These differences influenced the way that the Chinese script was borrowed to write these languages, and affected the subsequent history of their writing systems down to the current day.

Japanese has a fairly simple sound structure, with relatively few consonant and vowel sounds compared to most languages, and a low number of possible syllables. Modern Japanese has only fourteen consonant sounds and five vowel sounds. Throughout the history of Japanese, there have been on the order of a hundred basic syllables.[11]

Korean sound structure is more complicated than that of Japanese. There are a higher number of consonants (nineteen) and vowels (seven), and many more ways to combine these into different syllables. Korean today has no consonant clusters within a syllable, but it did have them in the past. In the Korean sentence above you may have noticed that the root of the verb 'read' is *ilk-*. When this root combines with a syllable beginning with a consonant, as in the dictionary form *ilk-da* 'to read', the [l] sound is not pronounced and the resulting pronunciation is "ikda." But if the following suffix begins with a vowel, the [k] moves over to the next syllable (and turns into a [g] sound), allowing the [l] to be pronounced. The verb form in the example sentence, *ilk-eotda*, is actually pronounced as the three syllables: "il+geot+da." Based on old spellings in Korean texts, we have good reason to believe that hundreds of years ago, syllables like *ilk* with an [lk] cluster were possible to pronounce in Korean.

In the past, both Korean and Japanese had tonal systems. Tonal contrasts are completely lost in most dialects of Korean today, including the standard one. In Japanese, the old tone system has evolved into an accentual system that linguists call "pitch accent." A major difference between the ancient tone systems of Japanese and Korean as compared to Chinese is that they were less crucial in distinguishing different words. In Chinese, just about every syllable can represent several different morphemes differentiated only by tone. In Japanese, there aren't many sets of words that are distinguished by pitch accent. One modern example is *sáke* 'salmon' vs. *saké* 'rice wine'. (The accent mark indicates which syllable is pronounced with a higher pitch.)

Don't worry if you haven't absorbed all the details about the grammar and pronunciation of Korean and Japanese. We'll refer back to these points as we need them in later sections.

Adaptation Methods of Chinese Characters: Korean

Imagine that you live in the Baekje kingdom in southwest Korea in the sixth century. You are training to be a scribe. Your teacher is an accomplished scholar who is well versed in the Confucian classics and able to read and write Classical Chinese. The spoken Korean that you and your teacher use to talk to each other has never been written down. Classical Chinese is the language of writing, and Korean is the language of speaking, and that's just how it is.

As a scribe in training, how do you go about learning the Chinese characters that will be the foundation of your ability to read and write Classical Chinese? It's really not so different from the way students all around the world today learn Chinese characters as second-language adult learners.

Because we live in a twenty-first-century world of writing and literacy, an English speaker who is studying Mandarin in the United States today can jot down a pronunciation and an English meaning on a piece of paper (like the flashcards I used in college; see figure 4.1) or type them into a computer or smartphone. But what if you are a fledgling scribe in ancient Korea who is trying to learn the script of the only writing system known in your time? You have no mechanism for writing down pronunciations and meanings of characters; the idea wouldn't even occur to you, because you haven't learned how to write yet. All you have are the characters themselves. You've got to bootstrap.

When learning a character, your teacher tells you the pronunciation (specifically, a Korean-accented imitation of a Middle Chinese pronunciation that has been passed down through several generations of Korean teachers) and the meaning (as expressed by a word in your native language, spoken Korean). Although you have no way to write them down, you can memorize them. And that's just what you do, over and over again for each character, hundreds and thousands of times. The work is hard, but eventually you learn to quickly recognize each character and say out loud its pronunciation and meaning.

TABLE 5.3 Some Chinese characters with their Korean pronunciations and meanings

CHARACTER	SINO-KOREAN PRONUNCIATION (*EUM*)	KOREAN MEANING (*HUN*)
十	*sip*	*yeol* 'ten'
食	*sik*	*meok-* 'eat'
見	*gyeon*	*bo-* 'see'
昆	*gon*	*mat* 'older brother'
月	*wol*	*dal* 'moon'
麗	*yeo*	*gop-* 'beautiful'

In this way, you are not only learning how to use the characters to read and write Classical Chinese. A side effect is that you are also associating a sound and a meaning—a Korean-accented Chinese syllable and a Korean word—with each character. This association is so strong and so deeply ingrained that you feel that they are inherent properties of each character itself. Characters, in other words, are things that naturally have Chinese pronunciations and Korean meanings.

This way of learning has created deep and lasting effects. The tradition of associating a Korean meaning and a Chinese-derived pronunciation with a Chinese character remains a fundamental way of thinking and talking about Chinese characters in Korea today. It's used in books and posters that teach Chinese characters to children, and is a basic feature of modern character dictionaries. The Korean word that translates the meaning of a character is called the character's *hun* ('gloss').[12] The Korean pronunciation is called the character's *eum* ('sound'). (We refer to these Korean flavors of Chinese character pronunciations as Sino-Korean pronunciations.) Among the examples in table 5.3 are some Chinese characters that we have seen before:

The pronunciations in the middle column originate as Korean-accented versions of Middle Chinese pronunciations. The meanings in the right-side column are native Korean words. (A hyphen, as in *bo-* 'see', indicates that the verb root is not a word by itself. It must occur in conjugated form by the addition of a suffix.)

Unlike the way a Chinese speaker learns characters, for a Korean learner of Classical Chinese, each character has a pronunciation and meaning that is understood via a *translated* form: its pronunciation is *adapted* into the sound system of Korean, and its meaning is *translated* into an equivalent Korean word. Even though the characters were originally only used to read and write the Classical Chinese language, the very act of learning them creates strong associations between characters and Korean words. For example, the character 月 is referred to by Korean speakers today as "dal wol," which is a shorthand label for "The character pronounced *wol* that means *dal* 'moon'." This way of conceiving of and talking about characters was a shared, common understanding among Korean-speaking scribes in ancient times.

These strong associations of written characters with Korean sounds and meanings are the foundation that make phonetic and semantic adaptation possible. The strong association between 月 and the Korean syllable pronounced "wol" makes it possible to adapt it phonetically to write a Korean syllable pronounced like "wol" in any word, which might have nothing to do with the meaning 'moon'. The strong association between 月 and the Korean word *dal* 'moon' makes it possible to adapt it semantically to write the Korean word for 'moon', which has no connection to the character's original Chinese pronunciation. In other words, the character can be used to represent spoken Korean by leaning on one of its two basic associations (sound or meaning) and ignoring the other one.

To go back to our thought experiment in which you are a scribe in training: these two methods would be effortless and natural to you after all the work you put into learning, memorizing, and using Chinese characters. Here's a schematization of the process that can help us better imagine what's going on:

KOREAN ASSOCIATIONS:

月 : {pronunciation "wol," meaning *dal* 'moon'}

Based on the pronunciation "wol," use 月 to write the Korean
syllable *wol* or a similar sound

SEMANTIC ADAPTATION:

Based on the meaning 'moon', use 月 to write the Korean word
dal 'moon'

The result of the phonetic adaptation is a graph that represents a sound
value only; it is a syllabograph, which could be used to write just part of a
longer word. The result of the semantic adaptation is a morphograph: it
represents a specific morpheme in Korean that has both a pronunciation
and a meaning. The pronunciation of that morpheme is not related to the
pronunciation that the character has in Chinese.

As a scribe in ancient Korea, your intuitive understanding of these basic
adaptations of Chinese characters is the key to writing your spoken Korean
language using Chinese characters. It's also going to be the key to readers
being able to understand what you've written, even if nobody has ever taught
them how to do it. As long as the readers have the same background knowledge as you, they will be able to interpret the characters correctly. That knowledge includes being a native speaker of Korean and associating the same
eum and *hun*—pronunciation and meaning values—with each character.

To illustrate this process in a more concrete way, let's go back to an English
analogy. Imagine that English is an unwritten language and that you are an
English-speaking scribe who is well trained in Classical Chinese, which is
the only written language you know about. You want to directly record the
following spoken English sentence instead of translating it into Classical
Chinese, and it suddenly occurs to you that you have a way to do it using
the Chinese characters that you already know:

(12) The moon in the sky shined brightly.

Because you are a literate scribe, you've memorized thousands of Chinese characters, associating with each one a sound and a meaning. The

sound is based on Chinese pronunciation but has an English accent (with no tones). Since you never interact with native Chinese speakers, only other English-speaking scribes who are literate in Classical Chinese, your English-accented pronunciation is shared by all of you. None of you even think of it as an accent, let alone a problem. It's just how one pronounces the characters. As for the meaning of each character, it is a conventional English translation of the Chinese morpheme written by the character. Among the thousands of characters you know are these:

因 : {"yin," 'because'}
月 : {"yue," 'moon'}
天 : {"tian," 'sky'}
照 : {"zhao," 'shine'}
明 : {"ming," 'bright'}
麗 : {"li," 'beautiful'}
得 : {"de," 'get'}[13]

(The tone marks have been removed from the Pinyin, to reflect the lack of tones in your "Sino-English" pronunciation.) It's a simple matter to write the English nouns, adjectives, and verbs of the English sentence using the Chinese characters that have equivalent meanings. It's something that feels quite natural:

The	moon	in	the	sky	shined	brightly.
一	月	一	一	天	照	明

You don't feel that you have much of a choice to do it any other way, because complex English syllables like *sky* and *bright* cannot be easily represented phonetically. There are no Chinese characters with pronunciations close to these English words, since no Chinese syllables have consonant clusters like *sk* and *br*. In any case, you are used to referring to the character 天 as "sky tian," so associating the word *sky* with this character is the most natural thing in the world.

But you never learned any characters that have associated meanings 'the', '-ed' or '-ly', because there is nothing in Chinese with equivalent meanings.

These are some of the many differences between English and Chinese grammar. So how can you write down these morphemes that have no translation equivalent in Chinese? In such a case, phonetic adaptation is the easiest choice, even though you must make do with approximating the English pronunciations rather than matching them exactly. Compare the underlined English words with the Mandarin pronunciations of the characters (it may be easier to hear the connection if you say the Mandarin syllables out loud).

The	moon	in	the	sky	shined	brightly."
得	—	因	得	—	— 得	— 麗
de		yin	de		de	li

Putting it all together, we get the following:

得	月	因	得	天	照	得	明	麗
de	MOON	yin	de	SKY	SHINE-de		BRIGHT-li	

which your readers will readily transform into "The moon in the sky shined brightly" when reading it aloud.

The line of characters <得月因得天照得明麗> may look superficially like Chinese on the page, but it's actually a written form of a spoken English sentence. Some of the characters are morphographs and some are syllabographs. As readers, how can we tell the difference? There is no way to know by looking at the shape of the graph. But we can tell by working out the meaning of the sentence. The way to work it out as a reader is to try out each character's sound and meaning value and figure out which ones yield sensible English in context.

Korean speakers used exactly this approach when they first figured out how to represent spoken Korean in writing. They used semantic adaptation of characters for nouns, verbs, and adjectives. They used phonetic adaptation for suffixes and "little words" that don't have obvious Chinese equivalents. The method is called *hyangchal*. It is precisely the pattern we see in the very earliest surviving Korean-language texts, which are written entirely in Chinese characters.

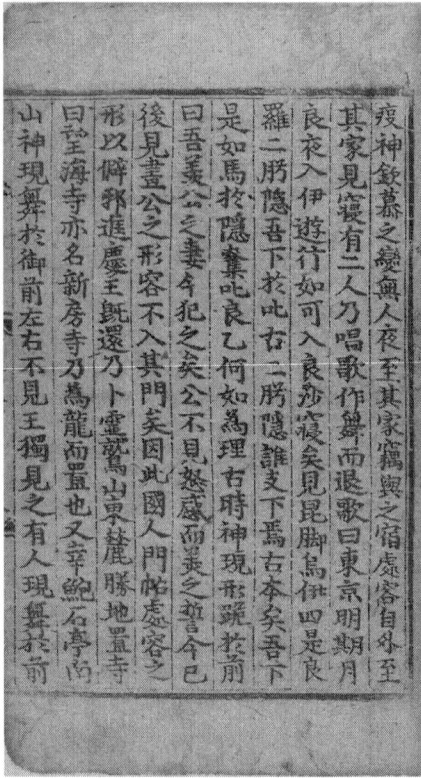

FIGURE 5.2. The "Song of Cheoyong." The Korean-language song begins near the bottom of the second line from the right, with the character 東, and ends halfway down the fifth column from the right with the character 古. The song is embedded in a surrounding narrative written in Classical Chinese. From a 1512 edition of *Tales of the Three Kingdoms* (Samguk yusa 三國遺事), a historical record compiled in the late thirteenth century. The edition is held by the Kyujanggak Institute for Korean Studies at Seoul National University and can be viewed at http://kyudb .snu.ac.kr/book/view.do?book_cd =GR36078_00, accessed February 7, 2024.

An Early Korean-Language Poem Written in Chinese Characters

Among the earliest examples we have of such texts are called *hyangga* 'country songs'. Some of them are believed to date from the seventh or eighth centuries, although the versions we have today are later copies. Only about two dozen of these early Korean poems survive today. They present many challenges of decipherment and interpretation for modern scholars. One of the best understood poems is called "Song of Cheoyong" (Cheoyongga). We have a thirteenth-century version in the book *Tales of the Three Kingdoms* (Samguk yusa). The poem is embedded within a mythical narrative, which is written in Classical Chinese (figure 5.2).

The story is about a man named Cheoyong, the son of the Dragon King of the Eastern Sea, who was serving as an official in the court of the Silla kingdom. His beautiful wife attracted the attention of the Smallpox Demon, a horrible monster responsible for afflicting the population with that terrible disease. One evening, Cheoyong returned home late at night to discover, to his shock, that his wife was in bed with the Demon, who had magically taken on the likeness of a handsome young man. But instead of becoming angry as one might expect, Cheoyong only sang a song, performed a dance, and then quietly left the room. Because of his politeness, the Smallpox Demon decided to return the favor and stop infecting the people of the kingdom. Cheoyong's deference had made him a hero.[14]

The song that Cheoyong sang in this extraordinary situation is the "Song of Cheoyong." Although it is written in Chinese characters, the language is clearly not Classical Chinese. It can only be understood as a written form of Old Korean. The text is as follows:

1　東京明期月良
2　夜入伊遊行如可
3　入良沙寢矣見昆
4　腳烏伊四是良羅
5　二肹隱吾下於叱古
6　二肹隱誰支下焉古
7　本矣吾下是如馬於隱
8　奪叱良乙何如爲理古

The corresponding English translation and hypothesized pronunciation in Old Korean are as follows:[15]

1	Under a bright moon in the capital,	*donggyeong balgi dala*
2	I returned home at night from carousing.	*bam deuli nolnidaga*
3	When I entered and looked in my bed,	*deuleosa jalay bogon*
4	There were four legs in it.	*gadali neoyh ileola*
5	Two belong to me,[16]	*du veuleun nayh ayeosgo*
6	But the other two—whose are they?	*du veuleun nuy hayeongo*
7	What once was mine,	*mideuy nayh ay damalan*
8	Having been stolen, what can be done?	*asal eosdi haligo*

Just as we saw with our English example about the moon in the sky, the Old Korean words are recorded in Chinese characters using a mixture of semantic and phonetic adaptations. The nouns and the verb roots are written semantically, using Chinese characters that are equivalent in meaning to the Korean words. Grammatical elements like the case-marking particles following nouns and the suffixes attached to verbs are represented by characters used phonetically. Let's take a detailed look at a few examples of this *hyangchal* technique.

In line 1, the Old Korean words for 'bright' and 'moon' appear bolded below:

1　東京明期月良　　*donggyeong **balgi dala***　　Under a bright moon
　　　　　　　　　　　　　　　　　　　　　　　　in the capital

We are already familiar with the characters that write the Chinese words meaning 'bright' and 'moon'. Here are their modern Korean pronunciation (*eum*) and meaning (*hun*) values:[17]

明 : Korean {"myeong," ***balk-* 'bright'**}
月 : Korean {"wol," ***dal* 'moon'**}

Bolding shows which of the values is being used in the poem.

We used these same two characters to write the English morphemes *bright* and *moon* in our thought exercise. Here they are doing the exact same thing, as semantic adaptations to write the Old Korean words *balgi* 'bright' and *dal* 'moon'.

What about the two characters that come after the ones representing 'bright' and 'moon'? That is, 期 after 明 'bright' and 良 after 月 'moon'? As expected, they are being used phonetically to represent grammatical endings. Let's focus on the one that comes after 明 'bright'.

The Old Korean root of the adjective meaning 'bright' is *balk-* (ancestral to modern Korean *balk-*). Remember that the *k* sound changes to a *g* sound in the suffixed form *balgi*.[18] The suffix is *-i*, so you might expect that the character 期 represents the sound of the suffix, [i]. But something a bit more complicated and interesting is going on here.

期 : Korean {"**gi**," --}[19]

The Korean pronunciation of the character 期 is "gi." Why is a character pronounced "gi" used to represent the suffix -*i* in *ba̠lgi*? It turns out that this character is being used to do two things at the same time. Only the [i] part of its pronunciation represents the suffix -*i*. The [g] part represents the very last sound of the root *ba̠lk*- (which is pronounced as [g] in this context).

But why? After all, the character 明 *already* represents the entire morpheme *ba̠lk*- meaning 'bright'. Why use a second Chinese character to repeat the sound of the last consonant?

The answer is that the use of a phonetically adapted graph to indicate the ending sound of the previous root, while also representing the sound of the attached suffix, is an efficient method of disambiguation. In this case, the [g] sound of 期 *gi* tells the reader that the preceding graph 明 represents a morpheme that ends in a [g] sound, and not any other morpheme or syllable that could theoretically be written with the same character. There are several reasons why this kind of explicit disambiguation is helpful. One is that characters can be used semantically or phonetically, but they look exactly the same in both uses. While context along with a native speaker's intuition about the language are usually enough to disambiguate, the text is clearer and easier to read if an explicit signal is given to the reader. The other reason is that Korean might have more than one word that can translate to the meaning of a single Chinese character. So a semantic adaptation of a graph could be used to write more than one Korean word. If that's the case, it's useful to disambiguate among those possibilities.

To give another analogy using English, earlier we saw the Chinese character 得 {"de," 'get'}. The English word *obtain* is just as appropriate a translation of the Chinese word as *get*. If this graph were used semantically to represent an English word in writing, how would the reader know if it was meant to write *get* or *obtain*? Or *acquire*? If I could somehow signal to the reader that the word written by 得 ends in a [t] sound, an [n] sound, or an [r] sound, that would do the trick.

Because the character 期 is pronounced "gi," it is a perfect choice for representing the adjective suffix -*i* and, at the same time, disambiguating the possible representations of the preceding 明 by specifying that what it writes ends in a [k/g] sound. In other words, it signals to the reader that 明 writes *ba̠lk*- and not any other Korean word meaning something like 'bright'.

There's a detail here that is important to stress: Although 明 represents *balk-* and 期 represents *gi*, the combination does not write *balggi* with two [g] sounds in a row. There is only one [g] sound in the word: *balgi*.

We actually do something similar in English writing. Have you ever thought about what the "st" is doing in the written English word *1ˢᵗ*? It seems obvious, right? It is spelling the [st] sounds. But if so, then does that mean that the *1* part writes *fir*? That doesn't feel right.

What's really going on here is that <1> is a morphograph. We use it to write two different words in English: *one* and *first*. In other words, this graph is ambiguous. The "st" notation is for disambiguation. It's telling you, the reader, that the preceding "1" writes a word that ends in the sounds [st], so it writes *first* and not *one*. The graph <1> writes *first*, but <1ˢᵗ> doesn't write *firstst*. This is exactly the reason why the "st" is typically superscripted, a way of signaling its special usage as a disambiguator of the preceding graph.

How to understand what the <st> is doing in *1ˢᵗ* isn't something you have to be taught—which is the reason you may have never thought about it before. It's a natural method of disambiguation that is readily understood by readers without the need for instruction. And it was employed by Koreans over a thousand years ago when they needed to disambiguate written Chinese characters.

Here are a few more examples of the *hyangchal* writing technique that we can observe in this poem. At the beginning of line 2, the Chinese character 夜 is semantically adapted to write the Korean word *bam* 'night'.

2 夜入伊遊行如可   ***bam deuli nolnidaga***   I returned home at night
                                                        from carousing

夜 : Korean {"ya," ***bam* 'night'**}

In line 8, the Chinese character 乙 is phonetically adapted to write the Korean case-marking particle *-l*, which indicates that the preceding noun phrase is a direct object.

8 奪叱良乙何如爲理古   *asal eosdi haligo*   Having been stolen,
                                                      what can be done?

乙 : Korean {"**eul**," --}[20]

And at the end of line 3, the two-character sequence 見昆 writes the Korean verb *bogon* 'see (and then)'[21]. The verb root 'see' is written with a semantically adapted graph, and the suffix *-gon* is written with a phonetically adapted one.

3　入良沙寢矣見昆　　*deuleosa jalay* **bogon**　　When I entered and
　　　　　　　　　　　　　　　　　　　　　　　　　　looked in my bed

見 : Korean {"gyeon," ***bo-*** '**see**'}

昆 : Korean {"**gon**," *mat* 'older brother'}

We won't go through the whole song line by line and character by character. These examples have already shown us just about everything we need to know to understand how Korean words are represented throughout the poem. Although there are exceptions, generally speaking, it is the case that nouns, adjective roots, and verb roots are written using Chinese characters for their meaning value. The case-marking particles following the nouns, and the suffixes attached to the adjectives and verbs are written using Chinese characters for their sound value. Sometimes those characters also reiterate the final sound of the preceding noun, adjective, or verb, as a disambiguating or specifying mechanism.

This may seem very cumbersome. You surely wouldn't design a Korean writing system from scratch that worked this way. But recall the knowledge base already shared by the community of literate Korean speakers at this time. They had a deep familiarity with written Classical Chinese, and they automatically associated each Chinese character with a Chinese sound (expressed in what we call Sino-Korean pronunciation) and a Korean word meaning. It was a simple extension of that knowledge base that allowed the spoken Korean language to be represented in writing.

Many kinds of information that people want to communicate can be translated into another language without much loss of information. It's not a surprise that the narrative story of Cheoyong, which began life as an oral Korean folk tale, is written down in Classical Chinese in the book *Tales of the Three Kingdoms*. But poems and songs are different from stories. They are greatly diminished when translated into another language. The rhythmic and sonic effects of a specific sequence of spoken words are essential to their expression. So it is also no surprise that within this story, the one part that is preserved as written Korean language is the *hyangga* itself, the eight-line song.

Direct Adaptation

Phonetic adaptation and semantic adaptation are the essential techniques of *hyangchal* writing. But there is also a third use of Chinese characters found in the *hyangga* poems. In "Song of Cheoyong," this third kind of adaptation occurs exactly once. It's at the very start of the first line:

1 東京明期月良   ***Donggyeong** ba̖lgi da̖la*   'Under a bright moon in the capital'

The first two characters, 東 and 京, are used in Chinese writing for the words meaning 'east' and 'capital'. Their Sino-Korean pronunciations, derived from Middle Chinese pronunciations, are "dong" and "gyeong." Here they are being used to write the proper noun *Donggyeong* 'Eastern Capital', the name of the modern-day city of Gyeongju, the capital of Silla in southeastern Korea.

Is this semantic adaptation or phonetic adaptation? That's an excellent question with a surprising answer. It seems to be both: The Sino-Korean pronunciations of the characters match that of the Korean word they write in the song. And the Chinese meanings of the characters match that of the Korean word being written. So what's going on here?

The answer is that this Chinese word meaning 'Eastern Capital' has been borrowed into Korean from Chinese. It is what scholars call a Sino-Korean word, a spoken word of Korean that is of Chinese origin. We mentioned earlier, when we saw our example sentences in modern Japanese and Korean, that a high percentage of the vocabularies of modern Japanese and Korean are words ultimately borrowed from Chinese, like those in table 5.2.

How did these Chinese words get into these non-Chinese spoken languages? The process was driven by literate elites. They began to insert some of the Chinese words they had studied into their speech. These eventually spread beyond this community into the speech of the general population, a process that took place over many centuries. The *hyangga* poems are from a time before these Chinese words had become pervasive in spoken Korean, but there are already a few. How would such words be written down? It was completely natural for them to be written with the same characters used to write them in Chinese. This isn't really an adaptation of the Chinese characters; it's more of a direct continuation of their usage in Chinese writing, carried into Korean and Japanese alongside the spoken words they represent. To use a term that is parallel to semantic adaptation and phonetic adaptation, we can refer to this as **direct adaptation**. In early Korean writing that uses Chinese characters, Sino-Korean vocabulary is written directly using the same characters that write the source word in Chinese.

In the early adaptation of Chinese characters to represent spoken Japanese in the first millennium, many parallels with developments in Korean are apparent. To what extent are these the natural outcome of the universal tendency toward semantic and phonetic adaptation, combined with the similar linguistic structures of Japanese and Korean? And to what extent is it due to the historical and cultural connection between Korea and Japan, and the many interactions between the literate elites of both places? These are questions that are not easy to answer with any certainty. We will be in a better position to consider them after learning about Japanese (in the next section) and comparing Korean and Japanese to Vietnamese and Zhuang (in the next chapter).

Adaptation Methods of Chinese Characters: Japanese

The main techniques of adaptation used in early Japanese writing are parallel to those seen in Korean *hyangchal* writing: semantic adaptation, phonetic adaptation, direct adaptation for words borrowed from Chinese, and disambiguation of the kind seen in 1*st*. But there are also some key differences between how writing developed and evolved in Korean and Japanese. One result is the mixed-script writing of modern Japanese, which intermixes morphographic *kanji* and syllabic *kana*.

In Korea, the *hyangchal* writing practices seen in *hyangga* died out and were forgotten. Now only a few dozen early examples survive. Because no tradition of how to read them was passed down through the generations, they are no longer fully understood. In Japan, the picture is quite different. Enormous numbers of texts survive, allowing us to trace the early development of Japanese writing. Moreover, an unbroken tradition of reading and interpreting those texts was inherited by modern scholars. As a result, the texts are not just well understood, but the details of how the language was represented through adapted Chinese characters are fully known.

Writing was probably introduced to the Japanese islands by literate scribes from the Korean kingdom of Baekje. Perhaps they explicitly taught Japanese scribes about semantic and phonetic adaptation. It's instead possible that the techniques were so intuitive that there was no need to teach them. Regardless of how it happened, the basic methods that were used to adapt Chinese characters to the written representation of spoken Old Japanese were the same as with Old Korean: semantic adaptation and phonetic adaptation. But in the history of Japanese writing, the use of these techniques appears to be a bit more chaotic, with more experimentation and variation than we see in Old Korean poems like "Song of Cheoyong." In the early period, we don't always see the same clear-cut alternation between semantically adapted graphs writing nouns and verb roots, and phonetically adapted graphs writing grammatical bits like suffixes. There is greater variety visible in these texts, although a similar underlying tendency is clearly present. After a period of experimentation, however, the Japanese writing system did eventually stabilize into that same familiar pattern.[22]

Not surprisingly, the most important text to help us understand early Japanese vernacular writing is a poetry collection. Administrative documents, legal contracts, inventories, and so on can be articulated in spoken Japanese, written down in Classical Chinese, and then translated back into spoken Japanese without loss of meaning. But song and poetry are different. The desire to record poetry and song in one's native language, so that it can be reproduced without change, was no doubt a key motivation for the adaptation of Chinese characters to write Japanese, just as it was for Korean.

The eighth-century poetry collection known as the *Man'yōshū* (Collection of ten thousand leaves) is a massive anthology containing approximately 4,500 poems, the earliest of which probably date to the mid-seventh century. They are written in Japanese using Chinese characters. As with the Korean *hyangga*, the characters are adapted both semantically and phonetically, with a tendency for grammatical elements like case-marking particles and verbal suffixes to be represented through phonetic adaptation. Noun and verb roots are represented by a mixture of methods: sometimes phonetically, sometimes with semantically adapted characters whose Chinese meaning is equivalent to the Japanese word being written.[23]

Like the Koreans, the Japanese considered each Chinese character to have an *on* ('sound') and a *kun* ('gloss'), which effectively tag or label the character and uniquely identify it.[24] These characters were all used in early Japanese texts to write native Japanese words by semantic adaptation:

CHARACTER	CHINESE	JAPANESE
山	{"shān," 'mountain'}	{"san," *yama* 'mountain'}
秋	{"qiū," 'autumn'}	{"shū," *aki* 'autumn'}
心	{"xīn," 'heart'}	{"shin," *kokoro* 'heart'}

Notice that the Sino-Japanese pronunciations listed first in the Japanese column bear a resemblance to the Chinese pronunciations (compare Sino-Japanese *san* and Mandarin *shān* for 山 'mountain'), while the native Japanese meaning equivalents do not (compare Japanese *yama* and Mandarin *shān*, both meaning 'mountain'). Not all Sino-Japanese pronunciations are obviously similar to the Mandarin pronunciations, however. That is because despite their common origin in Middle Chinese, they have been diverging for over a thousand years.[25]

The semantic adaptation of these graphs uses them to write native Japanese words that match the meaning of the Chinese words written by the characters but have very different pronunciations: 山 for *yama* 'mountain', 秋 for *aki* 'autumn', and 心 for *kokoro* 'heart', respectively.

Let's take a look at a few lines from the very first poem in the *Man'yōshū*. As with "Song of Cheoyong," keep in mind that these texts are well over a thousand years old, and the Japanese spoken language that they record was quite different in many respects from the Japanese spoken today.[26] (There are also many minor differences of interpretation among scholars that result in different understandings of the meaning of the poem, and therefore in the English translations. We don't need to be concerned about these, because they are not relevant to the general principles of script use that are our primary interest.)

Like the Korean-language "Song of Cheoyong," the written form of this Japanese poem can't be understood at all by Chinese readers. The language is Old Japanese. The text is as follows:

MAN'YŌSHŪ POEM #1 (FIRST FOUR LINES)

籠毛與美籠母乳
布久思毛與美夫君志持
此岳尓菜採須兒
家吉閑名告紗根

ENGLISH TRANSLATION:

Girl with your basket, with your pretty basket
With your spade, with your pretty spade
Picking greens on this hillside
I want to ask your home. Please tell me!

MODERN JAPANESE PRONUNCIATION:[27]

Ko mo yo miko mochi
Fukushi mo yo mibukushi mochi
Kono oka ni na tsumasu ko
Ie kikana norasane

The same text is given again below, with the characters grouped into words and Old Japanese pronunciations written beneath.[28] The morphemes that are represented by semantically adapted morphographs are capitalized. This will help you visualize the alternation between semantically adapted and phonetically adapted use of Chinese characters.

1	籠毛	與	美 籠	母乳
	KWO-mo	*yo*	*mi-KWO*	*moti*
	basket-TOP	EMPH	HON-basket	hold

2	布久思毛	與	美 夫君志	持
	pukusi-mo	*yo*	*mi-bukusi*	*MOTI*
	spade-TOP	EMPH	HON-spade	hold

3	此	岳尔	菜	採須	兒
	KONO	*WOKA-ni*	*NA*	*TUMA-su*	*KWO*
	this	hill-on	greens	pick-RESP+MOD	child

4	家	吉閑名	告紗根
	IPYE	*kikana*	*NORA-sane*
	home	ask	tell-RESP+REQ

Let's take a detailed look at the way some of the words are written. The native Japanese word *kwo* 'basket' is written with the Chinese character for 'basket' twice in line 1.

籠 : Japanese {"rō," ***kwo* 'basket'**}

"Rō" is the Sino-Japanese pronunciation of the character. It is historically related to the modern Chinese pronunciation "lóng." *Kwo* is the native Japanese word for basket. The usage in line 1 is semantic adaptation: the Chinese character writes a Japanese word with equivalent meaning.

In the same way, semantic adaptation is used for most of the nouns in this poem: 'hill', 'greens', 'child', and 'home' are all written with semantically adapted graphs. And as with Korean *hyangchal* writing, the case-marking particles that follow them are all represented by phonetically adapted graphs, like *-ni* after 'hill' meaning 'at, on'. At the second occurrence of the word for 'basket', an honorific prefix *mi-* is attached; this is written phonetically as well.

However, this tendency is not completely consistent. Contrast the representation of 'basket' using semantic adaptation with the representation of the Old Japanese word for 'spade', *pukusi*, at the start of line 2. Although it is a noun, it is written with three Chinese characters adapted phonetically:

布 : Japanese {"**pu**," *nuno* 'cloth'}
久 : Japanese {"**ku**," *hisa-* 'long time'}
思 : Japanese {"**si**," *omo-* 'think'}

The second time the word appears in the line, it is written with three entirely different characters (夫君志), which can do the same job because their pronunciations also match the Japanese word.[29]

Looking at verbs, we again mostly see the same pattern as in Korean *hyang-chal*. The verbs for 'hold', 'pick', and 'tell' use semantically adapted graphs for the verb roots: *moti*, *tuma*, and *nora*, respectively, and phonetically adapted graphs for the verbal suffixes on the latter two, *-su* and *-sane*.

持 *moti* 'hold'
持 : Japanese {"chi," ***mot-* 'hold'**}

採須 *tuma-su* 'pick-RESP+MOD'
採 : Japanese {"sai," ***tum-* 'gather, collect'**}
須 : Japanese {"**su**," *subekaraku* 'must'}

告紗根 *nora-sane* 'tell-RESP+REQ'
告 : Japanese {"kō," ***nor-* 'tell, inform'**}
紗 : Japanese {"**sya**," *usuginu* 'gauze'}
根 : Japanese {"kon," ***ne*** 'root'}

Where we see inconsistencies or deviations from the basic usage patterns, there is sometimes a poetic purpose that has come into play. Although the verb *moti* 'hold' is written as expected with the semantically adapted morphograph 持 at the end of line 2, at the end of line 1 this very same word is written phonetically using two graphs, one for each syllable: 母乳.

母 : Japanese {"**mo**," *haha* 'mother'}
乳 : Japanese {"nyū," ***ti*** 'milk; breast'}

Why write a verb root phonetically here? Well, looking at these two graphs, we can see that they are not just serving a phonetic function. Even though a reader would get the underlying word 'hold' purely from the sound value of the two characters, the meaning values of the characters simultaneously create semantic resonances in the mind of the reader. The particular characters selected by the poet for these syllabic sounds have related meanings, 'mother' and 'milk; breast', and are used in other contexts outside of this poem to write *mother's milk*. This kind of visual wordplay is possible with Chinese characters, because even when they are being used for their sound value, the conventional meaning values can still be manipulated and evoked in the minds of readers.[30]

There is something else to notice about the use of the second of the two characters (乳) as a syllabograph. The sound value it represents is the syllable "ti" (changed to "chi" in modern Japanese), which is part of the word *moti* 'hold'. But notice that "ti" is not the Japanese imitation of the Chinese pronunciation of the character, which is "nyū":

乳 : Japanese {"nyū," *ti* 'milk; breast'}

There is something a bit more complicated going on here. The character's sound value is derived through two steps of adaptation. First, the graph is understood as able to write the Japanese word with equivalent meaning to Chinese: Japanese *ti* 'milk; breast'. This is a semantic adaptation. Then the graph is again adapted, this time phonetically, so that it can be used to write the syllabic sound value "ti" in a different word entirely, one unrelated to the meanings 'milk; breast'. This kind of secondary adaptation was a common enough practice in early Japanese writing that it has been given a technical name in Japanese, *kungana*: phonetic adaptation based on Japanese meaning. How did readers know whether a character like 乳 was representing the Japanese syllable *nyū* (phonetic adaptation), the Japanese word *ti* 'milk; breast' (semantic adaptation), or the Japanese syllable *ti* (*kungana* two-step adaptation)? From a combination of context and native-speaker knowledge.

In the written form of the verb *nora-sane* 'please tell', there is another *kungana* usage. The last character (根) represents the syllabic sound *ne*, because that is the pronunciation of the Japanese word that is equivalent in meaning to the Chinese word written by the character.

根 : Japanese {"kon," *ne* 'root'}

Other Methods of Early Japanese Writing in Chinese Characters

Although the *Man'yōshū* shows us the general tendencies that would become solidified as writing developed, early Japanese texts also use other methods of writing with adapted Chinese characters. These alternative methods were eventually abandoned, presumably because they were not found to be as useful. The eighth-century *Kojiki* (Records of ancient matters) is a work of history and legend, which also contains poems.[31] The poems recorded in *Kojiki* are transcribed purely phonetically (as are some of the *Man'yōshū* poems). Each syllable of each Japanese word is written with a Chinese character whose pronunciation is similar to that syllable. There are no semantically adapted graphs like the use of 月 to write the Korean word for 'moon' or the use of 籠 to write the Japanese word for 'basket'. The first poem in *Kojiki* is about twelve words long, with a total of thirty-one syllables. It is written with a sequence of thirty-one characters, one per syllable, representing the sounds alone.

Interestingly, early Japanese texts contain some meta-analysis of writing. The preface to *Kojiki* (which is written in Classical Chinese) explicitly addresses the question of how best to represent Japanese in writing. The author of the preface, Ō no Yasumaro, said this: "If written entirely in characters used for their meanings, the words do not correspond to the sense; if written completely in characters used for their sound value, the text becomes much longer."[32]

What we see happening here in the eighth century is a recognition of the two basic methods of adaptation, semantic and phonetic, along with a conscious attempt to mix and match them to find the most effective way to make Japanese writing easy to read. And we can also see that, while it is entirely possible to represent spoken Japanese entirely through Chinese characters adapted phonetically, this was felt to be inadequate. Lurking behind the statement that "the text becomes much longer" is an implication that reading extended passages this way feels effortful.

Ō no Yasumaro also recognized the problem of ambiguity, especially in the rendering of names. Names present particular challenges, because while they may be meaningful, the reader cannot rely on linguistic context to decide on the representational value of graphs. In some places in *Kojiki*, graphs used semantically are followed by others used phonetically that represent the same word. This redundancy clarifies the intended pronunciation of the preceding graphs while still conveying meanings. Sometimes there are even explicit notes, written in Classical Chinese, that say things like "Read these two graphs by means of their sound value." In other words, the use of characters as phonetically adapted is called out for the reader.[33]

You may wonder why we don't see any early Korean texts that are written entirely phonetically, like the Japanese poems in *Kojiki*. One possible explanation is that such texts once existed but have not survived. In my view, a more likely explanation is that there are too many distinct syllables in Old Korean, many of which have sounds or sound combinations that are not easily approximated by Korean pronunciations of Chinese characters. This was not the case for Japanese, which has few sounds and few syllables. It is a simple matter to find a Chinese character whose Sino-Japanese pronunciation matches each Japanese syllable.

In the end, the "hybrid style" of writing won out: a mixture of semantically adapted and phonetically adapted graphs, more systematically employed than in the *Man'yōshū* and similar to what we see in Korean *hyangga*. This style first appears in the ninth century and becomes ascendant several centuries later.

The Development of Distinct Syllabaries

In the meantime, something very interesting was happening to the writing system that would lead to the creation of entirely new Japanese scripts. A single script was about to split into three.

The Chinese characters that were used purely for their phonetic value, as syllabographs, became conventionally written in a simplified form that was visually distinct from their source characters. These simplified forms were abbreviated through one of two processes: **cursivization** (in which strokes are smoothly joined together) or **part-selection** (keeping just one part of the character and discarding the rest).

Here are three examples of this process. In the *Man'yōshū*, the following three Chinese characters were frequently used via phonetic adaptation to write Japanese syllables:

天 : Japanese {"**ten**," *ama* 'sky'} for syllable *te*
加 : Japanese {"**ka**," *kuwae-* 'add'} for syllable *ka*
久 : Japanese {"**ku**," *hisa-* 'long time'} for syllable *ku*

We saw the last of these used to write the second syllable of *pukusi* 'spade' in line 2 of the *Man'yōshū* poem above.

As with Korean, when Chinese characters can be used semantically (to write local words as morphographs) or phonetically (to write sounds with no fixed meaning), the problem of ambiguity is always lurking in the background. Each character in a text potentially has two possible representations. The reader tries to determine which possibility is correct by relying on context. This ambiguity problem became permanently resolved in Japanese writing by **abbreviation**: changing the physical appearance of a graph when it was phonetically adapted. The result was the emergence of two brand-new scripts derived from Chinese characters: the two *kana* scripts known as *hiragana* and *katakana*. Some examples follow:

FULL FORM (*KANJI*)	CURSIVIZED (*HIRAGANA*)	PART-SELECTED (*KATAKANA*)
天	て *te*	テ *te*
加	か *ka*	カ *ka*
久	く *ku*	ク *ku*

The original full forms of the characters, called *kanji*, continued to be used as morphographs, to write verb and noun roots by semantic adaptation.

Remember the example of annotated Classical Chinese, which was marked up in such a way that a Japanese reader could convert the text into spoken Japanese (figure 5.1)? The *kanbun kundoku* method of text annotation had to squeeze Chinese characters into the small margins between columns of text. The part-selected abbreviations of characters that became the *katakana* script originate in this usage.[34]

Modern Japanese Mixed-Script Writing

The mixture of these scripts, with *kanji* used morphographically for verb and noun roots and *kana* used phonetically for suffixes, particles, and other grammatical elements, is called *kanji-kana majiribun* 'kanji-kana mixed writing'. It is the basis of modern Japanese writing.[35] To illustrate this, let's look again at the modern Japanese sentence from the beginning of the chapter:

Sachi-wa	*shinshitsu-de*	*ongaku-o*	*kii-te*
Sachi-TOP	bedroom-LOC	music-ACC	listen-and

musuko-to	*shinbun-o*	*yon-da*
son-COM	newspaper-ACC	read-PAST

'Sachi listened to music in the bedroom and then read a newspaper with her son.'

This is how the sentence is written in modern standard Japanese:
幸は寝室で音楽を聴いて息子と一緒に新聞を読んだ。

Let's match this up with the individual words. I've capitalized the elements that are represented morphographically; these are all written with *kanji*. The lower-case elements are written phonetically, with *kana*. To help you clearly see the difference, I've also <u>underlined</u> the *kana* graphs.

幸<u>は</u>	寝室<u>で</u>	音楽<u>を</u>	聴<u>いて</u>
SACHI-wa	*SHINSHITSU-de*	*ONGAKU-o*	*KIi-te*
Sachi-TOP	bedroom-LOC	music-ACC	listen-and

息子<u>と</u>	新聞<u>を</u>	読<u>んだ</u>
MUSUKO-to	*SHINBUN-o*	*YOn-da*
son-COM	newspaper-ACC	read-PAST

At the end of the first line, <て> is used to write the syllable *te*. Originally an abbreviated form of the character 天 meaning 'sky' in its reduced form, it is always a syllabograph. It has permanently lost its original semantic value.

Strictly speaking, the Japanese *kana* scripts aren't quite syllabic. In the example sentence above, most *kana* graphs are writing a single syllable, such as *wa*, *de*, *o*, and *to*. But in the two-syllable word *yonda* 'read', the graph <ん> represents just the single [n] sound at the end of the syllable *yon*. Japanese syllables come in long and short varieties. Those like *wa* and *o* are short; those like *yon* and *kii* are long. This distinction is important for rhythmic forms of artistic expression like poetry and music: long syllables count as two beats, compared to one beat for short syllables. Linguists analyze the long syllables into smaller units called **moras**. Short syllables have one mora each. But long syllables have two moras: *yon* = *yo* + *n*, and *kii* = *ki* + *i*. Because long syllables are written with two *kana* graphs, one for each mora, it is more technically accurate to describe *hiragana* and *katakana* as moraic rather than syllabic.

Notice too that the written Japanese sentence has no spaces between words. Readers do not need spaces, because the division of words is clearly discernible in the alternation between *kanji* and *kana*. When a *kanji* occurs after one or more *kana*, it nearly always represents the start of a new word.[36] Here's the sentence again, with *kana* underlined and arrows pointing to the start of each word.

幸<u>は</u>寝室<u>で</u>音楽<u>を</u>聴<u>いて</u>息子<u>と</u>一緒<u>に</u>新聞<u>を</u>読<u>んだ</u>。
　↑　　↑　　　↑　　　　↑　　　↑　　　↑　　　↑　　　　↑

There are a number of other disambiguating techniques that are found in Japanese writing. Some of them have clear parallels with Korean. We have already seen that one way early Korean *hyangchal* writing clarifies which of several possible value a morphographic character has is by reiterating part of its pronunciation, analogously to the role of <st> in the English written form *1st*. Scholars of writing call this kind of notation a **phonetic determinative**, because by specifying a sound value, it *determines* which of several possible values a morphograph has in a particular context.

This kind of disambiguation is seen frequently in the written forms of modern Japanese verbs: the last consonant sound or the last syllable of the verb root represented by a *kanji* morphograph is repeated using a following *kana* syllabograph. This repeated consonant or syllable is a phonetic determinative that disambiguates the value of the morphograph, clarifying which word it writes.

For example, there is a Japanese verb root *tabe-* meaning 'to eat'. It can be written morphographically with the Chinese character that represents the word 'to eat' in Classical Chinese, which we are already familiar with from chapter 1:

食 : Japanese {"shoku," *tabe-* 'to eat'}

The conjugated plain form of the Japanese verb is *tabe-ru*, with suffix *-ru* attached to the root *tabe-*. You might imagine that in modern mixed-script writing, the verb root *tabe-* would be written with the *kanji* <食>, and the suffix *-ru* would be written with the *hiragana* syllabograph <る>: <食る>.

TABLE 5.4 Examples of phonetic determinatives in English, Old Korean, and Modern Japanese

WRITTEN LANGUAGE	MORPHOGRAPH	WRITTEN SEQUENCE	VALUES OF GRAPHS	INTENDED READING	EXPLANATION
English	1	1ˢᵗ	*first* + "st"	*first*	"st" is a phonetic determinative indicating that the intended reading of <1> ends in [st]
Old Korean	明	明期	*balg* + "gi"	*balgi* 'bright' (with attached -*i* suffix)	The [g] part of 期 *gi* is a phonetic determinative indicating that the intended reading of 明 ends in [g]
Modern Japanese	食	食べる	*tabe* + "be" + "ru"	*taberu* 'eat' (with attached -*ru* suffix)	The *hiragana* graph べ *be* is a phonetic determinative indicating that the intended reading of 食 ends in [be].

But that's not how it's written. It is written <食べる>. The *hiragana* syllabograph <べ> represents the sound [be], and so reiterates the final syllable of the verb root *tabe-*.

You can think of the <べ> *be* in 食べる *taberu* 'to eat' as like the <st> in *1ˢᵗ*. It reiterates part of the sound of the morpheme written by the preceding *kanji* in order to disambiguate the usage of that *kanji*. (In addition to its morphographic use to write the Japanese verb *tabe-* 'eat', the *kanji* 食 can also write the verbs *ku-* 'eat; make a living' and the archaic *ham-* 'eat', among others.)

All of these details on phonetic determinatives can be hard to absorb if you don't know Korean or Japanese, so let's arrange them in a chart (table 5.4) for easier comparison.

In a mature writing system used by accomplished writers and readers, phonetic determinatives are not actively used to figure out what words are being written among multiple possibilities. For example, once we are accomplished readers of English, we don't look at 1st and think to ourselves "Does that <1> represent *one* or *first*? Oh, I see the <st>, so it must be *first*." Rather, we see 1st and read it off right away as "first," because we have conventionally associated the spoken word with that written form. Likewise, Japanese readers don't perceive the *kana* used in writing verbs as serving a disambiguating function anymore. The disambiguation strategies described here for Korean and Japanese were active when writers and readers were first developing the writing system. The techniques they came up with, consciously or unconsciously, led to conventionalized ways of writing individual words and created systematic patterns that were embedded within the writing system as a whole.

The point is not that disambiguation is happening constantly as we read. It's that disambiguating techniques are an essential part of the development of a writing system, and the results of those strategies persist in the writing system even after it is stabilized and conventionalized.

The Creation of New Characters

Much of the seemingly haphazard and complex process of script adaptation in early Japanese and Korean writing can be explained by the three basic techniques of semantic adaptation, phonetic adaptation, and disambiguation. The sequential alternation of semantic and phonetic adaptation made it possible for nearly all words and sentences of Old Korean and Old Japanese to be represented by borrowed Chinese characters.

But these techniques did not work in every situation. The most common difficulty that scribes encountered was nouns and verbs in their spoken languages for which no equivalent existed in written Chinese. If Chinese had no word with similar meaning, then there was no character available for semantic adaptation. What kind of spoken words might fall into this category? Those for local species of flora and fauna are a good example. A particular species of fish or tree found in Korea or Japan might not exist in China. There might also be cultural concepts that lack an equivalent word in Chinese.

In Japanese, it was always possible to represent such words phonetically, because of the simple syllable structure of the language. Even so, the patterned alternation of the writing system, and native-speaker feeling that verb and noun roots should be written morphographically, provided an incentive to write such words with morphographs. And in Korean, where some syllables were pronounced in a way that was very different from every existing Chinese syllable, the phonetic option wasn't always even available.

For this reason, in both Korea and Japan, a number of new characters were created. These did not exist in the mainstream Chinese written tradition, but they were formed using Chinese-character components and so had the "look and feel" of Chinese characters. Let's look at just two examples each from Korean and Japanese:

GRAPH	KOREAN WORD	SOURCE OF COMPONENTS (WITH CHINESE VALUES)
畓	*dap* 'rice field'	水 {"shuǐ," 'water'} + 田 {"tián," 'field'}
垈	*dae* 'housing site'	代 {"dài," 'era'} (SK "dae") + 土 'earth'

KANJI	JAPANESE MORPHEME	SOURCE OF COMPONENTS
峠	*tōge* 'mountain pass'	山 'mountain' + 上 'above' + 下 'below'
鱈	*tara* 'cod'	魚 'fish' + 雪 'snow'

The graph created to write *dap* 'rice field' combines the two Chinese characters for 'water' and 'field', the first atop the second, in a way that visually suggests a layer of water over a field. The graph created to write *dae* 'housing site' has the typical structure of a Chinese phonetic-semantic compound character. The component 土 means 'earth/dirt'. But instead of being on the left side, as would be typical, its position at the bottom of the character also suggests an iconic representation of an earthen foundation. The component 代 is being used purely for its sound value (Sino-Korean "dae") to specify the pronunciation of the word being written, 'housing site', also pronounced "dae." Its meaning in Chinese writing, 'era', is irrelevant to its function here.

The two Japanese-created *kanji*, like the Korean examples, have the "look and feel" of ordinary Chinese characters. The components 山 'mountain' and 魚 'fish' are commonly occurring meaning components in Chinese characters. Here they serve the same function: a mountain pass is a feature associated with mountains, and a cod is kind of fish. The other components of the characters look like they should be phonetic, but in fact there are no single Chinese characters whose Japanese pronunciations match the two-syllable pronunciations of the words *tōge* or *tara*. It is not possible to represent these words' sounds phonetically, so these other components are also being used for their semantic value.

What Is "Linear Adaptation"?

While many details of the historical development of writing in Japan and Korea differ, there are striking similarities in the ways Chinese characters were adapted to represent the ancient Japanese and Korean spoken languages.

Most basic is the use of two types of adaptation of existing Chinese characters: adaptation based on meaning and adaptation based on pronunciation. These ways of adapting characters of a morphographic writing system so they can be used to represent a different spoken language appear to be very natural, even automatic, for humans. We have already seen how the same techniques could be applied to creating a written representation of spoken English.

A second similarity, one that also seems to be universal, is the use of disambiguating techniques. The details vary considerably, but no matter which are used, the goals are the same: The first is to make sure a reader can determine if a graph is semantically or phonetically adapted. The second is to make sure that it is clear which word is represented by a semantically adapted graph that has multiple possible representations.

The early Korean and Japanese methods of adapting Chinese characters can be called **linear adaptation**, because they employ unmodified Chinese characters in linear sequence. Disambiguation is achieved linearly: through the alternation of semantic and phonetic adaptation that aligns with the grammatical structure of words and sentences, and through the use of phonetic determinatives immediately following the morphographs being disambiguated. This linear approach is visible in the examples in table 5.4.

Because every language has many fewer grammatical suffixes than roots, a relatively small number of phonetically adapted graphs is sufficient to represent all the suffixes. These become conventionalized as the writing system develops and stabilizes. In Japanese, disambiguation was further achieved by another development: the set of characters used phonetically was abbreviated and conventionalized to the point of turning into new scripts: *hiragana* and *katakana*. Once you have new scripts that are distinguished from Chinese characters, disambiguation of usage is automatically achieved, because the phonetically adapted graphs have a different visual appearance from the semantically adapted ones.

When one and the same Chinese character was used both semantically and phonetically, it came to look completely different in each usage. This can be illustrated with a simple example. Consider the modern Japanese word *futotteita* 'was fat'. It is a past-tense form of the verb *futo-* 'to be fat'. The word contains several suffixes attached to the verb root.

In written Modern Standard Japanese, the word looks like this: 太ってい た. The first graph <太> is a *kanji*, an unmodified Chinese character. The remaining four are all *hiragana*, simplified forms of what were originally phonetically adapted Chinese characters.[37] The character 太 has the following Chinese values:

太 : {"tài," 'great, large'}

It has been semantically adapted to write the verb root *futo-* 'fat' as a morphograph. This very same character was also phonetically adapted to write the syllable *ta*. In that usage, it was eventually cursivized into the *hiragana* graph <た>. It appears at the end of 太っていた to write the last syllable of the past-tense suffix *-ta*. Because it is written in its original form as a semantically adapted morphograph and in a cursivized form when functioning as a phonetically adapted syllabograph, there is no possible ambiguity between the two uses of the character. In fact, the modern Japanese reader will not be aware that these two graphs, so different in appearance and function, have any historical connection.

This still leaves the problem of disambiguating a graph that has two or more distinct representations based on its semantics. This could happen because two or more words in the vernacular language are roughly synonymous with a single word of Chinese, and therefore get written with the same character. (For example, the Chinese word *míng* 明 means 'bright, clear'. So two English words, *bright* and *clear*, could both be represented by the character 明 by semantic adaptation.) It can also happen when a character is adapted semantically to write a vernacular word and is also adapted directly to represent a Sino-derived word with a similar meaning. In these two kinds of cases, a phonetically adapted graph can serve as a phonetic determinative, like the <st> in *1ˢᵗ*. In Korean and Japanese, this was also done linearly, by appending the disambiguating graph. The most typical way of doing this was to reiterate the sound of the latter part of the word, sometimes just the last consonant.

One reason that early Japanese and early Korean writing are so similar in the ways they adapted Chinese characters is certainly related to their word, phrase, and sentence structures being very similar to each other, and very different from Chinese. Another reason may be the close cultural and historical connections between the peoples of the Korean Peninsula and the Japanese archipelago. It's likely that Classical Chinese writing was introduced to Japan from Korea, and that scribes moving between the two locations shared ideas and techniques for the written representation of local languages. To what degree were similarities of techniques in each place due to interactions between these groups, who may have learned from each other? And to what degree were they inevitably the result of patterns of linguistic structure? Most likely, both factors played a role.

One thing is sure: while semantic adaptation, phonetic adaptation, and disambiguation are the core of how Chinese writing was—and must inevitably be—adapted to write other languages, the specific patterns seen in the linear adaptation of characters to Japanese and Korean writing need not always occur. Vietnamese and Zhuang provide us with examples of writing systems in which these three core aspects played out in a very different way, one that led to a profusion of new graphs in a dazzling array of variant forms.

SIX

Composite Adaptation
Vietnamese and Zhuang

In 1988, the Beijing print and installation artist Xu Bing unveiled an art project called "A Book from the Sky." It featured, in several formats, a book over six hundred pages in length, covered densely in what at first glance appeared to be thousands of Chinese characters.[1]

If you know Chinese, there is something quite unsettling about these texts. All of the characters in them are fake. But they look real—or at least plausible. They appear in a traditional woodblock-print typeface and are composed of novel configurations of familiar parts: semantic and phonetic components that occur in the real script, along with brush strokes and stroke combinations like those found in real Chinese characters. For example, there are characters composed of 厂 over 正, of 刂 on the right side of 土, of 刂 on the right side of 刀, and of 左 with 力 at the bottom in place of 工. Most of the fake characters are more complex than these examples.

Encountering these texts, the first instinct of a reader of Chinese might be to presume that the characters appear strange but tantalizingly familiar because they are "difficult" characters that have been painstakingly extracted from obscure dictionary entries or ancient, long-neglected texts.

But they aren't. Xu Bing is deliberately playing with our instincts in order to convey an artistic message about our relationship to text and meaning.

Chữ Nôm, the native Vietnamese writing system based on adapted Chinese characters, fell out of use in the early twentieth century and is now only readable by a small number of specialized scholars. To a reader of Chinese, Vietnamese Chữ Nôm characters like the one top of the next page may appear no more real than Xu Bing's fanciful creations:

The character is composed of familiar, ordinary parts, but it is nowhere found within the history of Chinese writing. But these characters are not at all the same as Xu Bing's invented pseudocharacters. They are part of a real writing system for a real language. An understanding of the historical and linguistic context in which they were created and used reveals the logic and power of their structure.

English Written in Chinese Characters: Another Technique

We have used thought experiments about adapting Chinese characters to write spoken English as a way of understanding what actually happened in the history of Korean and Japanese writing. We made use of both phonetic and semantic adaptation to write an entire English sentence, *The moon in the sky shined brightly*, as <得月因得天照得明麗>.[2] The mixture of phonetically and semantically adapted Chinese characters creates potential ambiguities for readers. For each graph, the reader must pause, consider the character's conventional sound and meaning, and decide which way of reading it—semantically or phonetically—fits best into the English-language context. For example, recall the Chinese-based English sound and meaning values of the first two characters:

得 : {"de," 'get'}
月 : {"yue," 'moon'}

A reader must consider four possible ways to interpret these two characters in sequence:

- Phonetic, phonetic: representing one or more English words, or part of one longer word, that sounds something like "de-yue."
- Phonetic, semantic: representing an English word that sounds something like "de" followed by the English word *moon*: 'the moon'.

- Semantic, phonetic: representing the English word *get* followed by a word, or part of a longer word, that sounds something like "yue."
- Semantic, semantic: representing the English words *get* and *moon*: 'get moon'.

The second option, 'the moon', seems the most natural for an English speaker, but a reader can't be completely sure it's the best way of reading these two characters until they get further along into the sentence. Perhaps 'the moon' won't fit with what comes next in the sentence, and some other more plausible possibility will present itself.

Similar challenges were present for readers of the earliest Japanese-language and Korean-language texts. But keep in mind that aspects of writing become conventionalized. Once techniques of adaptation are put into place, certain conventions for the use of specific characters would be internalized by writers and readers very quickly, and would provide helpful guideposts in the reading process. The English word *the* is one of the most commonly occurring words in the language.[3] If the Chinese character 得 were consistently used for it, a reader's first instinct when seeing it would be to presume it is writing *the*. That presumption would be correct the majority of the time. As an experienced reader, you wouldn't even waste time thinking about the possibility of semantic adaptation—you'd just see <得> and think *the*. Similarly, Chinese characters writing concrete nouns like 月 and 象 would most often be used for the equivalent English words (*moon* and *elephant*) rather than for their sound value. Familiarity with these conventionalized tendencies makes reading much easier. The more you read, the more familiar the conventions of script usage become to you. Readers would develop a "default" interpretation of each graph, and would have to pause and reevaluate only in the rare case when that interpretation yields a nonsensical result. Over time, writers would naturally reinforce the most common ways of writing and avoid uncommon ways, in order to make things easier for their readers.

When it comes to Korean and Japanese, this kind of conventionalization of character usage would ultimately make reading far smoother than in this English example. That's because of the way sentences in those two languages tend to be structured. Recall these sentences from chapter 5:

Sachi-wa	*shinshitsu-de*	*ongaku-o*	*kii-te*
Sachi-TOP	bedroom-LOC	music-ACC	listen-and

musuko-to	*shinbun-o*	*yon-da*
son-COM	newspaper-ACC	read-PAST

'Sachi listened to music in the bedroom and then read a newspaper with her son'

KOREAN:

Jihye-neun	*chimsil-eseo*	*eumak-eul*	*deut-go*
Jihye-TOP	bedroom-LOC	music-ACC	listen-and

adeul-gwa	*sinmun-eul*	*ilk-eotda*
son-COM	newspaper-ACC	read-PAST

'Jihye listened to music in the bedroom and then read a newspaper with her son'

The basic pattern in each sentence is a sequence of noun phrases with following case-marking particles, followed at the end of the sentence by a verb with attached suffixes. If the case-marking particles (like Japanese *wa*, *de*, *o*, and *to*) and verbal suffixes (like *te* and *da*) are written with a small number of phonetically adapted characters that have become conventionalized in that usage, then the structure of the sentence is pretty clear to a reader. The particles act as guideposts showing where the nouns are, and the suffixes act as guideposts showing where the verbs are. The noun and verb roots are written with semantically adapted characters. In this way, the interpretation of the Chinese characters has a default value that works most of the time.

There are other ways to further reduce ambiguity too. In Japanese, phonetically adapted vs. semantically adapted characters became visually distinguished. The phonetically adapted graphs were reduced through cursivization or part-selection, turning into new syllabary scripts (*kana*). The semantically adapted graphs remained in their original complex form (*kanji*). That works well for Japanese. Because there aren't so many syllables in the language, all of them can be represented by just a few dozen phonetically adapted characters.

There are still other ways ambiguity can be reduced that were not employed in Chinese-character-based Korean and Japanese writing. For an English word like *moon*, if a writer were to simultaneously use one Chinese character for its meaning value and another for its sound value, the English target word could be specified by the two in combination without any ambiguity at all. The character that writes the Chinese word for 'door' (門) is pronounced "mén," which is similar to "moon." Suppose an English-speaking scribe who knows Classical Chinese combines it with the character for 'moon' (月), pronounced "yue." The result is a new, hybrid graph that looks like this: 腭.[4] A graph of this structure conveys a message something like: "I write an English word that means 'moon' (expressed by 月) and sounds something like [men] (expressed by 門)." There's no ambiguity anymore. There is only one word of spoken English in existence that satisfies these two criteria.

As a second example, consider the word *tongue*, which could be written with 堂 {"táng," 'hall'} based on sound or with 舌 {"shé," 'tongue'} based on meaning. One way to represent English *tongue* without any possibility of ambiguity would be to combine these two characters into a single graph: 舙, with the understanding that this represents an English word that has an equivalent meaning to the Mandarin word *shé* 'tongue' and a similar pronunciation to the Mandarin word *táng* 'hall'. The only English word that fits both criteria is *tongue*.

This kind of innovative combination graph is reminiscent of the phonetic-semantic compound graphs that were so important in the development of the Chinese script, and that continue to dominate it today. The key similarity is that both kinds of compound graph visually indicate something about both sound and meaning, which is the most unambiguous way of representing a word in writing. A crucial difference is that in Chinese compound graphs, the semantic component typically indicates a meaning category like 'celestial phenomenon' or 'body part', or a material like 'wood' or 'metal', rather than the precise meaning of the word being written. In the kind of compound characters we created for the words *moon* and *tongue*, the meaning component is more precise: its meaning in Chinese is a synonym for that of the English word being written.

The creation of new compound graphs of the 𦫼 type during the script-borrowing process is more than just a wild thought experiment for English or a figment of imagination in the inventive art of Xu Bing. It's an important part of the history of writing in Vietnam and adjacent areas of southern China.

Transmission of Chinese Writing to Vietnam and the South

Following the establishment of the first Chinese empire in 221 BCE, the Qín dynasty made military forays deep into the south, conquering areas inhabited by numerous non-Chinese peoples that Chinese histories refer to indiscriminately as "the Hundred Yue" (we should understand "hundred" here as simply meaning 'numerous, varied').[5] The area over which the Qín established a degree of military control encompassed parts of modern-day northern Vietnam. But in contrast to the Hàn dynasty's centuries-long control on the Korean Peninsula, this situation did not last long because of the Qín collapse. The succeeding Hàn dynasty did not immediately reestablish control. A Chinese military commander in the region named Zhào Tuó (Vietnamese Triệu Đà) seized the area and declared an independent kingdom in 204 BCE. The name of this kingdom is today pronounced Nam Việt in Vietnamese and Nán Yuè in Mandarin (the names mean 'southern Yue'). It is considered part of Vietnamese dynastic history and is known as the Triệu dynasty.[6]

While remaining nominally independent, the kingdom became a vassal state of the Hàn empire. In other words, it was allowed to function independently as long as it recognized the authority of the Chinese emperor.[7] Governed on a Chinese administrative model, Nam Việt/Nán Yuè employed Chinese writing for communication and record keeping. This was the first writing introduced into this area. Just as in Korea, a significant number of locals were absorbed into this administrative structure, and some of them were trained to read and write in Classical Chinese even as they spoke local languages, among which was the ancestor of modern Vietnamese. Indeed, their bilingual skills would be crucially important, because they could serve as go-betweens between the rulers and the general populace.

MAP 6.1. The Hàn empire's areas of control around northern Vietnam in the late second century BCE. Map by Ben Pease.

Eventually the Hàn dynasty absorbed the kingdom back into the empire as a province, and a significant Chinese-speaking population migrated into what is now northern Vietnam. Unlike the Korean Peninsula, which eventually gained independence from China, the northern part of Vietnam remained a part of China, and was home to a significant Chinese-speaking population, for a thousand years, until the early tenth century.

Chinese writing was widespread. Literacy meant being able to read and write Classical Chinese, regardless of one's spoken language. From the beginning of the seventh century, Chinese imperial civil service exams were administered in Vietnam as the basis for selecting government officials. To compete successfully, educated elites in the region were fully engaged in Chinese education, gaining a deep familiarity with Chinese language and culture and an intimate understanding of classical texts in history, philosophy, and literature. After Vietnam eventually became independent in the tenth century, the Chinese-speaking community was assimilated into the local culture and language. But Chinese remained the written standard language of Vietnamese government and educated elites right up until the early modern period, when a writing system using a script based on the Latin alphabet became official, as described in chapter 7.[8]

This history is intertwined with the history of the Zhuang and closely related peoples, whose written languages are the other subject of this chapter. But much less is known of that history than of the Vietnamese.

Zhuang is the name of the largest ethnic minority group in China, with a current population of over fifteen million. Today the Zhuang people live mostly in Guangxi in southwest China, which shares a border with Vietnam. The current Chinese government recognizes only a single language spoken by this ethnic minority, but in fact there are a variety of distinct non-Chinese languages spoken by the Zhuang people, all of which are related to each other and, more distantly, to the Thai language. (Nowadays, many Zhuang people are bilingual in Mandarin, or speak only Mandarin, however.) Although historical documentation is incomplete, it is likely that Zhuang speakers were living in roughly this same area during the great imperial expansion that conquered the area and northern Vietnam. Another officially recognized ethnic group of modern China, the Bouyei, speak a language very close to that of the northern Zhuang people. (In this book we will somewhat loosely use the term *Zhuang writing* to refer collectively to the closely related scripts used by the Zhuang and Bouyei peoples to represent their spoken languages.[9])

We know less about how Chinese characters and Classical Chinese writing were learned in these southern areas of China than we do for Japan and Korea. But we do know that Vietnamese and Zhuang speakers were taught and memorized Chinese characters in a way that is similar to how it was done in Korea and Japan: by imitating the pronunciation of Chinese speakers for their sound value, and memorizing an equivalent word in their native languages for the meaning value. The localized pronunciations of Chinese characters are called **Sino-Vietnamese** and **Sino-Zhuang**, parallel to Sino-Korean and Sino-Japanese.[10]

The use of Chinese characters to represent spoken Vietnamese in writing emerged much later than in Korea and Japan. There is no solid evidence of the practice prior to the fourteenth century. Given what we learned about the earliest examples of Korean and Japanese writing, it won't surprise you to learn that the most significant early corpus of Vietnamese-language texts is poetry, specifically the work of the great poet Nguyễn Trãi (1380–1442). The writing system employed in those texts is called Chữ Nôm 'Vietnamese characters', often abbreviated Nôm. The use of Chữ Nôm peaked in the eighteenth and nineteenth centuries, the period that the Columbia professor John Phan calls its "golden age."[11] One of the most famous works of Vietnamese literature, the early nineteenth-century epic poem "The Tale of Kiều," was composed in Chữ Nôm by Nguyễn Du (1765–1820).

We know less about the emergence of Zhuang writing than we do about Vietnamese Chữ Nôm. It is at least several hundred years old, but how much older is impossible to say with certainty. In Zhuang-speaking areas, we don't have clear evidence of the development of a widespread literary tradition like the ones in Korea, Japan, and Vietnam. Instead, surviving Zhuang texts are mostly restricted to a handful of genres. Texts written in the Old Zhuang script include cosmogonic songs, ritual Taoist religious texts, ceremonial and love songs, moral homilies, storytellers' tales, play scripts (including for marionette theatre), opera scripts, and legends written in verse.[12]

The Structure of Spoken Vietnamese and Zhuang

The grammatical properties of spoken Vietnamese and spoken Zhuang languages are very different from those of Japanese and Korean. In most respects, they are more similar to Chinese. This is important, because it is a major factor in the way that Chinese characters were adapted to write these languages spoken to the south of China. It explains why the results look strikingly different from what developed in Korea and Japan.

While the ancestor of ancient Vietnamese spoken two thousand years ago probably did not share all of the same properties as the modern language, by the time the Chinese character script was adapted to write Vietnamese in the fourteenth and fifteenth centuries, these features were present.

Some of the ways that Zhuang and Vietnamese are similar to Chinese languages and different from Japanese and Korean are as follows:

- The verb is in the middle of the sentence, not at the end.
- Words are invariant: there are no case-marking particles on nouns and no suffixes on verbs. Each word is always pronounced the same way no matter how it is used in a sentence.
- Most morphemes are one syllable long.
- There are complex tone systems that impose distinct pitch patterns on syllables, which are important for distinguishing words.

In comparison with the modern Japanese and Korean sentences used to illustrate some of the linguistic properties of those two languages, consider the following sentences in Mandarin and Vietnamese, which illustrate how similar their linguistic properties are to each other, and how different both are from the structure of Japanese and Korean.

MANDARIN:

Měilín	*zài*	*wòshì*	*tīng*	*yīnyuè*		
Meilin	at	bedroom	listen	music		

ránhòu	*hé*	*érzi*	*yìqǐ*	*kàn*	*bàozhǐ*
then	with	son	together	read	newspaper

'Meilin listened to music in the bedroom and then read a newspaper with her son'

VIETNAMESE:

Khiêm	nghe	âm nhạc	trong	phòng ngủ
Khiem	listen	music	in	bedroom

sau đó	đọc	báo	cùng	con trai
then	read	newspaper	with	son

'Khiem listened to music in the bedroom and then read a newspaper with her son'

One interesting feature of the Mandarin and Vietnamese sentences is that there is no tense marked on the verbs. Unlike in Japanese and Korean (and English), tense is not a required part of the grammar of a sentence. The time of the action is inferred from context.

For comparison, the equivalent Japanese and Korean sentences are as follows:

JAPANESE:

Sachi-wa	shinshitsu-de	ongaku-o	kii-te
Sachi-TOP	bedroom-LOC	music-ACC	listen-and

musuko-to	shinbun-o	yon-da
son-COM	newspaper-ACC	read-PAST

'Sachi listened to music in the bedroom and then read a newspaper with her son'

KOREAN:

Jihye-neun	chimsil-eseo	eumak-eul	deut-go
Jihye-TOP	bedroom-LOC	music-ACC	listen-and

adeul-gwa	sinmun-eul	ilk-eotda
son-COM	newspaper-ACC	read-PAST

'Jihye listened to music in the bedroom and then read a newspaper with her son'

All four of these languages have distinct historical origins, deriving from four different ancestral languages. For this reason, the basic vocabulary of each is unrelated to the others. For example, the basic verb roots for 'listen' in the four languages are as follows:

Japanese: *kik-*
Korean: *deut-*
Mandarin: *tīng*
Vietnamese: *nghe*

(The forms of these verb roots look a bit different in the Japanese and Korean example sentences because they change when conjugated.)

The similarities and differences that are most relevant to script adaptation are the ones involving grammatical patterns: whether and how word forms change (for example with the addition of suffixes) and how the words are arranged into phrases and sentences. But there is one aspect of vocabulary that plays a role as well.

Vietnamese and Zhuang, like Korean and Japanese, contain large numbers of vocabulary words that come from Chinese. Just as there are Sino-Japanese and Sino-Korean vocabularies (words of Chinese origin whose pronunciations have changed to fit the Japanese and Korean sound systems), there are also Sino-Vietnamese and Sino-Zhuang ones. In all of these languages, these words serve a function that is roughly equivalent to the Latinate words of English, most of which were borrowed from Old French in the centuries after the Norman conquest of England. Like Latinate words in English, these Chinese-derived vocabulary words are numerous and tend to be more formal than the native ones that have similar meanings.

Consider these pairs of words in modern English:

get	*obtain*
job	*occupation*
walk	*ambulate*
give up	*surrender*
shiny	*lustrous*

The ones on the left are inherited from the Old English spoken in England well over a thousand years ago. Those on the right were borrowed from a dialect of Old French, which inherited them from French's ancestor language, Latin. Notice that although the members of each pair have similar meanings, they convey a different feeling. The ones on the right probably strike you as more educated, more formal, or more appropriate to writing; the ones on the left more simple, more ordinary, more natural to informal speech.

Because of the long history of familiarity with Classical Chinese, leading to the borrowing of Chinese morphemes and their combination into compound words, languages in the region share a set of formal vocabulary words. The Sino-derived words of these languages are similar in pronunciation to each other, and to pronunciations in Mandarin and Cantonese, in just the same way that the Latinate words of English are similar in pronunciation to words in French, Spanish, and Italian. In the example sentences above, the words for 'music' are all related to each other, because they ultimately come from the same ancient Chinese source:

Japanese: *ongaku*
Korean: *eumak*
Vietnamese: *âm nhạc*
Mandarin: *yīnyuè*
Cantonese: *jam¹ngok*[6]

In medieval China, the first syllable was once pronounced something like "im," and the second syllable was once pronounced something like "ngawk," so together: "im ngawk." Although these pronunciations have shifted quite a bit in all five languages over many centuries, the similarities reflecting this common origin are still apparent. *Ongaku, eumak,* and *âm nhạc* are Sino-Japanese, Sino-Korean, and Sino-Vietnamese vocabulary words, respectively.

As writing systems developed for these spoken languages (and for Zhuang as well), it was natural to write the Sino-derived words using the same characters that write them in Chinese. This is what we have earlier called "direct adaptation" of Chinese characters, and we will see it again in our discussion of Vietnamese and Zhuang vernacular writing.

Adaptation Methods of Chinese Characters: Vietnamese

This short poem by Nguyễn Trãi illustrates Vietnamese Chữ Nôm writing:

1	雖浪罜波共英三	Tuy rằng bốn bể cũng anh tam,
2	固几賢冷固几凡	Có kẻ hiền lành, có kẻ phàm.
3	饒說吧停饒事磊	Nhiều thốt đã đành nhiều sự lỗi,
4	𠶊哊𠶊吏𠶊得宀	Ít ăn thì lại ít người làm.
5	奢華於曠铖庫	Xa hoa ở quãng nên khó,
6	爭竸宀恨摆貪	Tranh cạnh làm hờn bởi tham.
7	箕倘奴唯芇固怛	Kia thẳng nọ dùi nào có đứt,
8	得欣些舌買侯甘	Người hơn, ta thiệt, mới hầu cam.

All men are brothers living by the four seas—
Yet some are meek and gentle, some act wild.
He who talks much says much that will offend.
Eat less and you'll need fewer feeding you.
Spendthrifts live high and fall on days of want,
Contestants fight and feud because of greed.
A tug-of-war drags on, for rope breaks not.
Give way a bit—all will be well again.[13]

At first glance, this poem is visually similar to the ancient Korean poem "Song of Cheoyong." Both are eight-line poems of unequal line lengths, written in Chinese characters. But the similarity is largely superficial. "Song of Cheoyong" is written in Chinese characters that are part of the mainstream Chinese writing tradition. A modern-day, well-educated Chinese speaker will be able to recognize most if not all of the characters—or be able to quickly find them in a comprehensive modern Chinese dictionary. Because of this, an educated Mandarin speaker could even pronounce the Korean poem out loud in modern Chinese pronunciation, and identify the meanings of the Chinese words that are conventionally written by most of the characters.

However, the text of "Song of Cheoyong" would be meaningless to such a reader. Why? Because of the many characters that have been phonetically adapted to write Old Korean words or grammatical elements. If you don't know the Old Korean language, there is no way to understand what these characters are writing. It's true that those adapted semantically can be understood, so a Chinese reader might guess correctly that 月 in the poem means 'moon'. But without knowing Old Korean grammar, there is no way to understand the relationship between the word for 'moon' and the other words in the sentence. In short, there is simply no way for a Chinese reader to gain even a rough understanding of "Song of Cheoyong."

The untitled poem by Nguyễn Trãi known informally as "Poem 47"[14] is even more different from Chinese writing than Old Korean *hyangchal*, and even more impenetrable to a modern Chinese reader. Many of the characters in it do not even exist in the Chinese character script. For example, the third and fourth of the first line, 罙 and 波, are nowhere to be found in Chinese writing, either ancient or modern. No matter how well educated a Chinese speaker you might find, they will not be able to recognize or assign pronunciations to these characters. This is a feature of the Vietnamese Chữ Nôm writing system, as well as of Old Zhuang writing, that is not shared by Korean *hyangchal* or written Japanese.

Direct Adaptation

Some of the ordinary Chinese characters found in the poem are being used to write Sino-Vietnamese words. This is analogous to the characters writing *Eastern Capital* in "Song of Cheoyong." This is direct adaptation.

For example, the character at the end of line 6 has the following Chinese values:[15]

貪 : {"tān," 'greed, corruption'}

That word was borrowed into Vietnamese, whereupon the Sino-Vietnamese pronunciation (derived from an ancient southern Chinese pronunciation) became "tham."[16] In other words, the word became part of the vocabulary of spoken Vietnamese. When it appears in texts of written Vietnamese, it is naturally written with the same character as in Chinese.

Phonetic Adaptation

There is a very simple Chinese character at the end of line 1:

三 : {"sān," 'three'}

Looking at its shape, you can easily see the motivation for the original creation of this character in ancient China in order to write the Chinese word meaning 'three'. Its Sino-Vietnamese values are similar:

三 : {"tam," 'three'}

(Contrast this with the native Vietnamese word for three, which is *ba*.)

But here, the character is used to write the syllable "tam" in the word *anh tam* 'brothers'.[17] It has nothing to do with the number three. This is a simple case of phonetic adaptation: the character has been used for its Sino-Vietnamese sound value alone to represent a syllable of a Vietnamese word.

The fact that a Chinese character can be directly adapted or phonetically adapted creates the possibility of ambiguity. For example, the character writing the word 'to buy' in Chinese can represent two different words of Vietnamese:˘

買 : {"măi," 'buy'}   writes Sino-Vietnamese *măi* 'buy'
                             (direct adaptation)
買 : {"măi," 'buy'}   writes native Vietnamese *mới* 'new, recent'
                             (phonetic adaptation)

Occasional ambiguity of this type is not in and of itself a problem. Similar kinds of ambiguity exist in all spoken and written languages. Native speakers can usually resolve it based on real-world knowledge, context, and linguistic competence. Consider the English sentence "This movie is so awful, I just can't bear to keep watching." Whether you read this sentence or hear it spoken, there is no chance that *bear* will be interpreted as a noun referring to a kind of animal. But if this kind of ambiguity proliferates, it becomes more problematic. If nearly every written graph in a sentence can represent more than one possible word, context is less immediately helpful, and reading becomes more burdensome as the reader sifts through multiple combinations and possibilities in search of the most natural interpretation. In the previous chapter, we saw that features of the Korean and Japanese languages help reduce ambiguity in the interpretation of graphs. Commonly recurring structures like nouns followed by case-marking particles and verb roots with suffixes attached provide a framework that helps a reader to interpret the graphs. Conventions like phonetic adaptation for grammatical elements and semantic adaptations for noun and verb roots reinforce the most likely readings.

But the structure of Vietnamese spoken language is not like Japanese and Korean. There are no case-marking particles. There are no grammatical suffixes on nouns or verbs. The "signposts" that readers of those language relied on to correctly interpret the adapted Chinese characters simply aren't present in Vietnamese. So disambiguation was a more pressing need, and different solutions were hit upon by the scholars writing in Chữ Nôm.

One technique was quite simple: to explicitly mark rebus uses of characters. Sometimes, a small wedge-shaped mark ⟨ was added to a graph to indicate that it is being used for its sound value to write a Vietnamese word. Although the graph 買 (Sino-Vietnamese {"mãi," 'buy'}) was often used in unchanged form to write *mới* 'new, recent' by phonetic adaptation, it was also sometimes written this way to clarify its function: 買⟨. In contrast, when used to write the Sino-Vietnamese word *mãi* 'buy', the mark was never added.

New Phonetic-Semantic Compound Graphs

An entirely different technique resolved other cases of possible ambiguity. Consider the three graphs listed in table 6.1 that occur in "Poem 47." The compound graphs 罙, 嶅, and 辿 do not exist in the Chinese writing system. They are the graphs that will trip up a modern-day Chinese or Japanese reader. Each is a compound composed of two characters, one adapted for its meaning and the other for its sound, which in combination uniquely represent a Vietnamese word. They are structurally equivalent to the characters we invented for English words: 𨷹 for *moon* and 舙 for *tongue*. And because these compound graphs don't exist in the Chinese script, there is never any ambiguity about their representational value: they must be writing a native Vietnamese word, never a borrowed Sino-Vietnamese word.

Consider in more detail the Nôm graph <嶅> for *nhiều* 'many' that occurs twice in line 3 of the poem. The Sino-Vietnamese values of its two constituent characters are as follows:

堯 : {"nhiêu," 'lofty'} (Chinese {"yáo," 'lofty'})
多 : {"đa," 'many'} (Chinese {"duō," 'many'})

TABLE 6.1 The semantic and phonetic components
of three Chữ Nôm graphs in "Poem 47"

NÔM GRAPH	VIETNAMESE MORPHEME	SOURCE OF COMPONENTS
罤 – line 1	*bốn* 'four'	四 ('four') + 本 (SV *bổn*)
嶅 – line 3	*nhiều* 'many'	堯 (SV *nhiêu*) + 多 ('many')
乙少 – line 4	*ít* 'few'	乙 (SV *ất*) + 少 ('few')

In combination, the meaning value of the first character is ignored and the
sound value of the second character is ignored. Put another way, one component is adapted semantically and one phonetically. Together, the sound
and meaning values that are retained uniquely converge on a Vietnamese
morpheme.

In this case, the word *nhiều* 'many' satisfies the criteria of having a meaning that matches 多 'many' and a sound that matches 堯 *nhiêu*, which differs
from *nhiều* only by tone (as indicated by the tone mark ` over the vowel
<ê>). Like the phonetic-semantic compounds of the Chinese script, these
compound graphs like 嶅 function almost as little riddles, easily deciphered
by anyone who speaks Vietnamese and, by virtue of being literate in Classical Chinese, knows both the sound and meaning values of the component
characters. Of course, a reader only needs to solve the riddle the first time
they see the character. Once they learn the word it represents, they will read
it faster the next time.

Consider a second example of an innovated Nôm compound graph: <罤>.
(This character appears in line 1 of the poem.) What Vietnamese word sounds
like the bottom part <本> (Sino-Vietnamese *bổn*) and matches the meaning
of the top part <四> ('four')? To a Vietnamese speaker, the answer is obvious:
bốn 'four'.[18]

Semantic Adaptation—or Not

Semantic adaptation is extremely rare in Vietnamese Nôm writing, perhaps
even nonexistent. Only a handful of characters found in Nôm writing appear to have been semantically adapted. The example most often raised in

descriptions of Nôm writing occurs in "Poem 47" at the end of line 4. The graph 炰 writes the commonly occurring Vietnamese word *làm* 'to do, make'. Its form appears to be a part-selected abbreviation of the Chinese character 爲, taking just the top four strokes. Here are the values of 爲:

爲 : Sino-Vietnamese {"vi," 'be, do, act as'} (Chinese {"wéi," 'be, do, act as'})

It is reasonable to suppose that this character was semantically adapted to write the equivalent Vietnamese word *làm* 'to do, make'. It also makes sense that, because *làm* is a high frequency word and the graph 爲 is fairly complex with many strokes, the graph would become abbreviated for ease and speed of writing. The abbreviation would also serve to disambiguate the use of the graph for the native Vietnamese word *làm* from the direct adaptation of the whole character for the Sino-Vietnamese word *vi*.

But there are other hypotheses about the origin of this Nôm graph that don't involve semantic abbreviation, so scholars do not agree on the origin and motivation of this use.[19] Even if this is a genuine case of semantic adaptation, it is striking that this technique is so very rare in Nôm writing, when it is so common for representing verb and noun roots in early Korean and Japanese writing.

The scarcity (or even complete lack) of semantically adapted characters in Nôm writing is probably due to several factors, including the structure of the Vietnamese spoken language and the prevalence of Nôm-style phonetic-semantic compounds.[20]

Adaptation Methods of Chinese Characters: Zhuang

One thing that is so striking about Old Zhuang writing is how close it is structurally to Vietnamese Nôm writing. Similar methods of adaptation of Chinese characters were employed for the representation of Zhuang words. At the same time, spoken Zhuang languages are distinct from spoken Vietnamese, with completely different native vocabularies and sound systems. So while the methods of adaptation and character creation are the same, the particular combinations of phonetic and semantic parts seen in the two scripts are different.

This is exactly what we would expect. Recall that Zhuang and Vietnamese spoken languages have striking similarities in their features, even though they are not genetically related: both have mostly monosyllabic morphemes; both have invariant words that don't take suffixes or case-marking particles. To the extent that linguistic structure, and its relationship to Chinese linguistic structure, constrains and drives adaptation techniques, we would expect to discover similar patterns of adaptation. The geographic proximity of Vietnam and the Zhuang speaking areas also makes it quite possible that adaptation techniques were communicated between these communities as cultural practices.[21]

While many individual graphs are found only in one writing system or the other, the only significant *functional* difference between the two is the presence of semantically adapted characters in Old Zhuang writing. We speculated earlier that the lack of such graphs in Vietnamese Nôm was attributable in part to linguistic factors—that is, to characteristics of the spoken Vietnamese language. But this speculation is difficult to reconcile with the larger numbers of semantically adapted characters used in at least some Zhuang-speaking areas. It suggests that semantic adaptations, at least in small numbers, don't create too much ambiguity for script users. And this further suggests that other factors might be at play in the lack of such adaptations in Nôm. I don't have a good explanation for this disparity.

Let's take a look at some examples of Zhuang writing, and analyze the structure and use of a few graphs.[22]

Phonetic Adaptation

The graphs in table 6.2 are used to write native Zhuang morphemes that sound like, but have no meaning relationship with, the Chinese morphemes written by the characters. The Chinese pronunciations are listed to give you a general idea of those that would have been conventionally associated with Chinese characters by literate Zhuang speakers.

Semantic Adaptation

Semantic adaptation is much less commonly employed for Zhuang words than in early Korean and Japanese writing. But it does occur, and more frequently than in Vietnamese writing. In some Zhuang-speaking regions, it is rare, but in others it is not uncommon. Table 6.3 lists some examples.

TABLE 6.2 Phonetic adaptation in Zhuang writing

ZHUANG GRAPH	CHINESE MORPHEME	NATIVE ZHUANG MORPHEME
文	*wén* 'culture, literature'	*vun^z* 'person'
比	*bǐ* 'compare'	*bi* 'year'
明	*míng* 'bright'	*mwng^z* 'you'
眉	*méi* 'eyebrow'	*mi^z* 'have'

TABLE 6.3 Semantic adaptation in Zhuang writing

ZHUANG GRAPH	CHINESE MORPHEME	NATIVE ZHUANG MORPHEME
月	*yuè* 'moon'	*ndwen* 'moon'
夜	*yè* 'night'	*haem^h* 'evening'
人	*rén* 'person'	*vun^z* 'person'

TABLE 6.4 New phonetic-semantic graphs in Zhuang writing

ZHUANG GRAPH	ZHUANG MORPHEME	SOURCE COMPONENTS (CHINESE VALUES)
辈	*bi* 'year'	比 (*bǐ*) + 年 ('year')
胖	*ndwen* 'moon'	月 ('moon') + 年 (*nián*)

New Phonetic-Semantic Compound Graphs

As we saw with Vietnamese, in many cases two Chinese characters were combined in an innovative way to create an entirely new graph: one is adapted semantically, and one is adapted phonetically; together, they uniquely specify a spoken Zhuang word. Two examples are given in table 6.4.

Sometimes compound graphs use semantic elements that represent a category, rather than a translated equivalent meaning. These, as in table 6.5, are more like the phonetic-semantic compound graphs that developed in the history of Chinese, in which the semantic components represent categories rather than specific words or translated meanings.

If you look carefully at all the examples of Zhuang graphs that have been presented so far, you will notice repetition of some words. For example, 月 and 胖 both write *ndwen* 'moon'. All three techniques—phonetic adaptation, semantic adaptation, and compound graphs—are theoretically available for the representation of any Zhuang word. The script was never standardized or made consistent, so in practice it was quite common for a single Zhuang word to be written in many different ways, varying by time, region, or scribe. Different communities of writers and readers developed different conventions. Table 6.6 contains examples from earlier tables, arranged to show different ways of writing the same words.[23]

TABLE 6.5 More phonetic-semantic graphs in Zhuang writing

ZHUANG GRAPH	ZHUANG MORPHEME	SOURCE COMPONENTS (CHINESE VALUES)
霄	*mbwn* 'heaven, sky'	雨 (weather category) + 門 (mén)
侼	*mwng^z* 'you'	亻 (person category) + 名 (míng)

TABLE 6.6 Examples of variation in Zhuang writing

ZHUANG GRAPH	ZHUANG MORPHEME	TECHNIQUE
明	*mwng^z* 'you'	phonetic adaptation
侼	*mwng^z* 'you'	compound graph
月	*ndwen* 'moon'	semantic adaptation
胖	*ndwen* 'moon'	compound graph
文	*vun^z* 'person'	phonetic adaptation
人	*vun^z* 'person'	semantic adaptation

TABLE 6.7 The line 'What kind of year is this year?' written six ways

SOURCE BOOK	WRITTEN FORM OF SENTENCE *BI NEI^X BI GI^JMA^Z*
a. Matouzhen chapbook (l. 265)	皮女皮鸡马
b. Yellow chapbook (3a:4)	皮尼皮几马
c. Black notebook (l. 225)	辈尼辈鸡麻
d. Brown notebook (l. 225)	辈尼辈鸡马
e. Tiandong text (l. 137)	年呢年鸡麻
f. Taiping text (l. 305 p. 255)	辈呢辈几馬

The variation found in Zhuang writing is even greater than in Vietnamese Nôm writing because of the enormous regional differences in language and custom across the places where the script has been used. This regional variation is well documented by linguist and ethnographer David Holm: "We also discovered that there were typological differences in the scripts from various regions, with semantic readings of Chinese graphs much more common in the north-eastern counties, phonetic readings of standard Chinese characters preponderant in the central west, drastically simplified characters much more common in the east-central counties, and the frequency of Zhuang graphs with semantic indicators [i.e., categories] much higher in the southwest, near the border with Vietnam."[24]

Let's look at one final example showing both regional variation and a variety of techniques of character adaptation. It is a line from a song written in different ways in Zhuang songbooks from different regions.[25] The line represented in all six books is sung in the same way, as the same sequence of Zhuang words. But its representation in writing is different in all six books (table 6.7).

Bi nei^x bi gi^jma^z?
year this year what-kind
'What kind of year is this year?'

In these six texts, three different characters are used to write the Zhuang word *bi* 'year': one is semantic, one is phonetic, and one is composite:

皮 : Chinese {"pí," 'skin'}, phonetically adapted to write Zhuang {"bi," 'year'} (in a, b)

年 : Chinese {"nián," 'year'}, semantically adapted to write Zhuang {"bi," 'year'} (in e)

秕 : New phonetic-semantic compound character (in c, d, f), composed of:

年 : Chinese {"nián," 'year'} as semantic component

比 : Chinese {"bǐ," 'compare'} as phonetic component

Three different characters are used to write Zhuang *nei*[x] 'this', all phonetically adapted:

女 : Chinese {"nǔ," 'female'} (in a)

尼 : Chinese {"ní," 'Buddhist nun'} (in b, c, d)

呢 : Chinese {"ne," sentence-final particle expressing mood} (in e, f)

The characters used for the two-syllable word *gi*[j]*ma*[z] 'what' are all phonetically adapted:

鸡 : Chinese {"jī," 'chicken'} (in a, c, d, e)

马/馬 : Chinese {"mǎ," 'horse'} (in a, b, d, f)[26]

几 : Chinese {"jī," 'table'} (in b, f)

麻 : Chinese {"má," 'hemp'} (in c, e)

But this is only the tip of the iceberg when it comes to variation. The most widely used Zhuang-Chinese dictionary of the Old Zhuang script, *The Old Zhuang–Chinese Dictionary*, lists six ways of writing *nei*[x] 'this' and seven ways for *bi* 'year'.[27] Even this, however, is an incomplete indication of the true degree of variation. In his broad survey of graph forms across the entire region where the Old Zhuang script is used, Holm identified eighteen ways of writing *nei^x* 'this' and twenty-one for *bi* 'year'![28]

What Is "Composite Adaptation"?

In all four of the writing systems we have looked at—Korean, Japanese, Vietnamese, and Zhuang—the basic mechanisms of adaptation are the same: semantic and phonetic. This is a natural consequence of the way that people learn Chinese characters. Educational systems that create literacy in Classical Chinese encourage students to memorize sound and meaning values for each character. The sound values are localized, however. In other words, they are based on Chinese pronunciations but have changed through assimilation into a different language's system of pronunciation. Vowel and consonant sounds of Chinese that don't exist in the local language are modified into similar sounds that do.

The meaning values are also localized, in that they are expressed through a word that translates rather than precisely captures all nuances of their meaning. When a community of language speakers develops a conventionalized set of sound and meaning attributes associated with thousands of Chinese characters, it becomes a communal knowledge base. It is natural and inevitable that speakers of the local language who are literate in Classical Chinese will make use of those attributes as they adapt characters to write the words of their native language.

This process may sound complicated when it is described and explained, but history shows us that the process itself is so natural for the people engaged in it that it happens largely without conscious effort, as has occurred in the adaptation of the Chinese character script to write Korean, Japanese, Vietnamese, and Zhuang.[29]

It is in the secondary processes of disambiguation that we observe the greatest difference between two types of adapted writing systems: linear versus composite. And this is because we have two structural types of languages involved. Japanese and Korean are characterized by words that have suffixes. The alternation of semantically adapted graphs to write word roots and phonetically adapted graphs to write the attached particles and suffixes provides a disambiguating structure that did not require changes to the graphic structure of the characters.

But in Vietnamese and Zhuang, disambiguation was instead achieved through creation of new compound graphs, which combined a semantic and phonetic component in a novel way: **composite adaptation**. These graphs integrate, rather than append, a phonetic component. One advantage of this method is that any newly created graph that represents a native word's meaning with one Chinese character and its pronunciation with a second is always unambiguous.

Why do we not find linear disambiguation techniques in Zhuang and Vietnamese, as we do in Japanese and Korean? The answer lies in the structural differences of the spoken languages. Zhuang and Vietnamese lack suffixes and have one-syllable-long morphemes. The structural signposts that would guide a reader through a linear alternation between semantic and phonetic adaptation are not present. But a composite graph is never ambiguous, even in the absence of grammatical context. And unlike phonetic components that show only part of the pronunciations (like the "gi" that reiterates the [g] sound at the end of the Korean root for 'bright', or the "st" in English 1st), the Vietnamese and Zhuang composite graphs have a phonetic component that indicates the approximate pronunciation of the entire syllable. This degree of specificity further reduces any possible ambiguity.

Other Types of Adaptation

We've now seen the basic patterns and techniques that guided the adaptation of the Chinese-character script as it evolved into new scripts for other languages. As a broad generalization, we can say that the first successful attempts to record spoken versions of premodern Korean, Japanese, Vietnamese, and Zhuang were based on the same simple set of ideas: phonetic adaptation, semantic adaptation, and disambiguation. The particular ways that disambiguation happened were strongly influenced by structural features of the spoken languages involved. The resulting scripts and writing systems thus ended up looking quite different in each language. Japanese developed distinct scripts: morphographic *kanji* and syllabic *kana*. Zhuang and Vietnamese developed large numbers of newly invented compound graphs that never existed in Chinese writing.

In some sense, these differences are superficial, because they are all manifestations of the same underlying principles. The way they played out was affected by the linguistic structures of the languages involved, as well as by historical accident. As the Chinese script spread across Asia, they shaped the overall patterns of its adaptation to writing different spoken languages.

This is not to say that the entire history of these writing systems was simple and straightforward, and can be fully explained by reference to a few general principles. These can explain general trends, but there are also lots of unusual and interesting exceptions and variations. While they are not reflective of general tendencies, they do show the flexibility and creativity—even playfulness—that are made possible when adapting Chinese characters. Before ending the chapter, we'll look briefly at a few of the more interesting, if less common, ways that Chinese characters have been adapted, modified, and transformed.

The two Zhuang graphs in table 6.8 are compounds made up of two Chinese characters. But there is no semantic component. Both graphs approximate the syllabic pronunciation of the Zhuang word being written.

Upon first inspection, these characters seem unnecessarily redundant. Since one of the component characters already provides the pronunciation of the Zhuang word, the second would seem to be entirely superfluous. It doesn't give any additional useful information about pronunciation.

But there is an advantage: disambiguation. The combination of two components yields a distinct graph. By writing the Zhuang word for 'husked rice' with 屵 instead of with 三, the representation will never be in doubt.

TABLE 6.8 Double-phonetic Zhuang graphs

ZHUANG GRAPH	ZHUANG MORPHEME	SOURCE COMPONENTS (CHINESE VALUES)
屲	*san* 'husked rice'	山 {"shān," 'mountain'} + 三 {"sān," 'three'}
魴	*fang* 'ghost'	房 {"fáng," 'house'} + 方 {"fāng," 'square'}

TABLE 6.9 Another kind of Zhuang graph

ZHUANG GRAPH	CHINESE MORPHEME	ZHUANG MORPHEME
眉	*méi* 'eyebrow'	*mi^z* 'have'
冃	none	*ndwi* 'not have, empty'

三 could theoretically write the Sino-Zhuang word for 'three' by direct adaptation, the native Zhuang word for 'three' by semantic adaptation, or the native Zhuang word for 'husked rice' by phonetic adaptation. But 屵, which does not exist in the Chinese script, can only write a native Zhuang word meaning 'husked rice'.

The second example, in table 6.9, involves neither phonetic nor semantic adaptation. The Chinese character 眉 {"méi," 'eyebrow'} has been used for its sound value to write the similar-sounding Zhuang word *mi^z* 'to have' (table 6.2). That's a typical phonetic adaptation. It's the character 冃 in table 6.9 that is unusually interesting. To write the opposite word 'not have, empty', pronounced "ndwi" in Zhuang, the character 眉 'have' was manipulated. To signal the idea of something being missing, the two horizontal strokes inside the rectangular box were removed. The result is a new character that does not exist in the Chinese script.

While semantic and phonetic adaptations are at the core of all historical borrowings of the Chinese script, other methods like those seen above also play a role. In the next chapter, we'll see some examples of this kind of creative, even playful, manipulation and adaptation of Chinese characters, both inside and outside of China.

SEVEN

Chinese Characters in the Modern Era
Today's Written Chinese, Japanese, Korean, Vietnamese, and Zhuang

The historical, cultural, and linguistic properties of Chinese characters (and their Japanese counterpart, *kanji*) provide unique opportunities for playful creativity. Xu Bing's "A Book from the Sky" (chapter 6), for example, re-combines parts of Chinese characters in novel ways to create nonsense that appears superficially sensible, thereby deconstructing our notions of text and meaning. But Chinese characters also present opportunities for sensible play, and for thousands of years, users of the script have manipulated them in ways both novel and amusing.

Three features of Chinese characters contribute to the possibility of playful manipulation. The first is the fact that they are morphographic in function, so that each graph is associated with particular meanings (not just sound values). The second is that some of them contain parts that have semantic values. And the third is that, although Chinese characters are no longer clearly representational, script users possess shared cultural knowledge about the pictographic origin of some characters and parts of characters.

To see how these features allow for creative manipulation, consider the annual Original Kanji Contest jointly sponsored by the *Sankei Shimbun* newspaper and the Shirakawa Shizuka Institute of East Asian Characters and Culture at Ritsumeikan University in Japan. Each year, contestants are invited to submit their invented characters together with their proposed meanings and pronunciations. The grand-prize-winning original *kanji* of 2020, the first year of the global COVID pandemic, is shown in figure 7.1:[1]

Anybody who is literate in Chinese or Japanese would immediately recognize this as a modified version of this common character:

座

FIGURE 7.1. The 2020 Original Kanji Contest prize winner (from the 11th Sousaku Kanji (Original Kanji) Contest, *Sankei Shimbun*, December 24, 2020). Reproduced with permission, unauthorized reproduction and copying prohibited.

In Chinese writing, the character 座 represents the Mandarin word *zuò* 'seat'. In Japanese writing, it has been semantically adapted to write the root of the verb *suwaru* 'to sit'. Within this character are two occurrences of the character 人, which we have seen in earlier chapters. By itself, 人 writes the word for 'person' (Chinese *rén*, Japanese *hito*). In popular conception, these two occurrences of 人 within the character depict two sitting people. The modified version has changed the position of one of the seated figures, moving it to the lower right. What does it mean? The contestant, Akinobu Yamaguchi, submitted a phrase-long pronunciation for the character, built around the verb *suwaru*: *hanarete suwaru (sōsharu disutansu)* 'to sit apart (social distance)'.

The joke—black humor, really—is that the two "people" inside the *kanji* for 'to sit' can no longer be positioned adjacent to each other because of the risk of spreading infection. The shape of the new *kanji* reflects the new mode of socially distanced interaction imposed by the pandemic in 2020. Everyone familiar with Chinese characters gets the joke immediately, because of the salience of the 人 component and the presumption of its semantic value and positional meaning within the larger graph.

This kind of playful manipulation and interpretation of Chinese characters is nothing new. The same sensibility and impulse that we see in modern-day avant-garde art and public *kanji*-creation contests is also found in the *Man'yōshū*, the ancient Japanese poetry collection that is well over a thousand years old. A famous example of playful usage is the hidden occurrence of the character 出 (Chinese {"chū," 'go out'}) in poem 1,787 of volume 9. This character normally writes the root of the modern Japanese verb *deru* 'to go out', and in the ancient Japanese of the *Man'yōshū*, it wrote the root of the now-archaic Japanese verb *izu* 'to go out'. But where we expect this character to be present in the poem, we find instead the Classical Chinese phrase "山上復有山," which means 'a mountain atop a mountain'. The only way to make sense of this is to realize that if the character for 'mountain' (山) is placed atop that same character again, the result is something that looks like 出. So here we have a poetic phrase which is actually a riddle describing the shape of a character.[2] Substituting that covert character for the riddle yields the correct reading of the poetic line.

Playful interpretations and manipulations of characters make for excellent cocktail-party conversation. They are fun to think about and easily capture the imagination of those who are curious about Chinese and Japanese writing. But even though they garner a disproportionate amount of attention, they are atypical. They do not tell us much about the general patterns and principles that governed how the Chinese script developed, how it was borrowed, or how it functions. But they have played a role, if a marginal one. We'll talk about such characters in this chapter, in part because it's fun, but also because the full story of the script can't be told without them. But remember, it's important not to be distracted by the most colorful characters. As with people, they aren't usually the ones doing the bulk of the work.

With this in mind, let's examine a crazily complex character (figure 7.2). This character is used to write the name of a kind of noodle dish that comes from Shaanxi in China: *biángbiáng* noodles. (It is written twice in a row, once for each *biáng*.)

The origin of the name and the origin of the character are both obscure. It's likely that both were invented by enterprising proprietors of noodle shops.

FIGURE 7.2. The character *biáng*.

The name could be onomatopoetic in origin, perhaps an imitation of the sound of the uncooked noodle dough being smacked on the counter or of smacking lips enjoying a delicious meal. As for the character, it is clearly intended to be humorously complex. There are actually many different variants of this character found on noodle shop signs. The version of the character shown in figure 7.2 contains the following components, all of which recur in many other common characters, or are common characters themselves:[3]

辶 'journey'
穴 'cave'
月 'moon'
幺 'tiny' (twice)
言 'speech'
長 'long' (twice)
馬 'horse'
刂 'knife'
心 'heart'

If you search among them for a semantic component related to food or a phonetic component approximating the syllable *biang*, you will do so in vain. Component characters meaning 'moon', 'horse', 'speech', 'heart', and 'knife' are seemingly selected and arranged at random. The character is not structured at all like a normal one, and it is hopelessly impractical. Yet its complexity and impracticality are precisely what make it novel and interesting—and memorable. While people struggle to remember how to write the character, once seen, it is instantly recognizable forever after. There is some irony here, because while this character is effective precisely because of its playful arbitrariness, an entire script consisting of thousands of characters like this one would be impossible to learn or use.

In chapter 2, we saw how a new Chinese character, 鿬, was created to write the new Mandarin morpheme *tián*, meaning 'tennessine'. The structure of this character is modeled on the most common Chinese character type, the phonetic-semantic compound that contains one meaning component and one sound component. Throughout the history of Chinese writing, this has been the most common way to create new characters. But it is not the only way. The script has evolved—and will continue to do so—in creative ways. Technological and cultural shifts inevitably exert influence on Chinese-character-based scripts. In the modern era, the character-based scripts used to write Chinese and Japanese are changing under the influence of the internet, memes, texting, and increased exposure to global languages. Even though the focus of this book is on historical developments of the Chinese script as it spread and transformed in the premodern era, its full story is an ongoing one, and its ending has yet to be written.

How Are Japanese, Korean, Vietnamese, and Zhuang Written Today?

The Chinese-derived writing systems first employed to write the vernacular languages of Japan, Korea, Vietnam, and the Zhuang-speaking areas of China followed divergent pathways in the centuries leading to the modern era. The modern writing system for Japanese reflects an unbroken line of descent. Vietnamese and Korean writing underwent sharp breaks with the past in the early twentieth century. Zhuang writing is in an intermediate state.

The decades around the turn of the twentieth century were a time of tremendous political and cultural ferment in East Asia. Questions of reform—political, educational, military, economic, social, technological—dominated the discourse of elites concerned with modernization. Among the many issues that absorbed their attention was the matter of language reform, and specifically writing reform. In China, Japan, Korea, and Vietnam, beginning in the late 1800s, movements developed to replace Classical Chinese with written vernaculars and to abolish Chinese characters in favor of "phoneticization"—that is, the use of alphabets. While these are in theory separate issues (one is about which language is used in writing, the other about which script is used to represent that language), in practice they were intertwined. These movements reflected a widespread anxiety around character-based writing as a presumed source of weakness and inferiority in comparison with the West, as well as a desire to preserve vernacular languages against the encroachments of Western colonialism. Not all writing reform movements advocated outright abolition of characters; some proposed their reduction or simplification alongside an increased use of romanizations or native phonetic scripts (like *kana* in Japan and Hangeul in Korea). While not all of these reform movements succeeded, they had profound effects on modern writing systems. In some cases, their legacies continue to exert influence.

Japanese

Modern Japanese writing is striking in two ways. First, it is the only Chinese-character-based system outside of China that is stable and widely used today. The others that we have looked at in detail in preceding chapters are either no longer in use (Korean, Vietnamese) or are marginal (Zhuang). The second thing about modern Japanese writing that is so striking is the degree to which its modern incarnation has preserved the key characteristics of morphographic script borrowing that have been present for centuries.

Japanese books today look quite different from ancient texts (figures 7.3 and 7.4). They are typeset with modern punctuation and layout, and may use fonts that don't resemble ancient brush writing. The integration of the Latin alphabet into Japanese writing has also developed to the point that Latin letters (called *rōmaji* in Japanese) are sometimes considered a fourth script in the Japanese mixed-script writing system. Despite these superficial changes, the core structure of the writing is little different from the patterns established over a thousand years ago.

Generally speaking, semantically adapted Chinese characters (*kanji*) are used to write Japanese verb and noun roots, as well as the Sino-Japanese morphemes that are borrowed from Chinese. Phonetically adapted Chinese characters are used for grammatical particles and suffixes, as well as for many "little" words that lack concrete meaning. These phonetically adapted graphs have been simplified in form into new scripts (*hiragana* and *katakana*),

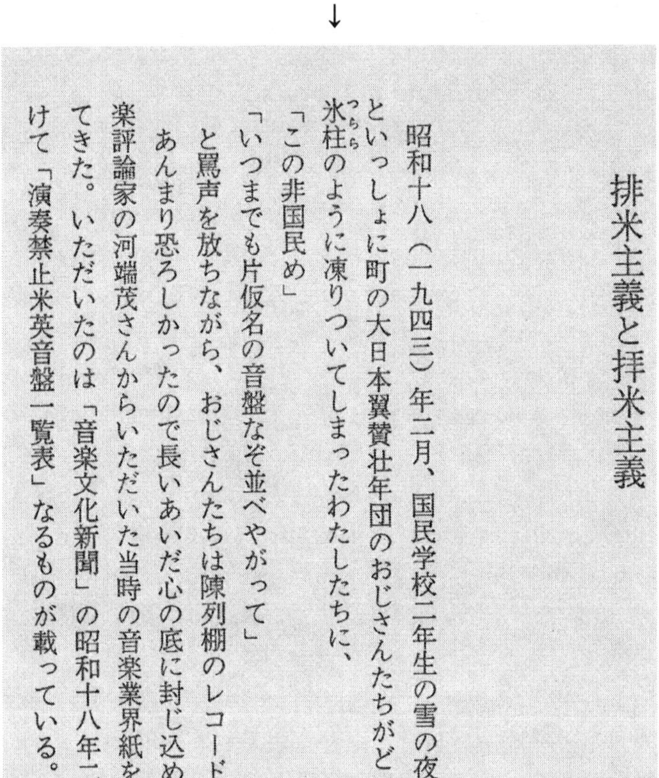

排米主義と拝米主義

昭和十八（一九四三）年二月、国民学校二年生の雪の夜、店の戸がはげしく叩かれ、吹雪といっしょに町の大日本翼賛壮年団のおじさんたちがどっと乱入してきた。びっくりして氷柱（つらら）のように凍りついてしまったわたしたちに、

「この非国民め」

「いつまでも片仮名の音盤なぞ並べやがって」

と罵声を放ちながら、おじさんたちは陳列棚のレコードを店の床に叩きつけて行く……。あんまり恐ろしかったので長いあいだ心の底に封じ込めてきたあの夜の記憶が、こんど音楽評論家の河端茂さんからいただいた当時の音楽業界紙を眺めているうちにまざまざと蘇ってきた。いただいたのは「音楽文化新聞」の昭和十八年二月一日号と二月十日号、二回に分けて「演奏禁止米英音盤一覧表」なるものが載っている。

217　排米主義と拝米主義

FIGURE 7.3. A page from Hisashi Inoue's *Nihongo nikki*, 217. The text of the novel is read in vertical columns from right to left.

so that their function as syllabographs is visually disambiguated from the morphographic *kanji*.

There are various other mechanisms that have evolved in the writing system to disambiguate, including the use of syllabographs to reiterate the final sound of a verb root at the same time it writes a suffix attached to that root. The possibility of ambiguity is still present in the script, but as we have seen over and over again, ambiguity is present in all writing systems, and native speakers can usually resolve it without too much difficulty. (Think about the potential ambiguity in the written English words *bear*, *mold*, *wind*, and *read*.)

That said, the use of morphographic *kanji* for both Sino-Japanese and native Japanese words does create the potential for more ambiguity than is present in most writing systems. An optional mechanism exists for reducing this ambiguity if the writer feels it is desirable: the use of *kana* graphs as annotations, written small alongside a *kanji* to specify its contextual pronunciation. These special-use *kana* graphs are called *furigana*. In English they are sometimes called *rubi* (or *ruby*) *text*. The practice of clarifying readings of morphographic *kanji* using syllabic *kanji* goes back to the earliest Japanese vernacular writing (before the latter had developed into *kana*) and is also a feature of the practice of marking up Classical Chinese texts so they can be read aloud into Japanese (figure 5.1). So this too is an old practice. Over the centuries, it has changed only in typographic appearance, not functionality.

All of these features of Japanese writing can be seen in the excerpt from *Nihongo nikki* (Japanese diary) by Hisashi Inoue (figure 7.3). At the top of the third line from the right, the two characters 氷柱 (Chinese {"bīng," 'ice'} + {"zhù," 'pillar'}) meaning 'icicle' are marked with small-size *furigana* spelling out the three syllables *tsurara* (つらら). This resolves the multiple possibilities for the word represented by the graph sequence <氷柱>, which can write the native Japanese word *tsurara* 'icicle' or the borrowed Sino-Japanese word *hyōchū* 'icicle'. And in this case, the linguistic context isn't sufficient to determine which way of reading is intended.

The existence in the modern writing system of two functionally equivalent syllabaries, *katakana* and *hiragana*, is in a sense redundant. They are interchangeable sets of graphs, each capable of representing all of the syllables of modern Japanese.[4] It's not hard to imagine an alternate history in which one of these two scripts fell out of use. Instead, what happened is that the visual difference between the two was ultimately exploited to convey additional information beyond pronunciation alone.

During certain periods in the past, *katakana* was the more commonly used form of *kana* in mixed-script writing, but in modern Japanese writing, it is *hiragana* that plays this role. *Katakana* is mostly reserved for writing borrowings into Japanese from foreign languages such as English, for sound effects, and to express emphasis (much as bolding, italics, or underlining does in English writing). In figure 7.3, *katakana* appears only once on the page. In the sixth line from the right, the word *rekōdo* (a borrowing of the English word *record*) is written in *katakana* as <レコード>.

In the Japanese translation of William Gibson's classic cyberpunk novel *Neuromancer* (figure 7.4), *katakana* is employed more frequently, reflecting the high density of borrowed English words in the Japanese text. As befitting a novel of experimental fiction, the writing here is deliberately innovative and unusual, and the script choices reflect that. In addition to *kanji*, *hiragana*, and *katakana*, roman letters (<T=A>, <DNA>) also appear, as does creative use of *furigana* that provides English readings for *kanji*. For example, at the top of the seventh line from the right, 冬寂 is annotated with *katakana* spelling *uintāmyūto*, expressing in Japanese pronunciation the name *Wintermute* of the original English text. In ordinary Japanese orthography, these two characters write Japanese morphemes for 'winter' and 'silent', so they would not be read with this English-derived pronunciation in the absence of the *rubi* annotation.

Another use of *katakana* is illustrated in the *Dragon Ball* panel in figure 7.5, where the sound effect *gyuaa-* is written in *katakana* script: <ギュアアッ>.

At this point, you might well be wondering: Why not just get rid of *kanji* and write Japanese using *kana* to represent the sounds of all the words? In fact, why not also eliminate one of the two *kana* scripts, and write all of Japanese just with syllabic *hiragana*? You would not be the first person to ask this question. One can imagine many advantages that these changes would bring. Japanese speakers would only have to learn several dozen graphs in order to become literate, instead of over a thousand *kanji*. They would no longer need to use complicated disambiguating strategies like *rubi* annotations.

But treating the Japanese writing system as a problem in need of a solution

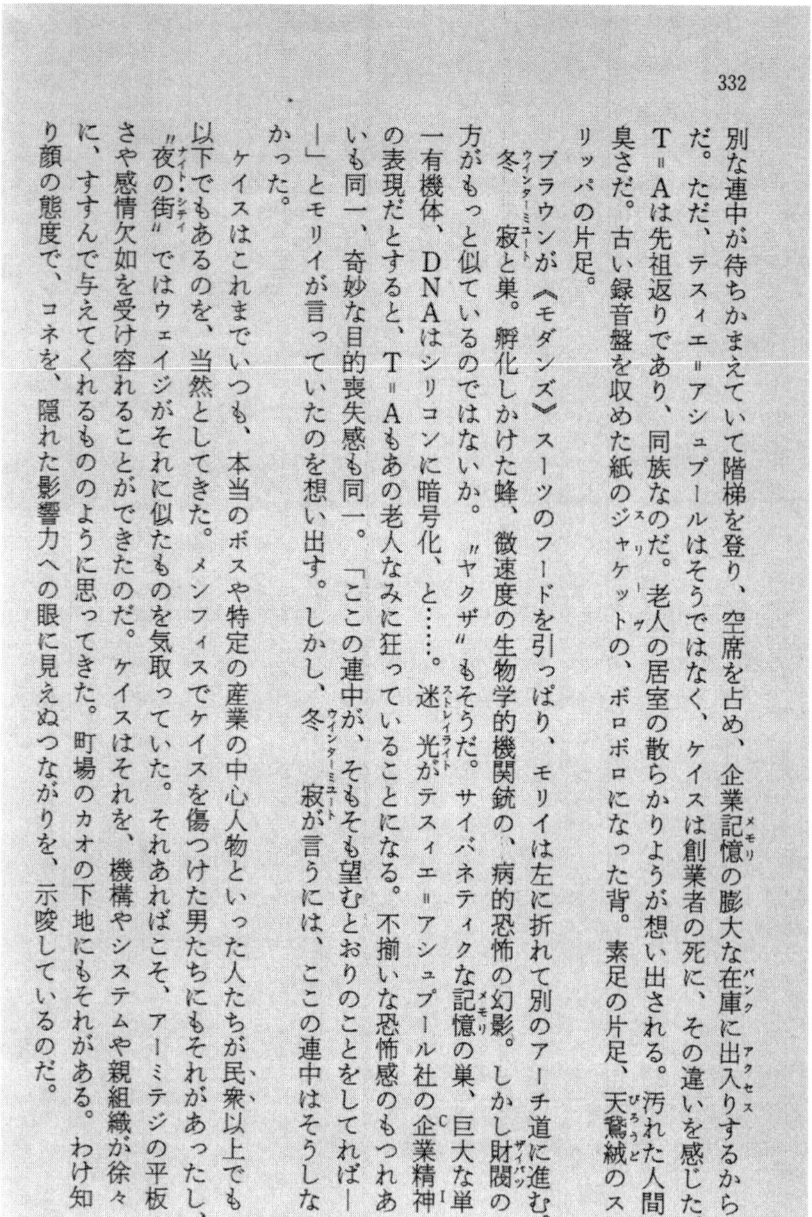

別な連中が待ちかまえていて階梯を登り、空席を占め、企業記憶の膨大な在庫に出入りするからだ。ただ、テシエ＝アシュプールはそうではなく、ケイスは創業者の死に、その違いを感じた。

T＝Aは先祖返りであり、同族なのだ。老人の居室の散らかりようが想い出される。古い録音盤を収めた紙のジャケットの、ボロボロになった背。素足の片足、天鵞絨のスリッパの片足。

ブラウンが《モダンズ》スーツのフードを引っぱり、モリイは左に折れて別のアーチ道に進む。冬寂と巣。孵化しかけた蜂、微速度の生物学的機関銃の、病的恐怖の幻影。しかし財閥の方がもっと似ているのではないか。"ヤクザ"もそうだ。サイバネティクな記憶の巣、巨大な単一有機体、DNAはシリコンに暗号化、と……。迷光がテシエ＝アシュプール社の企業精神の表現だとすると、T＝Aもあの老人なみに狂っていることになる。不揃いな恐怖感のもつれあいも同一、奇妙な目的喪失感も同一。「ここの連中が、そもそも望むとおりのことをしてれば——」とモリイが言っていたのを想い出す。しかし、冬寂が言うには、ここの連中はそうしなかった。

ケイスはこれまでいつも、本当のボスや特定の産業の中心人物といった人たちが民衆以上でも以下でもあるのを、当然としてきた。メンフィスでケイスを傷つけた男たちにもそれがあったし、"夜の街"ではウェイジがそれに似たものを気取っていた。それあればこそ、アーミテジの平板さや感情欠如を受け容れることができたのだ。ケイスはそれを、機構やシステムや親組織が徐々に、すすんで与えてくれるもののように思ってきた。町場のカオの下地にもそれがある。わけ知り顔の態度で、コネを、隠れた影響力への眼に見えぬつながりを、示唆しているのだ。

FIGURE 7.4. A page from the Japanese translation of the 1984 cyberpunk novel *Nyūromansā* (Neuromancer) by William Gibson, 332. The text is read in vertical columns from right to left.

FIGURE 7.5. A panel from the popular Japanese manga (comic book) *Dragon Ball*, from *Weekly Shōnen Jump*, no. 51, November 19, 1985, as reprinted in Toriyama, *Dragon Ball Full Edition*, 103.

is the wrong way to think about it. The current writing system must have some practical advantages for Japanese readers, or it would not have persisted through so many centuries of trial and error. Indeed, scientific studies suggest that the use of *kanji* in Japanese writing provides efficiencies for readers.[5] These may well compensate for the additional time and effort it takes for children to learn the *kanji* they need to become literate.

Modern Japanese writing, as unnecessarily complex as it may appear from the outside, works quite well. While nobody would have designed such a system from scratch, that doesn't mean its current incarnation, developed through a series of historical contingencies and organic improvements, should be considered a problem. Japan is a leading nation of the world—economically, scientifically, culturally, technologically. It would be hard to argue that its writing system has impeded the ability of its people or the country as a whole to excel in any sphere of modern life.

To be sure, the modern Japanese writing system can be frustratingly complex to adult learners approaching it as a second language. The mix of several scripts, the large number of *kanji* to learn, and the multiple representational values of many of those *kanji* all present enormous challenges to non-native learners. But an understanding of the historical processes of development explains the features we see in the modern writing system and why they came into existence. Modern Japanese writing results from the natural processes of semantic adaptation, phonetic adaptation, and disambiguation, processes that have happened every time the Chinese script has spread to write other languages. History demonstrates that these processes work. We have seen that they worked to enable spoken Old Korean to be represented in written form. Modern Japanese writing likewise continues to work well for its readers today.

Korean

Unlike Japanese, Korean writing has changed radically since Chinese characters were first adapted to write the vernacular language well over a thousand years ago. It seems at least possible that *hyangchal* writing could have developed into a modern mixed-script system very much like that used for Japanese today. Structurally, the way the writing functions in the poem "Song of Cheoyong," with its mix of semantically and phonetically adapted graphs, is very similar to what we see in modern Japanese writing. The only difference is that the phonetically adapted graphs of Korean *hyangchal* are not visually abbreviated into something resembling *kana*.

But even that difference is superficial. In the ancient Japanese *Man'yōshū* poetry collection, phonetically adapted characters still retain their original form. The writing looks a lot like *hyangchal*. And in various later kinds of Korean writing, as well as in glossing of Classical Chinese texts for reading aloud into Korean (analogous to the Japanese practice of *kanbun kundoku*, figure 5.1), we do see conventionalized abbreviations of phonetically adapted Chinese characters (table 7.1). These could have formed the basis of a *kana*-like phonetic script. But in Korea, the history of writing took a different path.

A singular event in the history of Korean writing took place in the mid-fifteenth century because of the decision of a powerful, intelligent, and ambitious king known today as Sejong the Great (1397–1450). This was the invention of the Korean alphabet, which ultimately completely remade the history of Korean writing. Half a millennium after King Sejong's innovation, Chinese characters now play only a marginal role in Korean writing.

TABLE 7.1 Examples of abbreviated Chinese characters functioning as syllabographs in premodern Korean writing

ORIGINAL CHARACTER WITH MANDARIN VALUES	SINO-KOREAN PRONUNCIATION	ABBREVIATED FORM	SYLLABIC SOUND
古 (*gǔ* 'ancient')	"go"	口	[go]
果 (*guǒ* 'fruit')	"gwa"	人	[gwa]
尼 (*ní* 'Buddhist nun')	"ni"	ヒ	[ni]
羅 (*luó* 'net')	"ra"	罒	[ra]

Excerpted from Chung, "Han'guk-ŭi kugyŏl," 168–71.

Could Korean writing have ended up more like Japanese if King Sejong hadn't invented an alphabet that provided a clear alternative?

It's certainly possible. The abbreviated Chinese characters functioning as syllabographs in table 7.1 never developed into a full script capable of representing every syllable of spoken Korean. But could it have? Not as easily as for Japanese. There are only around a hundred distinct syllables in Japanese, while there are many more in Korean. In addition, a lot of them are not particularly close in pronunciation to any syllables of Chinese. For this reason, selecting a subset of Chinese characters to represent all the syllables of Korean is challenging. This is not an insurmountable problem, but it isn't trivial either.

The poetic tradition embodied by the *hyangga* poems like "Song of Cheoyong" seems to have died out some time around the eleventh century, and even the ability to read and interpret these early vernacular writings subsequently was lost over time, along with the *hyangchal* writing technique itself.

Classical Chinese continued to be used, however. Alongside it, a stylized written language that had a simplified Korean grammatical framework and a large amount of Sino-Korean vocabulary also arose, called *idu*. It could be read aloud as a kind of highly formalized Korean, but it didn't correspond to the way people actually spoke. In *idu*, Sino-Korean vocabulary was written in Chinese characters (what we have been calling direct adaptation).

The limited number of native Korean grammatical elements present in this stylized language (case-marking particles, verbal suffixes, connecting words) were written with phonetically adapted characters. These were sometimes abbreviated (similar to what is seen in table 7.1), just as they were when used as marginal glossing marks to indicate where to insert Korean grammatical elements when reading Classical Chinese texts aloud into Korean.

But *idu* didn't do what *hyangchal* had once done. It never developed into a full written representation of ordinary spoken Korean. And once Classical Chinese ceased to be an official written language in Korea around the turn of the twentieth century, *idu* writing died out.

In the meantime, the Korean alphabet that King Sejong had invented in the mid-fifteenth century had not displaced Chinese writing, but it was used in a variety of nonofficial capacities, including Korean-style poetry, translations of Buddhist texts, Korean-language vernacular novels, and dictionaries, and for the annotation of pronunciations of Chinese characters. In the late nineteenth and early twentieth centuries, the need arose for a new national written language based on spoken Korean. Intellectuals seeking to create this modern written language naturally turned to this alphabet, originally called Hunmin Jeongeum ('proper sounds for enlightening the people'), now called Hangeul (often spelled Hangul).[6]

The new system of writing Korean that emerged after a period of experimentation in the early twentieth century was a mixed-script system but differed in a key respect from that of Japanese. Chinese characters were used only for Sino-Korean words, which meant there was effectively no ambiguity at all in their representation. They were all directly adapted, never semantically or phonetically. All other Korean words, not just grammatical particles but also native verb and noun roots, were written with the alphabet.

This mixed-script writing endured through more than half of the twentieth century in South Korea.[7] Afterward, the use of Chinese characters declined rapidly, as more and more Sino-Korean words were written in Hangeul instead. In North Korea, all Chinese characters were eliminated as a matter of government policy in 1949 (with exceptions for certain specialized uses). North Koreans today write entirely in the Hangeul alphabet.

It is interesting to compare a 1950 issue of a South Korean newspaper with one from this century. The older one is dense with Chinese characters, writing all the Sino-Korean words. In the headlines, Chinese characters out-number Hangeul use by a significant margin, reflecting the high percentage of Sino-Korean vocabulary present in newspaper-style language.

But today, some South Korean newspapers contain no Chinese characters at all, while others use only a handful. Their use is almost entirely restricted to headlines, where they serve a useful purpose as morphographs by disam-biguating homophonous morphemes. This is especially helpful in headlines, which are highly abbreviated to save space and provide less linguistic con-text for disambiguation. Chinese characters are also used, for branding and stylistic effect, in many product names. For example, the newspaper name *Chosun Ilbo* (The Chosun daily) is written in Chinese characters at the top of every issue, <朝鮮日報>, in the same font as it was in the 1950s. (Nowadays, however, it is written horizontally instead of vertically.)

Today, Korean students are still taught about Chinese characters. Korean speakers are still aware that their vocabulary contains "Chinese-character words" (what we have been calling Sino-Korean words), which they recognize as derived from Chinese. But the use of the characters themselves in everyday writing is hugely diminished, and most younger Koreans have little ability to write them. As their use diminishes, the motivation and opportunity for Korean speakers to learn, remember, and recognize them decreases, and this creates a feedback loop: the fewer characters that people know, the weaker the incentive becomes for writers and publishers to use any at all. It is certainly possible that Chinese characters will stop being a part of modern South Korean writing at all before too long.

On the other hand, Chinese characters are still culturally prominent, and this might extend their longevity. Their symbolic presence is ubiquitous in Korean public life, even if their use is marginal in ordinary writing. For ex-ample, characters are frequently employed in signage for a variety of reasons. They can signal a unique brand identity in advertisements and product names (as in the newspaper name *Chosun Ilbo*); they can convey connotations of elegance, erudition, nostalgia, or old-fashionedness; and they can help dis-ambiguate homophones in situations where linguistic context or space is lim-ited (such as newspaper headlines, signs, and technical writing). Moreover, Chinese characters occupy a place of prestige in the collective imagination and in cultural notions of proper education. Children's educational materials teaching basic characters are commonly sold in bookstores and stationery shops. Given the cultural value attached to Chinese characters, it's entirely possible that a limited number of them will persist within Korean writing, perhaps only a few hundred, which most Koreans will learn to recognize (if not to write) without too much difficulty.

Vietnamese

Even in its heyday, the lower status of Chữ Nôm as compared with Classical Chinese was one reason that it never became standardized. In the eighteenth and nineteenth centuries, when a profusion of literature was produced in Nôm, literary scholars creatively explored innovations for the script.[8] Given that Nôm was flourishing as a medium for expressing Vietnamese literary culture, it would seem to have been well positioned to displace Classical Chinese in the twentieth century, when vernacular writing displaced Classical Chinese throughout East and Southeast Asia. In fact, many Vietnamese nationalists deliberately used Nôm instead of Classical Chinese in the early years of the century as an expression of patriotic pride and anti-Chinese sentiment.

But Nôm was not the only readily available script that could be used to write Vietnamese. A standard romanized system had already been in use for several centuries. It was devised by Portuguese and French missionaries and colonialists, and its use had been largely limited to Catholic communities and colonial administrators. Based on the Latin alphabet and incorporating spelling conventions found in Portuguese and French writing, the script additionally made extensive use of diacritics to indicate distinct vowels and tones.

Throughout the first half of the twentieth century and into the second, the political situation in Vietnam was complex and fluid as the country vied for independence against the French and the Japanese. During the political realignments that took place in Asia after the end of the First World War, the Vietnamese independence movement selected the alphabetic form of writing over Nôm.[9] The romanized script spread quickly, already dominating Vietnamese writing by the 1920s. Over ensuing decades, the use of Nôm and knowledge of Chinese characters both rapidly declined. As in Korea, Vietnam's written landscape was completely transformed in a matter of decades.

Today, knowledge and use of Chinese characters and of Nôm writing are known only to academic specialists and calligraphers. But the influence of Chinese writing has not completely disappeared, even though characters are not used at all anymore. As in Korea, Vietnamese speakers retain a strong intuition about which words in their language are of Chinese origin and recognize them as distinct from native Vietnamese. Nôm script is still visible at historical and communal sites, attesting to its lasting impact on Vietnamese culture.

Zhuang

Usage of the Old Zhuang script had traditionally been limited to a small number of genres, and this has not changed in the modern era. As part of its policy toward ethnic minority peoples and languages, in the second half of the twentieth century, the Chinese government worked to develop functional writing systems for all of the officially recognized languages spoken in the country, including Zhuang. For some, like Mongolian and Tibetan, there were already well established, widely used writing systems. But most minority languages had been largely unwritten prior to the twentieth century. For these, the government created new writing systems by modifying Hanyu Pinyin to accommodate their sound systems. Even though Old Zhuang script already existed as an embodiment of the Zhuang cultural legacy, the decision was made to develop and promote a new alphabetic writing system. (The designation "Old" distinguishes the traditional script from the twentieth-century alphabetic ones devised for Zhuang). As a result of these language policy developments, today the Old Zhuang script is still used in specialized ways but will probably never develop into a widespread, standardized writing system.

Something else worth noting about the Old Zhuang script is that even within the limited scope of its use, it is not clear that it is functioning fully as a writing system. The creation and use of scriptural texts is often somewhat decoupled from the learning and recitation of its content, as David Holm explains:

> How such ritual texts are recited is something that is memorised by
> the acolytes (apprentices) of the master priests. . . . Acolytes from a
> young age listen carefully to their master's recitations and follow along,
> adding their voices to his in unison. By the time acolytes are considered

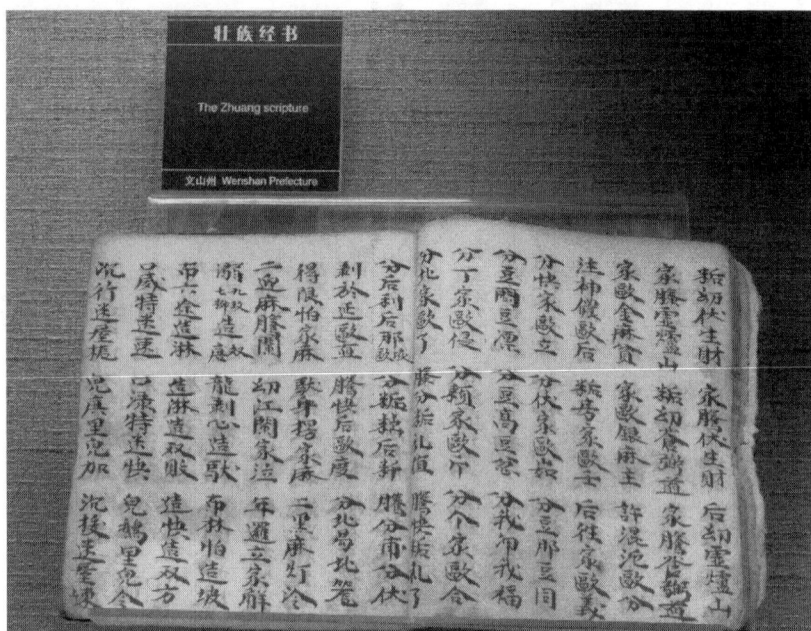

FIGURE 7.6. A Zhuang religious manuscript held in the Yunnan Nationalities Museum in Kunming.

ready for ordination as priests, they will have developed a high degree of familiarity with a range of liturgical texts, and be able to recite them from memory. *Thus the act of recitation in a ritual context, while it may involve turning the pages at more or less the right time, does not involve focussing on the pages of the manuscript, much less reading each character one by one.* Reciting the text, in other words, is a performative act. This is a very common situation among ritual practitioners in Southwest China.

On the other hand, the written content of the manuscripts is preserved quite carefully from generation to generation: each generation of apprentice priests is required to copy out carefully by hand all the ritual texts that his master gives him. The master's own copies of the manuscripts are normally burned along with the master's other personal belongings at the time of his death. I have seen copies of manuscripts in which the number of characters in each section was counted and the number written at the end of the section. This was clearly intended as a precaution against scribal omissions in copying. I have also inspected copies of manuscripts written by different disciples of the same priest, and found that they both replicate quite exactly the graphic composition of characters in the original. The textual tradition, in other words, is highly conservative.

The overall effect of this is that the recitation of texts and the transmission (copying) of texts are to a considerable extent de-coupled. That is, knowledge of how the texts are recited is conveyed orally, through the process of apprentices listening to recitations and replicating them in their own oral performance, while knowledge of the script in which the scriptures are written is effected by transcription (making manuscript copies). *These two modes for the transmission of cultural knowledge not only differ in quality, but are separated in time.* Oral recitation begins quite early in the process of participation in rituals—some acolytes learn to sing along when they are well under ten years of age, usually accompanying an older relative—whereas transcription of texts takes place when an apprentice undergoes ordination.[10]

One implication of this is that there are many fewer people who can produce new texts in Old Zhuang script than can copy and use existing texts. How long this writing system continues to be used and by how many people depends on cultural factors, including the survival of the cultural and religious practices that make use of it today, and of the symbolic value of the script as part of the ritual practice.

The Future of Chinese Characters Inside and Outside of China

By the third decade of the twentieth century, Chinese characters had been eliminated in Vietnam and had begun their long glide path to marginalization in Korea. In China and Japan, they survived, although the scripts underwent major changes.[11] But romanizations played an increasingly important role alongside those characters, one that was mediated through a series of technological changes.

It is difficult to imagine now, in this era of Unicode, high-resolution displays and printers, and adaptive-predictive character input systems, the degree to which technological changes in the twentieth century threatened—or were perceived to threaten—the survival of Chinese characters in China and *kanji* in Japan.[12] The anxiety expressed by Chinese intellectuals in the late nineteenth and early twentieth centuries about the drawbacks of Chinese writing surfaced once again in the 1970s through the 1990s as computerization became increasingly important.

Whether the invention of the telegraph, the typewriter, or the computer, each technological advance seemed to favor the alphabetically written languages of the Europeans.[13] The sheer quantity of Chinese characters, the lack of simple search and ordering algorithms, even the density of the characters that made them difficult to display in pixels on screens or in ink dots on a printed page, seemed life-threatening to Chinese writing.[14] Each technological advance brought a new chorus of voices demanding that characters be eliminated lest they doom their users to irrevocable technological and economic backwardness.

The historian Thomas Mullaney has pointed out that despite vocal advocacy for the elimination of Chinese characters in favor of sound-based scripts—more than twenty such proposals were made between 1890 and 1911—a series of brilliant and hard-working technologists in China, Japan, and beyond devised ways to ensure that character-based scripts would remain compatible with vital communication technologies, from the telegraph to the modern-day smartphone.[15]

Today the situation appears to have stabilized. Anxieties around character-based writing have dissipated. Suspicions about inherent incompatibility between characters and computing technology have been laid to rest. China and Japan have proven themselves on the world stage and demonstrated that their morphographic scripts are fully compatible with the modern era.

There is a long-standing tendency in the West to think of the alphabet as the culmination of progressively better writing systems. From the primitive "picture-writing" of ancient Egypt and Sumer, we have advanced to the rational phoneticization embodied by the Greek and Latin alphabets—or so the story goes. But the bigger historical picture doesn't favor the notion of alphabetic superiority. Egyptian hieroglyphs and Sumerian cuneiform were in successful use for thousands of years. Alphabetic writing—that is, scripts with letters representing both consonant and vowel sounds—has been in existence roughly as long as Chinese writing, and both are still in use today. While we cannot predict the future, it would be a mistake to assume that there is some overarching march toward progress and modernization that will inevitably eliminate the use of characters in China and Japan. That notion is a biased, Western-centric view that, in my opinion, has blinded too many scholars and laypeople from an objective assessment of the history of Chinese writing and Chinese characters.

Three Thousand Years of Chinese Characters: How Many More?

It's difficult to predict the future. But we can say with some confidence that the Chinese and Japanese writing systems don't appear to be in any sort of danger or crisis. This does not mean, however, that the script is unchanging. A morphographic script must change, because spoken languages shed and gain morphemes. New morphemes require new graphs. In addition, the creativity and innovation that have always been a part of Chinese character history have been supercharged by the internet, the rapid lifecycle of memes, the pressures of government censorship, and other factors. At the same time, the standardization of encodings has limited the speed at which the script can change and still be fully compatible with fonts, input methods, data searches, and other aspects of high-tech communication and storage. The discovery of tennessine was announced in 2010, but the character writing its Chinese name, 鿬, was made official only in 2017 and added to Unicode in release 11.0 in June 2018. It took several more years before major operating systems and fonts were modified to include support for the full set of codepoints in Unicode 11.0. Even today, many phones and computers will not be able to render this character properly. The complex character used to write *biáng* in *biángbiáng* noodles was added to Unicode 13.0 in March 2020. Prior to that time, it could not be encoded in Unicode-based text documents (except by the very unwieldy compositional formula ⿺辶⿳穴⿲月⿱⿲幺長⿱言馬幺長刂心).[16] While working on this book in January 2023, I found myself unable to input the character using my work computer, because I had not yet updated my system software to one containing the latest version of Unicode.

These technical challenges have not prevented new characters from being coined and disseminated, often in the form of graphic images or novel combinations of existing encoded graphs. In some cases, the characters are playful or even subversive. (For politically sensitive character creations, dissemination as images rather than text can be an advantage for evading automated censoring algorithms.[17])

For example, the name of Keio University in Japan is standardly written with two *kanji* that look like this: 慶應.[18] In Japanese they are pronounced "kei" and "ō," respectively, which happen to sound identical to the Japanese pronunciations of the names of the letters K and O. Notice that both of these characters have the component 广 in them (at the top and left). Taking advantage of all these facts, the two characters are sometimes rewritten playfully as 庆 庄, which makes them simpler to write. The characters' structures are completely normal. The only thing unusual about them is that the "K" and "O" parts, effectively phonetic components, come from a different script, the Latin alphabet.

Taking things a step further, these two novel *kanji* can be further abbreviated as 庆, a single *kanji* with a two-syllable pronunciation. This kind of integration of Latin letters into Chinese characters is increasingly common, which is hardly surprising given the familiarity that educated Chinese and Japanese speakers have with the alphabet.

Many newly coined characters are fleeting. Their creation is inspired by a cultural moment, a political event, a humorous meme. Most don't survive long enough to become part of the writing system. But some do, and each time one of them becomes embedded into the script, its unusual and innovative structure becomes a model for other characters of the same type. In this way, the nature of the script can subtly and gradually change over time. For example, we are likely to see more and more integration of Latin letters not just into Chinese writing but into the structure of Chinese characters themselves, as with the Keio University example. In my view, Chinese characters are far more likely to evolve than to disappear.

Today, Classical Chinese is no longer a common written language for East Asia and Vietnam. In China itself, it is still studied, and all high school students are exposed to it. But despite its cultural and historical importance, its mastery is no more a part of the ordinary Chinese person's education than is that of Latin and Greek in Europe and the Americas. The linguistic landscape that led Matteo Ricci to view Chinese characters as a kind of universal writing, symbols embodying ideas rather than words, vanished over a hundred years ago. It is, however, still the case today that Chinese characters are used to write modern Chinese and modern Japanese, often having similar meanings but very different pronunciations in the two writing systems. For example, the character 月 means 'moon' in both Chinese (where it's pronounced "yuè" in Mandarin) and Japanese (where it's pronounced "tsuki").

We've emphasized that characters write specific morphemes with specific pronunciations, and that we can't understand how characters were created and developed and adapted without recognizing their sound values. Yet today we can still observe that 月 writes different words for 'moon' in different languages regardless of any particular pronunciation. Does this mean that Ricci was correct that Chinese characters, even if only in theory, are so different from alphabetic writing as to potentially be a universal system of writing? Could this be a kind of shortcut that could allow people all over the world to easily learn to communicate with each other through writing?

In the next, final chapter, we will return to this idea, and reevaluate it given what we understand about the history, structure, and function of Chinese characters over the more than three thousand years of their existence, as they have spread and changed to write many different languages.

EIGHT

Universal Writing
The Impossible Dream

When I was a graduate student at UC Berkeley studying Chinese linguistics in the 1990s, I worked for a time as a research assistant to James A. Matisoff, a professor in the Linguistics Department specializing in languages of Asia. The project had its own office space with its own landline phone. You'd be surprised at the number of people who contact university academics out of the blue with all kinds of unusual questions and requests. One day, when I was working at the project office, the phone rang. On the other end of the line was a young man who eagerly explained to me that he was making a birthday card for his girlfriend, and he wanted it to be special. He planned to put a Chinese character on the card but, not knowing any Chinese, he needed help finding the right one.

For reasons that he didn't make clear, the character he was looking for was the one for 'horizon'. "If I give you my email address, can you send me the Chinese character that means 'horizon'?" he asked.

In Standard Mandarin there is a word meaning 'horizon'. It is *dìpíngxiàn*. The word is composed of three morphemes: {"dì," 'earth'}, {"píng," 'flat'}, and {"xiàn," 'line'}. It's a compound word that literally means 'flat line of the earth'. In Chinese writing, each meaningful element of spoken language—each morpheme—is represented by a distinct character. So the three meaningful elements of *dìpíngxiàn* are written with a sequence of three characters, one for each morpheme: *dì-píng-xiàn* 地平線.

In short, there is no single Chinese character for 'horizon'. I did my best to explain this. My best was not good enough. This fact was not just unwelcome; it was not comprehensible, because it contradicted his deeply held presumption about Chinese writing. Like Francis Bacon, he was convinced that each individual Chinese character represented an idea, and that for each basic concept in our universe there must exist a single corresponding Chinese character.

But would it even be possible for a system of characters of this kind to exist? A thought experiment along these lines raises all kinds of daunting practical and philosophical questions. How many "ideas" or "things" are there in the universe, and which ones are "basic"? Do our spoken languages have single words corresponding to all basic ideas? Are basic ideas immutable, or do they vary across time, space, and cultures? For example, is 'toast' a basic idea? Is 'toothbrush' a basic idea? Is 'dodecahedron'? 'Disgruntlement'? 'Romantic love'? Is the slight indentation between the bottom of your nose and your upper lip a basic idea?

Anyone who has engaged in the task of translation from one language to another has had to grapple with issues like this. The answers to these questions have implications not just for how we conceptualize our universe and how we understand human thought. They also bear on what kinds of writing systems are possible, and whether a universal system of communication could ever be invented.

How Do You Make a Universal Writing System?

Chinese writing is not picture writing. It is not possible to create a true writing system through representational pictures alone. This is because human languages do not simply consist of linearly arranged nouns and verbs referring to real-world objects and events that can be depicted by drawings. They are replete not just with abstract nouns and verbs (*equality, privacy, dissatisfaction, ponder, evaluate, represent, chillax*) but with words and functional components that express qualities (*red, basic, intentional*), grammatical relationships (*to, of, for*), and syntactic categories (*-ed, -s, -er*). If writing is to adequately represent speech in visual form, and thus be capable of preserving and transmitting narratives, poems, songs, philosophical arguments, legal judgments, dialogues, and so on, it must be able to represent all of these things. This is simply impossible to do with representational images. Extract any medium-sized paragraph from your favorite novel or essay — or from this book—and think about which words, prefixes, and suffixes could be depicted through small, simple drawings. Or whether the whole passage could be adequately conveyed with one or more complex images.

Consider this example, a brief excerpt from American writer Edgar Allan Poe's classic 1843 short story "The Tell-Tale Heart":[1]

> But even yet I refrained and kept still. I scarcely breathed. I held the lantern motionless. I tried how steadily I could maintain the ray upon the eye. Meantime the hellish tattoo of the heart increased. It grew quicker and quicker, and louder and louder every instant. The old man's terror *must* have been extreme! It grew louder, I say, louder every moment!—do you mark me well? I have told you that I am nervous: so I am. And now at the dead hour of the night, amid the dreadful silence of that old house, so strange a noise as this excited me to uncontrollable terror.

Many of the words in this passage are clearly not amenable to pictorial representation: *yet, refrained, scarcely, so, as, uncontrollable*, and so on. Setting these words aside and considering the more concrete vocabulary, even if you could come up with a good drawing to represent the word *ray*, how would you distinguish it from drawings for *beam* and *shaft*? You could in theory come up with an arbitrary convention to distinguish drawn representations of these three words for an emanation of light. But this problem recurs again and again. How would you draw a distinction between *nervous, anxious, worried, distressed, ill at ease*? Continuing to make arbitrary variations in pictorial representations runs into the problem that humans don't have the ability to memorize tens of thousands of arbitrary images and match them with words of spoken language.

The basic problem is that spoken languages contain too many words and grammatical components that are not amenable to visual representation. The only way to get from a set of pictographs to a full writing system is through rebus use. And rebus use depends on pronunciation. And pronunciation of words varies from language to language. The word for 'say' sounds different in Mandarin and Swahili and Spanish and Lushootseed and on and on. The rebus use of the written representation for the word meaning 'cloud' to also write the word meaning 'say'—something that happened in the history of

Chinese writing—only works in a language that has a similar pronunciation for these two words. It doesn't make any sense for English speakers. In other words, the development of a full writing system depends crucially on the specific language that is to be written.

What if we tried a different approach to a universal method for the communication of ideas—by avoiding anything that is language specific, by avoiding reliance on rebus use, but also sidestepping the problem of pictorial representation. What if instead of using pictures as the basis for communication of ideas, we composed graphs for ideas out of elemental meaning components? We would first come up with a set of a few hundred basic notions, categories, and properties, which can combine in various ways to represent the meanings of anything humans need to talk about. Each basic notion could be represented by pictures, or abstract symbols, or numbers. There would be few enough symbols that even if they were arbitrary in form, people could memorize them. These would include graphic representations of basic materials (metal, wood, plastic, cloth, etc.), categories of objects (plant, rock, living creature, man-made tool, etc.), kinds of motion (iterative, punctual, durative, repetitive, etc.), categories of action (eating, moving, thinking, etc.), and a number of other categories that are basic to human experience. You would then combine these graphs into the unique combinations needed to express an idea. Maybe the graph for 'spoon' would combine the graphic components for *man-made object, metal, round,* and *eating.* Maybe the graph for 'jogging' would combine the graphic components for *moving, repetitive, fast,* and *legs.*

It's an attractive idea in theory, but all practical attempts to put it into practice have foundered.[2] In fact, the effort is hopeless. One problem is that basic concepts are culturally determined, so there is no one set that covers all cultures and human experiences. How many basic ideas are there for different kinds of colors? Is bamboo a basic building material, like wood? Is nanofiber on the same level as cotton? Is 'sedan' a different concept from 'hatchback', or is 'automobile' the right level of granularity? Is 'tangerine' a different concept from 'orange'? Is 'tongue scraper' a more or less basic concept than 'toothbrush'? How do you express the idea of 'toaster' for a culture that doesn't make toast?

But let's assume we could somehow find a way to universally represent all the ideas we need, in a way that would be transparent to a speaker of any language. What order should the written graphs be placed in? How should the grammatical relationships among them be expressed? These too are questions with language-specific answers. Some languages have verbs at the beginning of sentences, some in the middle, and some at the end. Some languages use case-marking particles after nouns, and some use prepositions before nouns. The more you try to develop a universal system of writing, the more entangled you become with the grammatical structures of particular spoken languages.

In the end, the only way to create a writing system with all the communicative power of language is to commit a spoken (or signed) language to writing. The result can be read and understood only by people who have learned that language, and who therefore have knowledge of its vocabulary, its grammar, and its distinctive syntactic categories.

What about our example of 月 being able to write the word for 'moon' in many different languages? As we now know, this is an example of semantic adaptation. It depends on the ability of individual humans, with knowledge of the Chinese writing system and their own spoken language, to determine which words in one language are good translations of words in the other. In other words, it's not because the particular graphic form <月> inherently embodies the concept *moon*. It's because it represents a word in one language that someone has decided is similar in meaning to a word in another language. This kind of adaptation is sufficient to create ways of writing *some* words in one's spoken language. In our thought experiments, we used it to write English words like *moon, sky,* and *elephant* using Chinese characters.[3]

But semantic adaptation cannot work to fully write another language using Chinese characters. This is why every example we've seen of Chinese script borrowing—from Korean *hyangchal* to Japanese *kanji-kana* mixed-script writing to Vietnamese Nôm—makes extensive use of phonetic adaptation.

But what about Matteo Ricci's observation of written Chinese functioning as a universal writing system? How can we reconcile this observation with all the objections raised above? Indeed, Ricci's idea has persisted across the centuries with remarkable tenacity. In the nineteenth century, a group of reformers called the Romanization Association worked to develop a romanized script for Japanese that could replace *kanji*. The Italian ambassador to Japan reportedly expressed opposition to the idea, saying that "the scripts of other nations represent words but contain no meanings [i.e., they are sound-based alphabets]. The Chinese script creates meaning in the form of its graphs and is capable of encompassing a great many ideas. Hence if the myriad nations used this script, then they would communicate in ideas."[4]

What exactly is it about the use of Chinese characters that has conveyed this false impression—this impossible idea of a universal, idea-based script—to so many observers who so firmly believe it to be true?

Matteo Ricci and the Universality of the Chinese Script (Revisited)

Let's try to answer this question by turning to some fragments from an anonymous diary written in the thirteenth century. In 1241, one of the many grandsons of Genghis Khan, a Mongol military commander named Qadan, led a force of Mongols in attacks against various Eastern European nations, including areas of modern-day Poland, Czechia, Hungary, and Croatia. One of the low-ranked Mongol soldiers (whose name is lost to history) became separated from his company in the confusion of battle and was captured by Croatian forces. Eventually released from captivity, he ended up traveling throughout much of Europe over subsequent decades, eventually dying in France without ever making his way home. For this Mongolian soldier, born in an area that is now part of northern China, his sojourns in Europe were the first time he encountered writing in the Latin alphabet. One of his surviving diary entries reads as follows:

It is the use of Rome, and all the other kingdoms of Civilized Europe, to write in what they call "Latin." This marvelous language expresses not spoken words but Things or Notions. That this must be so is apparent, because any book written in Latin will be understood not only by the inhabitants of Rome and its surrounding regions where numerous dialects are spoken but also by the Franks, the Anglo-Saxons, the inhabitants of Scandinavia and the Low Countries, even the Iberians, who all read it as ably as the Romans. While the tongues of these peoples are so different that they cannot communicate in speech, they can all understand written Latin, and engage in complex discourse by means of Latin books. If only the educated of all races of the world were to adopt Latin, we would be able to transmit our ideas to people of other countries in writing, though we would not be able to speak to them.

This statement seems preposterous, of course. We already know how it is that educated medieval Europeans could read Latin, despite speaking different languages. The reason they could communicate with each other in Latin is because *they had all learned Latin*, which took many years. They studied the vocabulary, memorized the meanings of the words, and mastered the grammatical rules for constructing sentences. No European who hadn't studied Latin would be able to look at an individual word of written Latin and magically understand the concept represented.[5]

I have, of course, been playing games with you. The passage above is completely fictional. Perhaps you recognized in it echoes of the quotations from Ricci and Bacon that you saw in chapter 1. This is what Ricci said about Chinese writing:

> Any book written in Chinese . . . would also be understood by the Japanese, the Koreans, the inhabitants of Cochin China, the Leuchians and even by people of other countries, who would be able to read it as well as the Chinese. While the spoken languages of these different races are as unlike as can be imagined, they can understand written Chinese because each individual character in Chinese writing represents an individual thing.

Written Classical Chinese could be read and understood by all these people speaking different languages because *they had all learned Classical Chinese*. There is no magical property in a Chinese character that conveys a basic concept directly to the mind through its visual form alone. Show the graph <象> to someone who has never seen it before, and they will never guess it represents an elephant.

Everyone who can read Classical Chinese has learned the script through the painstaking process of memorizing the words (or morphemes) that each character represents, and by learning the specific grammatical rules of Classical Chinese. Neither its vocabulary nor its grammar is universal. It takes many years of education to achieve the ability to communicate in Classical Chinese, and in this respect, it is no different from the time it takes to learn to read and write any written language, including Latin and English.

What Ricci had observed was not some incredible property of Chinese writing that might make it quickly adaptable as a universal writing system. What he had actually observed, but failed to fully understand, was something important about the East Asian societies of his era: that acquiring literacy meant learning Classical Chinese, and that this was a deeply embedded and culturally valued practice, which justified the years of effort it entailed.

Based on what we've learned, we might take the liberty of correcting the last sentence of Ricci's statement as follows:

> While the spoken languages of these different races are as unlike as can be imagined, they can understand written Chinese because *they have spent many years learning the Classical Chinese language: its vocabulary (specific words with specific sounds and meanings), the characters used to write the vocabulary, and its grammar (rules for arranging those words in structures that express their relationships to each other).*

Ricci himself put in many years of effort doing the same thing.

Ricci continued: "If this were universally true, we would be able to transmit our ideas to peoples of other countries in writing, though we would not be able to speak to them." Ricci believed Chinese could be a universal form of communication for people speaking different languages. Well, in a sense he was right: Any written language is potentially universal insofar as, in theory, everyone could take the time to learn it well enough to communicate using it. This is precisely the idea behind such proposed global languages as Esperanto. But, sadly, there are no shortcuts. No writing system is instantly intelligible by virtue of representing ideas directly, obviating the need to learn the unique complexities of a foreign language.

Not that people haven't tried. There have been many attempts to create universal systems of written communication.[6] But the more expressive and sophisticated these invented writing systems become as vehicles of communication, the farther they get from universality. This is because to approach the power, flexibility, and precision of spoken language, they must begin to incorporate cultural and grammatical structures that are not universal but differ from language to language and community to community.

Does this seem disappointing? I would venture to say it's not disappointing but inspiring. As we've seen, it's precisely the linguistic specificity of writing—the association of Chinese characters with spoken words, having pronunciation and meaning—that created the possibility of using those characters to write other languages—Japanese, Korean, Vietnamese, Zhuang—through language-specific adaptations. The development of those vernacular written languages enabled the creation of literatures where none existed before, opening up new dimensions for the creation and expression of cultural knowledge. A world in which just one form of written communication existed, divorced from any spoken language, would be a sterile one indeed, in which the imaginative power of Poe's writing to convey an interior psychological state could not exist, and the rich literary cultural traditions of Japanese, Korean, Vietnamese, and Zhuang peoples would never have come into being.

The Legacy of Chinese Characters

Like Chinese characters, the other three writing systems that were independently invented by our species—Sumerian cuneiform, Egyptian hieroglyphs, and Mesoamerican hieroglyphs—were all in use for thousands of years, and were borrowed and adapted across time, space, and language. But of these milestone inventions, only Chinese characters remain in use today. In this book, we have traced the pathways of their long, forking journey. We began with their origin over three thousand years ago as pictographic representations of spoken words, through their development into a fully functioning writing system for the ancient Chinese language, preserved on divinatory bones and shells. We learned that the rebus principle, which is inseparable from specific pronunciations, was crucial to that process. And we saw how phonetic components played an integral role in the formation of Chinese characters, attesting to the tight connection between written characters and spoken pronunciations. We have dispelled the myths that Chinese characters represent pure ideas, whether as pictures or as abstract symbols.

We saw how written Classical Chinese, which persisted for over two thousand years in China even as the spoken varieties diverged considerably from it, was exported to surrounding countries as their official written languages. Speakers of non-Chinese languages were taught to read and write through an educational process that involved memorizing characters with two clearly defined attributes: sound and meaning.

While these two attributes are bound together in the conventional use of Chinese characters to represent morphemes and words, they can also be disassociated. And this is precisely what people who natively spoke one language (such as Japanese) and were literate in Chinese did. Using a character for its sound alone (phonetic adaptation) or meaning alone (semantic adaptation) to represent sounds and words of the vernacular language was the key step. This made it possible to recast the Chinese script into new writing systems for Japanese, Korean, Vietnamese, and Zhuang. Through our thought experiments on how to write English using Chinese characters, we have observed that this kind of dissociation and adaptation appears to come naturally to humans when working with a morphographic script. And, crucially, it is only possible because characters *don't* represent things or ideas directly: it's because they represent specific sounds and meanings that can be translated into specific words of other languages.

Finally, we saw that these universal processes of semantic and phonetic adaptation are further shaped by specific features of the languages involved, which constrain and motivate further adaptations of the script. One of the prime drivers of this process is the need or desire for disambiguation, which can be achieved in many different ways. The specific linguistic features of the languages involved favor some over others, resulting in real structural differences among the new Chinese-character-based scripts and writing systems for those other languages.

Finally, we saw how political, social, and cultural upheavals around the globe in the early twentieth century disrupted and reshaped writing systems. These events not only ended the role of Classical Chinese as a standard written language in China as well as neighboring countries, they put an end to the character-based script in Vietnam and set Korean writing on a century-long glide path toward the elimination of Chinese characters. Only in China and Japan do we see, after considerable soul-searching, a recommitment to Chinese characters as an integral part of their writing systems. That commitment was challenged by technological concerns, but from our current vantage point in the third decade of the twenty-first century, we see how those apprehensions, born of technological shifts, have been addressed by further technological advances.

The story of Chinese characters, of their adaptability and flexibility, of their metamorphoses and reconfigurations, is more complex in all its details than can be explored in a single book. It is also a story that does not yet have an ending. How the rest of the story unfolds we can only wait and see.

Glossary of Linguistic and Technical Terms

abbreviation: Reduction of the size and/or complexity of a graphic form. Both **part-selection** and **cursivization** are kinds of abbreviation.

abjad: A **script** in which each **graph** represents a consonant, and there are (more or less) no stand-alone graphs to represent vowels. Also called a **consonantary**. Examples of abjads are the Hebrew and Arabic scripts.

alphabet (adjective form: alphabetic): A **script** in which each **graph** represents (more or less) a consonant or vowel sound; the graphs are called **letters**.

case-marking particle: A grammatical element appended to a noun phrase to indicate the role that the phrase plays within the sentence. In languages that use case-marking particles, such as Japanese and Korean, they specify that noun phrases are functioning in such roles as subject, object, destination, recipient, and so on.

character: A nontechnical, commonly used term for the **graphs** of the Chinese **script** as well as their borrowed or modified forms.

composite adaptation: A type of **script** adaptation in which **graphs** adapted semantically and those adapted phonetically are composed into compound graphs in order to represent the words of the language for which the script is being adapted.

consonant cluster: A sequence of two consonant sounds within the same syllable, with no intervening vowel sound. For example, the English word *ban* has no consonant clusters, while the English word *bland* has a cluster at the beginning and a cluster at the end.

consonantary: See **abjad**.

conventionalization: The elimination of variation in the structure of graphic forms in favor of a single norm. It typically accompanies **abbreviation** and **stylization** as **writing systems** evolve.

cursivization: The **abbreviation** of graphic forms by linking together separate strokes, as when writing quickly with a brush or pen. Cursivization yields simpler graphic forms that have fewer strokes.

direct adaptation: Along with **semantic adaptation** and **phonetic adaptation**, this is one way that a Chinese **character** can be used to write something in another language, in which the spoken Chinese **morpheme** originally written by the character is borrowed into the other language, and the same character is used to write it.

disambiguation: A method of modifying a graphic form to specify which of several spoken linguistic elements it is meant to represent in writing. In a **morphographic script**, it is possible for a single **graph** to represent two (or more) spoken **morphemes**. Disambiguation results in two distinct graphic forms, one for each morpheme.

graph: A basic unit of writing, for example, the letter <b>.

homophones: Spoken words with identical pronunciations, like English *bear* (n.) and *bear* (v.) or *pair* and *pare*. Words with similar pronunciations are called near-homophones, like *bear* and *pair*.

ideograph: A visual form that represents a concept, idea, or meaning without representing a specific word or words of a language. An example is the No Smoking symbol. By definition, ideographs are not writing. Chinese **characters** are sometimes incorrectly described as ideographs.

letter: A **graph** of an **alphabetic script**. Letters represent individual consonant and vowel sounds.

linear adaptation: A type of **script** adaptation in which **graphs** adapted semantically and those adapted phonetically are placed in linear sequence in order to represent the words of the language for which the script is being adapted.

Mandarin: This word can refer to several different but related concepts. *Mandarin* is used by linguists to designate a wide range of spoken forms of Chinese that share similar features and are spoken across northern, northwestern, and southwestern China, including the capital Beijing. The term is also used to refer to a specific variety, Modern Standard Chinese, the official spoken language of China. With this narrow meaning, it is equivalent to the terms Standard Mandarin, Putonghua, and Guoyu. Third, it can refer to the common spoken language of government officials during the Míng and Qīng dynasties, which is a predecessor to Modern Standard Chinese.

Middle Chinese: A variety of medieval northern Chinese dating to approximately the sixth through tenth centuries. There is some dispute over whether Middle Chinese was actually a spoken language, or is better understood as a set of standardized reading pronunciations of Chinese **characters**. Some scholars prefer the term *Medieval Chinese* when referring to spoken language of the time.

mixed-script writing system: A **writing system** that normally uses two or more **scripts** at the same time. Most writing systems use only a single one. Japanese is notable in that three scripts are normally used together in running text.

mora (adjective: moraic): A unit of spoken language that is longer than a single sound but may be shorter than a syllable. It corresponds to a beat in metered use of language. In some languages, such as Japanese, there are long and short syllables: long ones, like *kan* and *kō*, count as two rhythmic beats in poetic meter, while short ones, like *ka* and *ko*, count as one. Short syllables contain one mora, and long syllables contain two.

morpheme: An indivisible, meaningful unit of spoken language. Morphemes have meaning and pronunciation, and cannot be divided into smaller meaningful units. Some morphemes are words, and some can only function as parts of words. Examples of morphemes in English are words like *run, banana, tall*, and *so* and grammatical affixes like *-ly, un-*, and *-ing*. Many words are composed of two or more morphemes, like *classroom, runner, rejection*, and *unlawful*. Morphemes exist in all languages as the building blocks of words.

morphograph (adjective: morphographic): A **graph** that differs from **letters** and **syllabographs** in that it represents (more or less) a meaningful part of language (**morpheme**), not just a sound sequence.

Old Chinese: The earliest recoverable stage of spoken Chinese, spoken roughly during the first millennium BCE.

oracle bone inscriptions: Ancient Chinese written texts found inscribed on cattle scapulae and turtle plastrons, which were used in royal divination rituals. The oldest that are extant date to approximately 1250 BCE.

part-selection: The **abbreviation** of a graphic form by eliminating part of it.

phonetic adaptation: Along with **semantic adaptation** and **direct adaptation**, this is one way that a Chinese **character** can be used to write something in another language. In phonetic adaptation, the character is used to write sounds in the language that are similar to the conventional pronunciation of the Chinese character.

phonetic component: In a compound **morphograph** of the type commonly seen in Chinese writing and Vietnamese Chữ Nôm writing, the phonetic component is the part of the **graph** that indicates or suggests the pronunciation of the **morpheme** that the graph represents.

phonetic determinative: Something that is added to a **graph** to specify part or all of its sound value in a particular context. If a **morphograph** can be used to represent two different **morphemes** (like a picture of an eye to represent the words *eye* and *see*), the phonetic determinative uses a sound value to specify which word is represented in a particular usage context.

phonetic extension: The use of a **morphograph** conventionally associated with one word or **morpheme** to write another based on its sound value alone. This is a technical term for **rebus** usage.

phonetic-semantic compound: A type of **graph** seen in Chinese, Vietnamese, and

Zhuang writing formed from two components, a **phonetic component** and a **semantic component**. The vast majority of **characters** used in the Classical and modern Chinese **writing systems** are phonetic-semantic compounds.

phonology: The sound system of a language. The phonology of a language is the set of distinctive sounds that occur in the language, as well as the structural patterns for how those sounds can be arranged into larger groupings like syllables.

pictograph: A picture that functions as a **morphograph** in a **writing system**. A pictograph is a picture used to represent *the word for the object depicted*. Its function is not to represent an object, but to represent a word of spoken language.

rebus: The use of a **graph** or picture for its sound value alone to represent a different word or part of a word. An example is the use of a picture of an eye to represent a word with a similar sound but an unrelated meaning, like *I*.

reduction: The simplification of a graphic form by reducing its internal complexity. This is similar, but not identical, to **abbreviation**.

script: A set of **graphs** that function together in writing. For example the Latin alphabet, consisting of the letters from <A> to <Z>, is a script.

semantic adaptation: Along with **phonetic adaptation** and **direct adaptation**, this is one way that a Chinese **character** can be used to write something in another language. In semantic adaptation, the Chinese character is used to write a word or **morpheme** in the language that has a meaning similar to the conventional meaning of the Chinese character.

semantic component: In a compound **morphograph** of the type commonly seen in Chinese writing and Vietnamese Chữ Nôm writing, the semantic component is the part of the **graph** that indicates or suggests the meaning or category of meaning of the **morpheme** that the graph represents.

Sino-Japanese, Sino-Korean, Sino-Vietnamese, Sino-Zhuang: The elements in Japanese, Korean, Vietnamese, and Zhuang that are of Chinese origin. The terms are commonly used to refer to two different aspects of these languages: first, vocabulary of Chinese origin used in the written or spoken varieties of these languages, and second, the conventional pronunciations of Chinese **characters** that are employed by speakers of these languages.

structural mismatch: A situation in which the **graphs** of a **script** do not align well with the linguistic units of a language. Structural mismatch is common when a script used for one language is adopted to write a different language. In such a situation, a script or the rules for using it might be modified to reduce the degree of mismatch.

stylization: A change in the form of **pictographs** that reduces or eliminates their pictorial quality.

syllabary (adjective: syllabic): A **script** in which each **graph** represents (more or less) an entire syllable; the graphs are called **syllabographs**.

syllabograph: A **graph** of a **syllabic script**. Syllobagraphs represent spoken syllables.

Unicode: A digital encoding standard developed in the early 1990s to specify unique codepoints for all of the world's writing systems, so that textual information can be shared across computing platforms. Unicode is constantly being expanded as emojis, historical scripts, and rare and unusual characters are added. If a **graph** is not in Unicode, it is difficult to enter, display, or transmit it reliably across computers and digital networks.

vernacular writing: A **written language** that reflects the local spoken language.

writing system: One or more **scripts** and the language-specific conventions for how their **graphs** are used to represent spoken language, for example, in the English writing system, <c> represents [k] or [s]. A conventionalized or standardized writing system is also called an orthography.

written language (vs. spoken language): A language in written form, including its vocabulary and grammatical rules. Note that different **writing systems** can be used to represent the same written language. For example, Turkish was written with the Arabic script prior to 1928 and thereafter in the Latin script. While written languages are based on spoken languages, they tend to be more conservative. For this reason, they may diverge from their spoken-language source over time.

Notes

Conventions

1 These are the northern pronunciations of Hanoi; the southern pronunciations of Saigon differ in some key respects.

2 If the vowel letter already includes a diacritic on top of it, then the tone mark is placed above it. For example, the six tones marked on the vowel *â* are *â, ấ, ẩ, ẫ, ẩ, ậ*.

3 To emphasize that these are not to be pronounced as consonant sounds, I have deviated from the standard orthography by superscripting the tone letters. For example, the Zhuang word meaning 'horse' is normally written <max>, but I transcribe it as <ma^x>. The superscript <x> is not pronounced; it merely indicates that the syllable "ma" is pronounced with a falling tone.

4 Schuessler, *Minimal Old Chinese*. Simplifications include the removal of glottal stop symbol [ʔ] and the diacritic [^], the replacement of [ŋ] with [ng], and a number of other minor adjustments to make these ancient reconstructed pronunciations easier for the average reader to pronounce.

ONE *What Are Chinese Characters?*

1 Fontana, *Matteo Ricci*; Spence, *Memory Palace*; Hsia, *Jesuit in the Forbidden City*.

2 Ricci, *China in the Sixteenth Century*, 446.

3 Bacon, *Advancement of Learning*, 215–16.

4 Rogers, *Writing Systems*, 4–5. Mayan writing is the best understood and most widely developed of the early Mesoamerican scripts.

5 Two examples of script creation of this type are the invention of the Korean alphabet by King Sejong in the fifteenth century and of the Cherokee syllabary by Chief Sequoyah in the nineteenth century.

6 Kornicki, *Languages, Scripts, and Chinese Texts*; Kin, *Literary Sinitic and East Asia*.

7   For more on this broad cultural sphere, sometimes referred to as the Sino-graphic cosmopolis, see the books published by Brill and edited by Ross King, David Lurie, and Marion Eggert under the series title Language, Writing and Literary Culture in the Sinographic Cosmopolis.

8   Daniels and Bright, *World's Writing Systems*, sections 3, 4, and 22.

9   Natural human languages occur in two modalities: signed and spoken. Both types of language are equally complex and highly patterned in grammatical structure. Both are acquired naturally by children who grow up in a community of language users, without the need for formal instruction. Unfortunately, the historical record provides us with very little detailed information about sign language usage prior to the modern era. Nevertheless, it is likely that sign language use is equally as old as spoken language use for our species. So far as I am aware, there is no evidence for the invention or development of written representation of sign language until the twentieth century. The most widely used today is SignWriting, invented by Valerie Sutton in 1974. Sign language does not play a role in the development and spread of Chinese characters in the premodern era. For that reason, in this book I will be focusing on the relationship between spoken language and writing.

10 Consider Papua New Guinea, a country estimated to have over eight hundred spoken languages, as well as at least one sign language. Nearly all are unwritten.

11 Academics in some other disciplines prefer to group both kinds of visual communication under the label "writing" but use qualifying terms to distinguish between them. Some scholars use the technical terms *nonglottographic writing* and *glottographic writing* to make the distinction. In the end, which specific labels we use for the two kinds of visual communication aren't as important as making a clear conceptual distinction.

12 This definition follows that of Rogers, *Writing Systems*, 2.

13 As mentioned earlier, this definition can be easily extended to include written representation of signed language. One way to do this would be to define "utterance" to encompass both modalities of natural language: spoken and signed. Because written representation of sign language does not seem to have existed prior to the twentieth century, it does not play a part in the premodern invention and development of writing systems.

14 The emoji is encoded in the Unicode standard as U+1F319 'crescent moon'.

15 Scholars typically formalize this distinction by referring to the set of variant shapes as a *grapheme*. Its distinct manifestations are called *allographs*. For simplicity, I will only use the word *graph*. For more on this notion, see Meletis, *Nature of Writing*, 107–19.

16 The Latin alphabet is also called the Roman alphabet.

17 Peter T. Daniels, "The Study of Writing Systems," in Daniels and Bright, *World's Writing Systems*, 3–12, presents an influential six-way categorization; Joyce and Borgwaldt, "Typology of Writing Systems: Introduction" provides an overview of various proposals for writing system typologies.

18 People often casually use the word *alphabet* to talk about any kind of writing, but in this book we will use it in the narrower technical sense defined here.

19 Until recently, the term *logographic* (from the Greek roots for 'word' and 'writing') was more widely used for the type of writing system in which graphs represent meaningful units. However, the term *morphographic* is more precise, as it specifies that the relationship is one of graph to morpheme, rather than of graph to word.

20 As we saw earlier, from a historical perspective, these shapes are not arbitrary. Recall that our letter <M> comes ultimately from an image of water via the Phoenician alphabet. But for modern learners of the Latin alphabet, the shapes are effectively arbitrary.

21 The Pinyin transcription system is not part of the regular Chinese writing system, and is not intended to replace Chinese characters. It is used in dictionaries to indicate Modern Standard Chinese pronunciations, as an aid to help young children who are still learning to read and write, for signage intended for foreigners, and in contexts inside and outside of China where Chinese characters are inconvenient.

22 A notable exception in English are the pronouns, many of which have different forms such as *he* (subject), *him* (object), and *his* (possessive) and *I, me,* and *my*. If we substitute *they* for *dogs* in the example sentences here, we get **They** chase cats and Cats chase **them**.

23 Unger, *Ideogram*; McDonald, "'Ideograph'"; Du Ponceau, *Dissertation*. Unger provides a more elaborated explanation of why Chinese characters cannot be ideographs. McDonald presents a brief and insightful overview of the historical background and cultural discourse underlying the perception of Chinese writing as ideographic, and references additional scholarship on the topic. The most famous and brilliantly articulated refutation of the myth is that of Du Ponceau in 1838.

TWO *Chinese Writing*

1 For more on the history and structure of Egyptian writing, see Stauder, "Scripts."

2 A stele is a vertically oriented monument. They are typically made of stone or wood and inscribed with images and/or text. They are intended to be prominently visible and long-lasting, and often have commemorative function.

3 The horizontal line at the top reads (from right to left): "The gift that Anubis gives for his burial in the Necropolis" (Orly Goldwasser, email message to author, September 25, 2023). Note that there are also pictures on the stele. There were many visual and linguistic clues available to an Egyptian reader to allow them to easily recognize the distinction between pictures and writing.

4 On the question of whether this crucially important transition can be attributed to the creative invention of individuals or if it emerges organically through precursors to true writing, see Smith, "Are Writing Systems Intelligently Designed?"

5 The hyphen in *-ing* shows that this morpheme must attach to something on its left when forming a word, like *going*. Similarly, the hyphen in *un-* shows that it must attach to something on its right when forming a word, like *unkind*.

6 For a full translation, see Keightley, *Sources of Shang History*, figure 12 (between pages 182 and 183). Keightley's book is an excellent general introduction to the oracle bone inscriptions.

7 Keightley, *Sources of Shang History*. We know that the carving was made after the bone was cracked, because the location of the graphs is carefully chosen to avoid the cracks.

8 The translation is modified from that found in Keightley, *Sources of Shang History*.

9 I have tried to keep phonetic symbols to a minimum in this book, but when writing out ancient pronunciations, it is sometimes impossible to avoid. The symbol <ə> represents a vowel sound like that in *but*, the first syllable of *banana*, or the second syllable of *photograph*. The name of this sound and of the symbol used to represent it is *schwa*.

10 Ancient Chinese pronunciations are known to us through the work of twentieth-century historical linguists. Their reconstruction presents enormous challenges. We not only lack audio recordings, but we don't have an alphabetic spelling that can give us valuable clues about individual consonant and vowel sounds. Historical linguists have used a variety of tools and data to piece together the pronunciations. They include analysis of rhyming poetry, knowledge of pronunciations of Chinese words borrowed by other languages, correlations with modern pronunciations in various Chinese languages, and the analysis of Chinese character components and functions described in this chapter. A good introduction to the methods applied to these sources of evidence to arrive at reconstructed pronunciations of the language stage we call Old Chinese can be found in Baxter, *A Handbook of Old Chinese Phonology*.

11 And vice versa. The use of a picture of a bee to write the verb *be* is a natural rebus in English but would make no sense at all in other languages.

12 These semantic components are often informally referred to as radicals. However, the term radical is imprecise and can also be used to label character components that do not have semantic function. For this reason I will avoid it.

13 This is the so-called "traditional" form of the character. If you know some Chinese and this character is not familiar to you, don't worry. An explanation of the difference between traditional and simplified characters is coming later in this chapter.

14 What this early form represented visually isn't entirely clear, and scholars are not uniform in their opinion. One hypothesis is that it is a drawing of a carpenter's square.

15 In Modern Standard Chinese, both 'square' and 'fragrant' are pronounced *fāng*.

16 Notice that in chapter 1, five of the six characters writing morphemes with meanings related to speaking are phonetic-semantic compounds. Those five (説, 講, 討, 論, 訴) all contain the semantic component 言 'speech'. Other characters appearing in this book that have the same semantic component are 認 {"rèn," 'recognize'} (table 2.1) and 訪 {"fǎng," 'to visit'} (table 2.2).

17 The twentieth century saw many politically motivated policy changes in Chinese language and writing, some of which are described in more detail later.

18 *Dream of the Red Chamber* or *A Dream of Red Mansions*, also known as *Story of the Stone* (Shítóu jì), is an eighteenth-century work of fiction by Cáo Xuěqín (1710–65). It is one of the most popular works of Chinese fiction ever written, and is widely read and studied today.

19 The sentences are from an article titled "'Gia Zhengrhen'—Meiguo de Techan" in *Sin Wenz Zhoukan* (New Writing Weekly), no. 21 (April 29, 1950). These and other publications demonstrated that it was perfectly possible to write Chinese using an alphabet. For more on this and other proposed romanizations, see Dorothea Wippermann, "Transcription Systems, Overview," in Sybesma et al., *Encyclopedia of Chinese Language and Linguistics*, vol IV, 396–404.

20 Gotelind Müller, "Esperanto," in Sybesma et al., *Encyclopedia of Chinese Language and Linguistics*, vol. II, 192–94.

21 Hanyu Pinyin was hardly the first romanization of Mandarin intended as a tool for recording and teaching standard pronunciations. Dozens of systems already existed, developed by both Westerners and Chinese, some in wide use. For example, the Wade-Giles system was once the standard in the English-speaking world. Hanyu Pinyin has now supplanted them all. The name comes from the words *Hànyǔ* 漢語 'Chinese language' (literally 'speech of the Han ethnicity') and *pīnyīn* 拼音 ('spelling'). See Dorothea Wippermann,

"Transcription Systems: Hànyǔ pīnyīn 漢語拼音," in Sybesma et al., *Encyclopedia of Chinese Language and Linguistics*, vol IV, 424–32.

22   The terms *simplified* and *complex* are somewhat misleading, as they imply that the simplified character script is easier to learn and use. Although the "simplified" characters are written with fewer strokes, it's not clear that they are truly simpler in a broader sense. For more on this question, see Handel, "Can a Logographic Script Be Simplified?"

23   A Cheng, *Chess Master*, 6–7. This is a bilingual edition with Chinese (in traditional characters) and English on facing pages. The translation of this passage is: "It all seemed very odd to me, but I still picked up one of my cannons and moved it to the centre line. Before I had the time to put it down he moved his knight, rapping the piece down on the board even faster than I could put mine down, so I deliberately moved my cannon past the centre line."

24   On the blogging site qq.com, a user named Crystal posted an article in Chinese headlined "It's unbelievable! I've never studied traditional characters, so how can I read them with no problem?" The first half of the headline is written in simplified characters, the second half in traditional characters (http://mp.weixin.qq.com/s/KEF6h3tUDOEWWy3ZNAolEw, posted August 14, 2023). The article examines why, to her surprise, Crystal found it easy to read traditional Chinese characters when traveling to Hong Kong and Taiwan, or when reading movie subtitles. Among the reasons Crystal gives for this lack of difficulty are (1) the overall similarity in shape of most traditional and simplified counterparts; (2) the methods of simplification tend to follow systematic patterns; (3) the majority of commonly used characters are no different in the simplified and traditional scripts; and (4) context helps clarify which words are intended.

25   Matthew M. Anderson, "Number of Characters," in Sybesma et al., *Encyclopedia of Chinese Language and Linguistics*, vol. 3, 255–59.

26   One of the most important early dictionaries in Chinese history, the famous *Shuōwén jiězì* of 100 CE, contained somewhat under ten thousand characters. This suggests that the number of characters in active use in the script has been relatively stable over time.

27   Notably, the dictionary *Zhōnghuá zìhǎi* has over eighty-five thousand distinct character entries.

28   One might compare the *Oxford English Dictionary*. Intended as a historical record of English, the second edition, published in 1989, contains nearly three hundred thousand main entries. Many of the words are ancient, obsolete, rare, dialectal, technical, variant, or otherwise not part of the vocabulary of an ordinary modern English speaker and writer. It would be misguided to claim that English today has three hundred thousand words simply because

they appear in this dictionary. In fact, speakers of English today know and use about a tenth as many words.

29   Over larger time scales, we can see that the Latin alphabet isn't fixed. For example, the letters <W> and <Z> were not part of the alphabet used by the ancient Romans, and the additional letter <Ñ> has been added to the Spanish variant of the Latin alphabet. But the pace of change for an alphabet or a syllabary is glacial compared to a morphographic script.

30   For example, the word that was coined for 'text message', *duǎnxìn*, is made up of the two existing morphemes, {"duǎn," 'short, brief'} and {"xìn," 'letter, message'}. *Duǎn* is written 短 and *xìn* is written 信, so *duǎnxìn* is accordingly written 短信.

31   Zhou, "Chinese Names of New Elements." This character, along with the characters for elements 113 (nihonium), 115 (moscovium), and 118 (oganesson), was selected by the China National Committee for Terminology in Science and Technology at a naming conference held in January 2017. The participants in the naming conference included not just scientists but also experts in Chinese writing.

THREE   *Classical Chinese*

1   We may well get the same mistaken impression when we think of Ancient Greek in relation to Modern Greek, or Classical Arabic in relation to Modern Arabic.

2   There are many uncertainties about how Old Chinese was pronounced in the first millennium BCE. Different scholars have different hypotheses. The details of these reconstructed pronunciations aren't important for our purposes in this chapter, however. The main thing to notice is how different the pronunciation was then from any of the modern pronunciations.

3   The period is used to show that the translation of a single Chinese word requires two or more words in English. In this case, the single word *nə* means 'and so'.

4   Though not without changes! All three of the Spanish, Italian, and French writing systems employ modified forms of the alphabet used in ancient Rome. In some cases, new letters (like <J>) have been added; in other cases, letters have been modified by diacritical marks, like Spanish <Ñ> (which represents a sound similar to the "ny" of English, as in *cañón* 'canyon'). And in all three writing systems, the sound values associated with some of the letters have changed. For example, the letter <C> was always pronounced [k] in Latin. In French, it is sometimes pronounced [s] as in *merci* 'thank you'; in Castilian Spanish, it is sometimes pronounced like the English "th" of *think*,

as in *Barcelona*; and in Italian, it is sometimes pronounced like the English "ch" of *church*, as in *ciao* 'hi; bye'.

5   The two written languages coexisted for a while during this transition. One striking example of the use of the two languages together is in the famous 1918 short story "Diary of a Madman" by Lu Xun, one of the early twentieth-century's great Chinese writers, who was an advocate for vernacular writing. The conceit of the story is that the narrator is presenting excerpts from a discovered diary. The diary entries are written in modern Chinese, the vernacular. But the story's narrator provides a framing introduction written in Classical Chinese. The contrast between the two written languages is an important literary device that is connected to the story's themes about societal transformation and upheaval.

6   Premodern Chinese punctuation was less elaborate. See Matthias Richter, "Punctuation, Premodern," in Sybesma et al., *Encyclopedia of Chinese Language and Linguistics*, vol. 3, 501–6.

7   McDull says, "McMug, recently I've had some strange sounds constantly echoing inside my head, but I don't even know what those sounds mean . . ." McMug replies, "That strange? Let me hear what the sounds are like."

8   For an overview on the creation of a Buddhist canon in Chinese, see chapter 3 of Ostler, *Passwords to Paradise*.

9   I use the term *Koreans* very loosely here. The ethnic, linguistic, and cultural affiliation of the peoples in northern Korea at that time with the peoples we know as "Korean" from later periods of history is unclear. It is entirely possible that the language or languages spoken in the region during the Hàn dynasty were not directly ancestral to later documented forms of Korean. Scholars have proposed many different hypotheses, but a lack of evidence makes it difficult to determine the linguistic landscape of the ancient Korean Peninsula with any certainty. See Georg, "Other Isolated Languages of Asia," 151–52.

10   The situation with Japanese is somewhat more complicated than I have implied. The "straight-through" reading illustrated here, variously known as *bōyomi*, *chokudoku*, or *ondoku* reading of Classical Chinese, became restricted to just a few types of texts and cultural contexts, like the chanting of Buddhist sutras. The more common way of reading Classical Chinese texts was a method called *kanbun kundoku*, which mechanically transformed the written Chinese text into stylized Japanese. However, as Kin Bunkyō observes in his book *Literary Sinitic and East Asia*, it is presumed that straight-through reading was more common in the first few centuries of literacy in Japan, even though we have little in the way of recorded evidence (p. 32). *Kanbun kundoku* is discussed a bit more at the beginning of chapter 5.

FOUR *Sound and Meaning*

1 Ötkür, *Iz*. The Arabic script is the current official script for Uyghur in the People's Republic of China. Widely used up until the twentieth century, it was reinstated as the official script in 1982 after a series of experiments with other scripts. The Cyrillic script, official in China in the 1950s, is still used by Uyghurs living in Kazakhstan and other Central Asian regions outside of China. The Cyrillic-influenced Latin script was introduced in China in the late 1950s and actively promulgated by the government in the early 1960s, but it was not widely liked or adopted and fell out of use when the Arabic script was reinstated. The purely Latin script is not intended to displace the Arabic script but is instead an official transliteration that was standardized in the early 2000s for ease of use in computer-based applications and communications. It replaces the Cyrillic letters in the Cyrillic-influenced Latin script with Latin letters, such as <q> replacing <к>. For more on the history of the scripts, see Duval and Janbaz, "Introduction to Latin-Script Uyghur."

2 Translation by Talant Mawkanuli (email message to author, February 3, 2023). I am indebted to Prof. Mawkanuli for transcribing this passage into the different scripts for me.

3 The lack of a representation of the vowel *i* in my example is intentional. While we use the vowel *i* in the spelling of the word *shirt*, there is no distinct "i" sound in the pronunciation. You can verify this by pronouncing the "sh" and "r" sounds in sequence.

4 Chinese has no articles corresponding to English *the* and *a*.

5 An example is the Adlam script developed by two brothers, Ibrahima and Abdoulaye Barry, when they were teenagers in the 1980s, in order to write Fulani, a language spoken by millions of people in West and Central Africa. It has become widely used. See Waddell, "Alphabet That Will Save a People."

FIVE *Linear Adaptation*

1 Hàn is the name given to the dominant ethnic group of China, making up over 90 percent of the modern-day population of China. The dozens of other ethnic groups with Chinese citizenry include Mongolians, Uyghurs, Tibetans, Zhuang, Hmong, and many others. These peoples have been assimilated, culturally and linguistically, to varying degrees. As a recent example of language death and cultural assimilation, consider Manchu, a language once spoken by millions of people in what is now northeast China, including the ruling aristocracy of the Qīng dynasty. It recently became extinct there upon the death of the last native speakers born in the twentieth century. The descendents of

Manchu speakers, who still claim Manchu ethnicity, are now Chinese-speaking. For more on the complexities of ethnicity and language in China, see Dwyer, "Texture of Tongues."

2   Kim Byung-Joon, "Introduction of Chinese Characters," 30.

3   Yoon, "Creation of *Idu*," 104.

4   Lurie, *Realms of Literacy*. Lurie's book thoroughly examines all of the historical and archeological evidence related to the arrival and development of writing during this early period.

5   Some scholars place Korean into a small family called Koreanic, which includes the closely related language of Jeju Island. Whether Korean is characterized as a single language with no relatives or a member of a small language family depends on whether the varieties spoken on Jeju Island and other peripheral areas are considered dialects of Korean or distinct languages. See Georg, "Other Isolated Languages of Asia," 151.

6   Why "Middle Chinese" and not "Old Chinese"? Because there is an even earlier stage of Chinese that we call "Old Chinese," the common ancestor of all the modern Chinese languages.

7   Giving examples from modern languages as a way of understanding the structural features of their ancient ancestors presents an incomplete picture. However, it has some advantages for us. We can use familiar transcriptions of pronunciation and avoid having to learn the complex system of phonetic notation that would be needed to represent ancient pronunciations. The examples also use modern vocabulary that will be familiar to those who have some experience with these languages. And we can avoid the uncertainty that scholars face when speculating to fill in gaps in our knowledge about the ancient languages involved.

8   Japanese and Korean are so remarkably similar in their grammatical structure that linguists continue to debate whether the two share a common ancestral language. There are several competing hypotheses to explain the similarities. One is that they are genetically related, both deriving from an ancient common ancestor of Korean and Japonic, perhaps spoken in northern China or on the Korean Peninsula. Another holds that the languages lack a common origin but became more similar because their speakers interacted in ancient times. This posits that the ancestor of modern Japanese was once spoken somewhere on the Korean Peninsula, before its speakers migrated to the Japanese archipelago. During that time, there would have been interaction between this ancestral Japanese and the geographically adjacent ancestor language of modern Korean, accounting for some of their shared features. For a brief summary of the competing hypotheses, see Georg, "Other Isolated Languages," 151; and Whitman, "Relationship Between Japanese and Korean," 24–25.

9   Some Korean sounds change automatically depending on what sounds are next to them. For example, [k] changes to [g] in certain contexts. When the verb root *ilk-* 'to read' is followed by the past-tense suffix *-eotda*, the result is *ilgeotda*.

10 For examples of Norman French words that became part of English, see chapter 6.

11 The actual number of syllables is considerably higher if long vowels, doubled consonants, and the *-n* ending are counted. But even taking nonbasic syllables into account, the overall number is low compared to many languages.

12 A *gloss* is a brief explanation or definition; the word is related to the word *glossary*. The *hun* isn't meant to capture the full range of meanings of the Chinese morpheme written by the character; it's a conveniently concise label to help Korean speakers remember the character's meaning.

13 The Mandarin pronunciation of this word is closer to "duh" than to "dee." So "duh" is the sound you associate with this character.

14 For more on the unusual aspects of this tale—featuring a culture hero who is more passive than aggressively heroic—see McCann, "Story of Ch'ŏyong."

15 The translation is based on Kim Young Wook, "A Basic Understanding of *Hyangga* Interpretation," *Korea Journal* 50, no. 2 (June 2010): 83 and Ki-Moon Lee and Ramsey, *History of the Korean Language*, 58, with my modifications. I have adjusted the transcription of Old Korean pronunciation used by Ki-Moon Lee and Ramsey, 57–58, to be compatible with the modern Korean transcription system used throughout this book. The vowel written *a* no longer exists in modern Korean; its pronunciation was probably somewhere between "ah" and "uh."

16 That is, they are the legs of a person who "belongs" to the narrator: his wife.

17 The modern pronunciations differ somewhat from the Old Korean pronunciations, but they are similar enough for us to see how these characters were being used to write the Old Korean words of the poem.

18 The suffix is present on the adjective because the root by itself cannot be used to describe a following noun. The grammar requires a suffixed form of the adjective here.

19 The meaning of this character in Chinese is 'period of time'. It does not have a traditionally associated native Korean word to express its meaning.

20 In Chinese, this character writes the second of the ten heavenly stems, a sequence of ten Chinese characters of unknown origin that constitute a cycle used for calendrical and counting purposes. They are already found on the earliest Chinese texts, the oracle bone inscriptions, over three thousand years ago. There is no native Korean word that has equivalent meaning.

21 The suffix -*gon*, translated as 'and then', is used to connect two verbs in sequence. It indicates that a second action will follow.

22 It is entirely possible that there was a wider variety of early experiments in the adaptation of Chinese characters to written Korean too. But if so, they did not survive or have not yet been discovered. The textual record in Japan is much richer and more robust than in Korea, where gaps in surviving materials and reading traditions suggest that the historical record we have is incomplete.

23 The poems, written by numerous authors, are so varied in style that it is impossible to make any generalization about writing mechanisms that applies to all of them. Many of them contain complex oral and graphic puns, double meanings, and playful manipulations. What is presented here is necessarily an oversimplification. See Lurie, *Realms of Literacy*, chapter 6 for more details and additional references.

24 There is a great deal of complexity in both the *on* (sound) properties and *kun* (meaning) properties associated with Chinese characters in Japanese. Unlike in Korean and, as we will see in the next chapter, Vietnamese, most Chinese characters have multiple sound values in Japanese. This is because the Chinese pronunciations were adapted into Japanese at several different times in history. The earlier medieval set of pronunciations is called *Go'on* 'Go pronunciations', and the later medieval set of pronunciations is called *Kan'on* 'Kan pronunciations'. Their differences are due to different pronunciations of Chinese connected to different times and places. For example, the character <山> has two pronunciations, "sen" (the earlier Go'on) and "san" (the later Kan'on). In order to reduce complexity, I have generally chosen the more commonly occurring pronunciation in my examples. In the case of <山>, "san" is the more common pronunciation found in modern Japanese.

25 The various transcription systems can make the pronunciations look more different than they really are. Pinyin <x> in *xīn* 'heart' represents a Chinese sound very similar to Japanese [sh] in *shin*.

26 The description here is taken from Frellesvig, *History of the Japanese Language*; and Vovin, *Man'yōshū*, 16–19. I have made some minor adjustments to the translation.

27 This is the pronunciation that is used in Japan today when reciting this poem aloud.

28 The grammatical details are not relevant to the analysis of the representational value of the graphs.

29 You may have noticed that the first occurrence of the word spade is *pukusi*, while the second is *bukusi*. The change of [p] to [b] is a normal process in

Japanese that consistently occurs under particular circumstances. In this case, it is related to the presence of the prefix *mi-*.

30 The semantic resonances of the phonetically adapted characters sometimes are thematically connected to the content of the poem, adding depth or nuance. In other cases, however, they seem to be entirely independent of the poem, in which case they might simply be playful flourishes. Or the resonances may be absent altogether, because the semantic values of phonetically adapted characters have been attenuated through repeated conventionalized usage. This aspect of variability in Japanese writing of the *Man'yōshū* presents enormous yet fascinating challenges for modern interpretations and analyses of the poems. See Lurie, *Realms of Literacy*, 281–91.

31 Both this book and another eighth-century text, *Nihon shoki* (Historical records of Japan), contain a brief discussion of the origin of writing in Japan. They attribute the arrival of writing to a scribe who brought knowledge of Classical Chinese to the Japanese court from the Korean Peninsula. For more on these texts, see Lurie, *Realms of Literacy*, 105ff. For additional evidence that Korean scribes were likely present in Japan as early as the fifth century, see Lurie, *Realms of Literacy*, 91–92.

32 Translated by Christopher Seeley, *History of Writing in Japan*, 43–44.

33 Lurie, *Realms of Literacy*, 230.

34 All three *katakana* graphs listed above (テ *te*, カ *ka*, and ク *ku*) appear to the right of Chinese characters in the first (rightmost) column of figure 5.1.

35 Although technically redundant in function as syllabaries, the distinction between the two scripts (*hiragana* and *katakana*) has proven useful, as they have been employed for different purposes in the modern era. *Hiragana* is the more common phonetic script. *Katakana* is somewhat specialized: it is used to write words borrowed from other languages (such as English); to render sound effects, onomatopoeia, and other specialized vocabulary; and to provide visual contrast for emphasis (equivalent in some ways to the use of *italics*, underlining, or ALL CAPS in English writing). Understanding the different functions of these two scripts is essential for mastery of Japanese literacy, but is not relevant to the main conceptual points of this book.

36 The exception is when a word has a prefix attached to the root. Prefixes are generally written in *hiragana*.

37 The sound values of the last three *kana* are: [te] <て>, [i] <い>, and [ta] <た>. The first one, <っ>, indicates that the following consonant is doubled. Thus, the four *kana* together spell *tteita*.

SIX *Composite Adaptation*

1   To see images from the exhibit, visit "Book from the Sky," Xu Bing, accessed August 23, 2023, https://www.xubing.com/en/work/details/206?type=project (click "Book from the Sky" on the left).

2   Refer back to chapter 5 (page 113) for a detailed breakdown of the function of each character.

3   The exact frequency depends on what data source and counting method you use. Many studies that look at large selections of English-language texts list *the* as the fourth most frequently occurring word of written English.

4   Note that these invented graphs for writing *moon* and *tongue* can only make sense as written English. Their structure would not make sense for writing words for 'moon' and 'tongue' in Mandarin, Cantonese, Japanese, Korean, French, Spanish, or any other language in which these words sound different from the English words.

5   For more on this topic see Brindley, *Ancient China and the Yue*, especially chapters 7–9.

6   Keith Taylor, *Birth of Vietnam*; Kiernan, *Việt Nam*. The brief summary of early Vietnamese history presented here is based primarily on information in these two books.

7   "Yuè" is the modern Mandarin pronunciation of the word that is historically the same as the first syllable of Vietnam. Indeed, the modern name Vietnam (Việt Nam) means 'south of Yue'—the same two words as in the kingdom name Nam Việt, but in reverse order.

8   Phan, "Lacquered Words."

9   The ethnolinguistic situation in southern China and northern Vietnam is even more complex than has been described here (Yongxian Luo, "Zhuang," in Diller, Edmondson, and Luo, *Tai-Kadai Languages*, 317–77). One of the officially recognized ethnic minorities of southern China, called Jing, Gin, or Kinh, are descended from ethnic Vietnamese. There are also ethnic minorities in northern Vietnam, called Nùng and Tày, that are closely related to the Southern Zhuang people. As in so many parts of the world, language and ethnicity do not line up neatly with national borders or government classifications.

10 David Holm, in *Mapping the Old Zhuang Character Script* (45), explains that in the Zhuang-speaking areas of central Guangxi, a system of reading pronunciations of Chinese characters developed during the Míng and Qīng dynasties (fifteenth through nineteenth centuries). It "was used for learning the script, reciting school texts and classical texts, and similar purposes. It later came to be used more broadly . . . Phonologically this pronunciation

was based on [the local Chinese dialect] Pínghuà, but it took on a modified form suitable for Zhuang learners of Chinese." This is an example of the kind of conventionalized set of character pronunciations that formed the basis for phonetic adaptation of characters by Zhuang-speaking people at different times and places.

11 Phan, "Lacquered Words," 392.

12 David Holm, "The Old Zhuang Script," in Diller, Edmondson, and Luo, *Tai-Kadai Languages*, 417; Holm, "Typology of Readings," 248. "Cosmogonic" means related to the origin of the universe.

13 Translation by Huỳnh Sanh Thông (1926–2008), as quoted in Nguyễn, "Graphemic Borrowings from Chinese," 415.

14 It is the forty-seventh poem in the set of untitled poems called *Bảo kính cảnh giới* within the larger poetry collection *Quốc âm thi tập* (Poetry collection in the national language), of which it is the 174th poem. https://www.nomfoundation.org/nom-tools/QATT/QATT?poem_id=174&uiLang=en, accessed on November 2, 2023.

15 As elsewhere in the book, I'm presenting "Chinese values" using the modern Mandarin pronunciation and a simple English word or phrase reflecting the character's meaning in Classical Chinese.

16 In Vietnamese spelling, <th> represents a sound like English [t] as in *tie*, not English [th] as in *thigh*.

17 *Anh tam* 'brothers' is itself a compound word made up of two morphemes, meaning 'older brother' and 'younger brother'.

18 The character 𠀧 from the beginning of this chapter is structured similarly. It was created to write the native Vietnamese word *ba* 'three'.

19 One hypothesis is that 𬭼 is not an abbreviation of 爲 but of 濫 (Sino-Vietnamese *lạm* 'overflow'), which is used to write *làm* 'do' by phonetic adaptation. See Handel, *Sinography*, 142 for more details.

20 Handel, *Sinography*, 161–62.

21 This same question of the degree of influence of linguistic structure versus cultural diffusion applies to the similarity of techniques seen in Korea and Japan. Korean and Japanese are structurally similar to each other and spoken in geographic proximity, and they have adapted Chinese characters in remarkably similar ways. In *Mapping the Old Zhuang Character Script*, Holm notes that there are very few innovated compound graphs that are found in both Vietnamese and Zhuang writing. But the lack of overlap in specific graphic forms doesn't necessarily mean that there was no influence in techniques and practices between the two communities.

22 Example Zhuang words in this chapter are cited from Holm, "Typology of Readings"; Holm, *Mapping the Old Zhuang Character Script*; and Wáng, *Cóng*

Hànzì dào Hànzì Xì Wénz. In the standard Zhuang romanization, tones are indicated by appended "silent" letters, which have been superscripted in this book to more clearly show that they are not pronounced. For example, the Zhuang words in table 6.2 are normally romanized as *vunz, bi, mwngz,* and *miz.*

23   For details on which Zhuang-speaking regions or communities these different forms are found in, and the pronunciations of the words in the local dialects, see Holm, *Mapping the Old Zhuang Character Script.*

24   Holm, "Graphic Variation," 9.

25   Holm, "Graphic Variation," 21–22. Holm (36) describes the importance of songbooks in traditional Zhuang culture. Song contests and "song markets" were prevalent. Young men would keep small songbooks in their pockets. Young men and women performed songs together, as part of a cultural practice in which singing at song markets played a role in the selection of marriage partners. For an explanation of the different source books in table 6.8, see Holm, "Graphic Variation," 15–18.

26   Both the traditional-character form 馬 and the simplified-character form 马 appear.

27   The entries are on pages 366 and 21 of the dictionary, respectively.

28   Holm, *Mapping the Old Zhuang Character Script,* 144–45, 603.

29   And other languages too, which are beyond the scope of this book.

SEVEN *Chinese Characters in the Modern Era*

1   The website of the contest is https://sousaku-kanji.com. The grand-prize-winning entry (as well as other award winners) from 2020 can be seen at https://sousaku-kanji.com/archive/contest_11th.html, accessed August 23, 2023.

2   The character 出 has nothing to do with mountains in its origin. But its modern form very much looks like a stack of two 山 characters. That superficial resemblance is sufficient for the riddle phrase to work.

3   This version of the *biáng* character was encoded in Unicode version 13.0 as codepoint U+30EDE. Its "simplified" equivalent 𰻝 is codepoint U+30EDD. In the simplified character, the two components 長 'long' and 馬 'horse' appear as 长 and 马, respectively.

4   There are actually some slight differences in usage that make the two scripts not entirely isomorphic. The most notable difference is that Japanese long vowels are marked with a length sign in *katakana* but by writing a second vowel symbol in *hiragana.*

5   Insup Taylor, "Psycholinguistic Reasons," 314. Taylor observes that "study after study shows that texts are easier to read in Kanji-Hiragana mixed script than in all Hiragana."

6   Iksop Lee and Ramsey, *Korean Language*, 13. The modern name of the alpha-
      bet was coined in the early twentieth-century by Ju Sigyeong (1876–1914),
      a linguist who worked on standardization of modern Korean language and
      writing. The name literally means 'great writing'. Because Korean also has a
      homophonous word *Han* meaning 'Korean', and because the word *han* 'great'
      is obsolete, the name is commonly thought to mean 'Korean writing'.

7   Ki-Moon Lee and Ramsey, *History of the Korean Language*, 288–89.

8   Phan, "Lacquered Words," 392–93.

9   For an analysis of the cultural and political factors involved, see Phan, "Crisis
      in the Cosmopolitan," 247–48. Phan observes that "the success of [the alpha-
      betic script] Quốc Ngữ over the 1920[s] and 1930s resulted from a number
      of factors, not least of which was the dismantling of the civil service exam in
      1919, the Western education of a new generation of Vietnamese intellectuals,
      exposure of Vietnamese intellectuals to notions of nationalism and statehood
      (both within Vietnam and abroad), and even the circulation of Western
      fiction (notably French and Russian) as an expression of the pedestrian, the
      everyday, and the 'vernacular' in a social and political sense."

10   Holm, *Mapping the Old Zhuang Character Script*, 61–62 (emphasis added).

11   In mainland China, the major change was the introduction of the simplified
      character script. In Japan, it was the reduction in number of the standard set
      of *kanji* to be learned in school (currently numbering 2,136), some of which
      were simplified.

12   Prior to the invention of Unicode (a universal standardized text encoding
      intended to support all of the world's scripts and writing systems), most com-
      puter systems and fonts were based on English and designed to encode only
      128 or 256 characters. This number of codepoints was sufficient to accommo-
      date all the letters of many alphabetic scripts but woefully inadequate for the
      storage and transmission of Chinese characters.

13   For more on the history of Chinese typewriting and computing, see Mul-
      laney, *Chinese Typewriter*, and Mullaney, *Chinese Computer*.

14   Alphabetical order is a ubiquitous way of ordering and searching for written
      forms. In Chinese dictionaries over the centuries, many different organizing
      and ordering schemes have been used. Today many dictionaries arrange
      characters in alphabetical order by Pinyin spelling. But even in these, whether
      printed on paper or stored electronically, it is necessary to have a method to
      look up unfamiliar characters when the user does not know the pronuncia-
      tion. These methods are based on the number and type of strokes found in
      the characters and/or the functional components that recur across characters.
      For more information, see chapters 5–10 of Chen et al., *Literary Information
      in China*.

15	Mullaney, "QWERTY in China," S35. Today there are a number of input systems designed to make it easy to enter Chinese text into computers and smartphones. Many of these are based on pronunciation: users type in Pinyin, and the system inserts appropriate characters, making use of dictionary data and predictive text algorithms. There are also ways to enter text by "drawing" the character shapes on the touchscreen. For an overview, see Thomas S. Mullaney, "Character Input," in Chen et al., *Literary Information in China*, 36–47.

16	Unicode has a mechanism for describing Chinese characters that are not encoded, even ones that don't exist. The mechanism is to precede character components with a symbol that specifies how they are to be spatially combined. For example, ⿰ means "combine the following two characters side by side."

17	Some recent innovative and subversive characters used on the internet or on public signage have been described and explained in Li and Zhu, "Tranßcripting."

18	The university takes its name from the era name in effect at the time it was adopted, in 1868.

EIGHT *Universal Writing*

1	The full short story can be found at https://poemuseum.org/the-tell-tale-heart as well as in numerous published collections of Poe's short stories.

2	Proposals for universal languages became popular in seventeenth-century Europe. Just to give one example, the English philosopher and scientist John Wilkins developed a scheme for universal ideographic writing in his 1668 publication *An Essay Towards a Real Character, and a Philosophical Language.* The proposal established a set of symbols for different concepts that could be combined in various ways. A modern rethinking of this idea is found in Blissymbolics, invented by Charles K. Bliss in the mid-twentieth century and still actively promoted today: https://www.blissymbolics.org, accessed November 3, 2023.

3	Even in this case, we cannot say that the character has a fixed meaning across languages. The connotations, uses, and cultural implications of near-equivalent words vary from language to language and change over time. The nouns *love* (English), *àiqíng* (Mandarin), *amor* (Spanish), and *koi* (Japanese) all have different senses and shades of meaning. The semantic adaptation of a character is based on the judgment of a human being at a particular time that two words in two different languages have similar meanings. But when that character is used to write the word in Language A, it expresses all the nuances and scope of meaning of that word. When used to write the word in Language B, it expresses a different set of nuances and connotations. And if those words shift their meanings over time—as words do—the scope of meaning of the character in each writing system will further diverge. In other words, the character doesn't represent an unchanging, fixed idea across time and space but represents meaning only through the words that it writes.

4   This anecdote is recounted by Vedal, *Culture of Language in Ming China*, 226.

5   The same is of course true for the international educated elites who communicate effectively in written English today.

6   For just two examples of such attempts across the centuries, see Wilkins, *Essay Towards a Real Character*; and de Bono, *De Bono Code Book*, as discussed in McDonald, "'Ideograph'," 275.

Bibliography

I have endeavored to provide as many English-language references as possible for the convenience of the reader who wishes to do further reading. Much good scholarship on the topics discussed in this book has been published in other languages; references to many of them can be found in the bibliographies of the English-language books and articles listed here.

A Cheng. *The Chess Master* 棋王. Translated by W. J. F. Jenner. Hong Kong: Zhōngwén Dàxué Chūbǎnshè, 2005. Chinese-English bilingual edition.

Bacon, Francis. *The Advancement of Learning*. 1605. Reprint, Auckland: Floating Press, 2010.

Baxter, William H. *A Handbook of Old Chinese Phonology*. Berlin: Mouton de Gruyter, 1992.

Brindley, Erica Fox. *Ancient China and the Yue: Perceptions and Identities on the Southern Frontier, c. 400 BCE-50 CE*. Cambridge. Cambridge University Press, 2015.

Chen, Jack W., Anatoly Detwyler, Xiao Liu, Christopher M. B. Nugent, and Bruce Rusk, eds. *Literary Information in China: A History*. New York: Columbia University Press, 2021.

Chung, Jae-young 鄭在永. "Han'guk-ŭi kugyŏl" 韓國의 口訣 [Korean gugyeol]. *Kugyŏl yŏn'gu* 口訣研究 17 (2006): 129–89.

Confucius. *Rongo* 論語 [Analects]. Tokyo: Shibunkai, 1967.

Daniels, Peter T., and William Bright, eds. *The World's Writing Systems*. Oxford: Oxford University Press, 1996.

Davies, W. V. "Egyptian Hieroglyphs." In *Reading the Past: Ancient Writing from Cuneiform to the Alphabet*, introduced by J. T. Hooker, 74–135. Berkeley: University of California Press; London: British Museum, 1990.

De Bono, Edward. *The De Bono Code Book*. London: Viking, 2000.

Diller, Anthony, Jerold Edmondson, and Yongxian Luo, eds. *The Tai-Kadai Languages*. New York: Routledge, 2008.

Du Ponceau, Peter S. *A Dissertation on the Nature and Character of the Chinese System of Writing, in a Letter to John Vaughan, Esq*. Philadelphia: McCarty and Davis (for the American Philosophical Society), 1838.

Duval, Jean Rahman, and Waris Abdukerim Janbaz. "An Introduction to Latin-Script Uyghur." Lecture presented at the Middle East & Central Asia Politics, Economics, and Society Conference, University of Utah, September 7–9, 2006. https://web.archive.org/web/20061022113840/http://www.uyghurdictionary.org/excerpts/An%20Introduction%20to%20LSU.pdf.

Dwyer, Arienne M. "The Texture of Tongues: Languages and Power in China." In *Nationalism and Ethnoregional Identities in China*, edited by William Safran, 68–85. Portland, OR: Frank Cass, 1998.

Fontana, Michela. *Matteo Ricci: A Jesuit in the Ming Court*. Lanham, MD: Roman & Littlefield, 2011.

Frellesvig, Bjarke. *A History of the Japanese Language*. Cambridge: Cambridge University Press, 2010.

Georg, Stefan. "Other Isolated Languages of Asia." In *Language Isolates*, edited by Lyle Campbell, 139–61. New York: Routledge, 2018.

Gibson, William. *Nyūromansā* ニューロマンサー [Neuromancer]. Translated by Kuroma Hisashi 黒丸尚. Tokyo: Hayakawa Shobō, 1986.

Handel, Zev. "Can a Logographic Script Be Simplified? Lessons from the 20th Century Chinese Writing Reform Informed by Recent Psycholinguistic Research." *Scripta* 5 (September 2013): 21–66.

———. *Sinography: The Borrowing and Adaptation of the Chinese Script*. Leiden: Brill, 2019.

Holm, David. "Graphic Variation among Traditional Song Texts in the Zhuang-Speaking Areas of West-Central Guangxi". *Scripta* 12 (2021) 7–45.

———. *Mapping the Old Zhuang Character Script: A Vernacular Writing System from Southern China*. Leiden: Brill, 2013.

———. "A Typology of Readings of Chinese Characters in Traditional Zhuang Manuscripts." *Cahiers de Linguistique - Asie Orientale* 38, no. 2 (2009): 245–92.

Hsia, P. Po-chia. *A Jesuit in the Forbidden City: Matteo Ricci, 1552–1610*. Oxford: Oxford University Press, 2010.

Inoue, Hisashi 井上ひさし. *Nihongo nikki* ニホン語日記 [Japanese diary]. Tokyo: Bungei Shunjū, 1993.

Joyce, Terry, and Susanne R. Borgwaldt. "Typology of Writing Systems: Introduction." In *Typology of Writing Systems*, edited by Susanne R. Borgwaldt and Terry Joyce, 1–11. Amsterdam: John Benjamins, 2013.

Keightley, David N. *Sources of Shang History: The Oracle-Bone Inscriptions of Bronze Age China*. Berkeley: University of California Press, 1978.

Kiernan, Ben. *Việt Nam: A History from Earliest Times to the Present.* Oxford: Oxford University Press, 2017.

Kim Byung-Joon. "The Introduction of Chinese Characters into Korea: The Role of the Lelang Commandery." *Korea Journal* 50, no. 2 (June 2010): 8–34.

Kim Young Wook. "A Basic Understanding of *Hyangga* Interpretation." *Korea Journal* 50, no. 2 (June 2010): 72–96.

Kin Bunkyō. *Literary Sinitic and East Asia: A Cultural Sphere of Vernacular Reading,* edited by Ross King. Leiden: Brill, 2021.

Kornicki, Peter Francis. *Languages, Scripts, and Chinese Texts in East Asia.* Oxford: Oxford University Press, 2018.

Lee, Iksop, and S. Robert Ramsey. *The Korean Language.* Albany: State University of New York Press, 2000.

Lee, Ki-Moon, and S. Robert Ramsey. *A History of the Korean Language.* Cambridge: Cambridge University Press, 2011.

Li Wei and Zhu Hua. "Tranßcripting: Playful Subversion with Chinese Characters." *International Journal of Multilingualism* 16, no. 2 (2019): 145–61.

Lurie, David B. *Realms of Literacy: Early Japan and the History of Writing.* Cambridge, MA: Harvard University Asia Center, 2011.

McCann, David R. "The Story of Ch'ŏyong, a Parable of Literary Negotiation." *Korean Studies* 21 (1997): 31–53.

McDonald, Edward. "The 'Ideograph' and the 漢字 *hànzì*: A Cross-Cultural Concept with Two Mutually Invisible Faces." *Translation & Interpreting Studies* 13, no. 2 (2018): 271–92.

Meletis, Dimitrios. *The Nature of Writing: A Theory of Grapholinguistics.* Brest: Fluxus Editions, 2020.

Mullaney, Thomas S. *The Chinese Computer: A Global History of the Information Age.* Cambridge, MA: MIT Press, 2024.

———. *The Chinese Typewriter: A History.* Cambridge, MA: MIT Press, 2017.

———. "QWERTY in China: Chinese Computing and the Radical Alphabet." *Technology and Culture* 59, no. 4 Supplement (October 2018): S34–S65.

Nguyễn Đình-Hoà. "Graphemic Borrowings from Chinese: The Case of Chữ Nôm—Vietnam's Demotic Script." *Bulletin of the Institute of History and Philology* 61, no. 2 (June 1990): 383–432.

Norman, Jerry. *Chinese.* Cambridge: Cambridge University Press, 1988.

Ostler, Nicholas. *Passwords to Paradise: How Languages Have Re-invented World Religions.* New York: Bloomsbury, 2016.

Ötkür, Abdurehim. *Iz* [Trace]. Ürümchi: Shinjiang Xäliq Näshriyati, 2000.

Phan, John. "A Crisis in the Cosmopolitan: Colonization and the Promotion of the Vernacular in an Early-Twentieth-Century Vietnamese Script Experiment." In

Cosmopolitan and Vernacular in the World of Wen 文: *Reading Sheldon Pollack from the Sinographic Cosmopolis*, edited by Ross King, 245–88. Leiden: Brill, 2023.

———. "Lacquered Words: The Evolution of Vietnamese under Sinitic Influences from the 1st Century BCE through the 17th Century CE." PhD diss., Cornell University, 2013.

Ricci, Matteo. *China in the Sixteenth Century: The Journals of Matthew Ricci, 1583–1610*. Translated by Louis J. Gallagher. New York: Random House, 1953.

Rogers, Henry. *Writing Systems: A Linguistic Approach*. Malden, MA: Blackwell, 2005.

Schuessler, Axel. *Minimal Old Chinese and Later Han Chinese: A Companion to Grammata Serica Recensa*. Honolulu: University of Hawai'i Press, 2009.

Seeley, Christopher. *A History of Writing in Japan*. Leiden: Brill, 1991.

Smith, Adam. "Are Writing Systems Intelligently Designed?" In *Agency in Ancient Writing*, edited by Joshua Engelhardt, 71–93. Boulder: University Press of Colorado, 2013.

Spence, Jonathan. *The Memory Palace of Matteo Ricci*. New York: Viking Penguin, 1984.

Stauder, Andréas. "Scripts." In *The Oxford Handbook of Egyptology*, edited by Ian Shaw and Elizabeth Bloxam, 868–96. Oxford: Oxford University Press, 2020.

Sybesma, Rint, Wolfgang Behr, Yueguo Gu, Zev Handel, C.-T. James Huang, and James Myers, eds. *Encyclopedia of Chinese Language and Linguistics*. Leiden: Brill, 2015.

Taylor, Insup. "Psycholinguistic Reasons for Keeping Chinese Characters in Korean and Japanese." In *Cognitive Processing of Chinese and Related Asian Languages*, edited by Hsuan-Chih Chen, 299–319. Hong Kong: Chinese University Press, 1997.

Taylor, Keith. *The Birth of Vietnam*. Berkeley: University of California Press, 1983.

Toriyama, Akira 鳥山 明. *Dragon Ball Full Edition* ドラゴンボール完全版. Vol. 4. Tokyo: Shueisha, 2003. From *Weekly Shōnen Jump* 1985 #51, November 19, 1985.

Tse, Brian 謝立文, and Alice Mak 麥家碧. *Mak⁶Dau¹ Sampler hou²siu³ bou⁶wai⁶* 麥兜*Sampler*好笑部位 [McDull Sampler: The funny parts]. Hong Kong: Bliss, 2001.

Unger, J. Marshall. *Ideogram: Chinese Characters and the Myth of Disembodied Meaning*. Honolulu: University of Hawai'i Press, 2004.

Vedal, Nathan. *The Culture of Language in Ming China: Sound, Script, and the Redefinition of Boundaries of Knowledge*. New York: Columbia University Press, 2022.

Vovin, Alexander. *Man'yōshū: A New English Translation Containing the Original*

Text, Kana Transliteration, Romanization, Glossing, and Commentary, Book 1. Leiden: Brill. 2017.

Waddell, Kaveh. "The Alphabet That Will Save a People from Disappearing." *The Atlantic*, November 16, 2016.

Wáng Fēng 王锋. *Cóng Hànzì dào Hànzì xì wénzì: Hànzì wénhuàquān wénzì yánjiū* 从汉字到汉字系文字: 汉字文化圈文字研究 [From Chinese characters to Chinese-character-based writing systems: A study of writing in the Sinographic sphere]. Beijing: Mínzú Chūbǎnshè, 2003.

Whitman, John. "The Relationship between Japanese and Korean." In *The Languages of Japan and Korea*, edited by Nicolas Tranter, 24–38. New York: Routledge, 2012.

Wilkins, John. *An Essay Towards a Real Character, and a Philosophical Language.* London: Sa. Gellibrand, 1668.

Yoon Seon-tae. "The Creation of *Idu*." *Korea Journal* 50, no. 2 (June 2010): 97–123.

Zhou, Shan-Gui. "Chinese Names of New Elements with Z = 113, 115, 117 & 118." *Nuclear Data News* 核データニュース, no. 118 (October 2017): 12–18. http://www.aesj.or.jp/~ndd/ndnews/pdf118/No118-03.pdf

Zhū Xī 朱熹. *Sì shū jí zhù* 四書集注 [Collected commentaries on the Four Books]. Reprint, Shanghai: Shāngwù Yìnshūguǎn, 1906.

Character Locator

To help the reader locate Chinese characters and Chinese-character-derived graphs, occurrences of these graphs in the text are listed here, ordered by the English glosses that accompany them in the text. Pronunciations in various languages are also provided. Note that only characters that are given as examples or discussed as objects of analysis are listed. Characters in dynasty names, place names, book titles, and personal names are not included, nor are characters that occur only in passages of text, such as the excerpt from *The Chess Master* (Qí Wáng) on page 60 and the example sentences on page 70.

Characters that appear in the text only as part of a longer word are not given individual entries. For example, in this book 品 appears only as part of 食品. Accordingly, there is no separate entry for 品, which will be found only in the entry **food product** 食品.

Simplified Chinese characters, if they differ from the traditional versions used in the book, are provided following a slash. See pages 58–61 for an explanation of traditional and simplified characters. If the Japanese character form differs from the Chinese, it is provided just before the Japanese pronunciation, as in the entry for **icicle**.

For all mainstream Chinese characters, the Modern Standard Chinese pronunciation is provided whether or not it appears explicitly in the text. Pronunciations in other languages are given only if they occur in the text.

The pronunciations are labeled as follows:

[Ch] Standard Chinese = Mandarin
[C] Cantonese
[J] Japanese
[K] Korean
[V] Vietnamese
[Z] Zhuang
[E] English

above 上 *shàng* [Ch], 135

acquire. *See* **get**

act. *See* **be**

add 加 *jiā* [Ch], *ka, kuwae-* [J], 129–30

all 凡 *fán* [Ch], 93–94

ancient 古 *gǔ* [Ch], *go* [K], 179

autumn 秋 *qiū* [Ch], *shū, aki* [J], 123

basket 籠 *lóng* [Ch], *rō, kwo* [J], 125,
 128. *See also* **winnowing basket**

be, do, act as$_1$ 爲/为 *wéi* [Ch], *vi, làm*
 [V], 157, 221n19

be, do, act as$_2$ 灬 *làm* [V], 157, 221n19

beautiful 麗/丽 *lì* [Ch], *yeo, gop-* [K],
 84, 109, 112–13

because 因 *yīn* [Ch], 112–13

bedroom 寢室/寝室 *qǐnshì* [Ch], 寝
 室 *shinshitsu* [J], *chimsil* [K], 105, 131

below 下 *xià* [Ch], 135

biangbiang noodles 𰻞/𰻝 *biáng* [Ch],
 170, 187, 222n3

breast. *See* **milk**

brief. *See* **short**

bright 明 *míng* [Ch], *myeong, balk-*
 [K], 112–13, 116–18, 133, 138, 159–60.
 See also **you**$_1$

broken 破 *pò* [Ch], 23

brother. *See* **older brother**

brothers 英三 *anh tam* [V], 154, 221n17.
 See also **three**$_2$

Buddhist nun 尼 *ní* [Ch], *ni* [K], 162,
 179. *See also* **this**$_2$

buy 買/买 *mǎi* [Ch], *mãi* [V], 154–55.
 See also **new, recent**

candy. *See* **sugar**

cave$_1$ 洞 *dòng* [Ch], 64

cave$_2$ 穴 *xué* [Ch], 170, 187

chicken 雞/鸡 *jī* [Ch], 162. *See also*
 what$_1$; **what**$_3$

cloth 布 *bù* [Ch], *pu, nuno* [J], 125

cloud 雲/云 *yún* [Ch], 47, 53, 59. *See
 also* **say**$_3$

cod 鱈 *tara* [J], 135

collect. *See* **gather**

compare 比 *bǐ* [Ch], 159, 162. *See also*
 year$_1$

compassionate 仁 *rén* [Ch], 20

corruption. *See* **greed**

cow 牛 *niú* [Ch], 44, 54

culture, literature 文 *wén* [Ch], 159.
 See also **person**$_2$

diet, restrict one's food intake 節食/
 节食 *jiéshí* [Ch], 25. *See also* **food
 and drink**

dining hall 食堂 *shítáng* [Ch], 21, 25

discuss 討論/讨论 *tǎolùn* [Ch], 26,
 211n16

do. *See* **be**

door 門/门 *mén* [Ch], 143, 160

dragon 龍/龙 *lóng* [Ch], 4

drink. *See* **food and drink**

each 各 *gè* [Ch], 63, 64

earth$_1$ 土 *tǔ* [Ch], 135

earth$_2$ 地 *dì* [Ch], 190. *See also* **horizon**

eastern capital 東京/东京 *dōngjīng*
 [Ch], *donggyeong* [K], 120

eat$_1$ 食 *shí* [Ch], *shoku, tabe-* [J], *sik,
 meok-* [K], 20–21, 25, 26, 109, 132–33

eat$_2$ 吃 *chī* [Ch], 26

edible sugar 食糖 *shítáng* [Ch], 21, 25

elephant 象 *xiàng* [Ch], 44, 47, 52, 54,
 93, 94, 141, 196. *See also* **resemble**

era 代 *dài* [Ch], 135

evening. *See* **night**

eye 目 *mù* [Ch], 44

eyebrow 眉 *méi* [Ch], 159, 166. *See also*
 have

fat. *See* **great, large**
female 女 *nǚ* [Ch], 162. *See also* **this**₁
few₁ 尐 *ít* [V], 155, 156
few₂ 少 *shǎo* [Ch], 156
field 田 *tián* [Ch], 62–63, 135. *See also* **rice field**
fish 魚 *yú* [Ch], 44, 54–55, 135–36
flat 平 *píng* [Ch], 190. *See also* **horizon**
food and drink; one's diet 飲食/饮食 *yǐnshí* [Ch], 25
food product 食品 *shípǐn* [Ch], 25
four₁ 四 *sì* [Ch], 87–88, 91, 94, 156
four₂ 罙 *bón* [V], 155–56
fragrant 芳 *fāng* [Ch], 53, 64
fruit 果 *guǒ* [Ch], *gwa* [K], 179

gather, collect 採 *cǎi* [Ch], *sai, tum-* [J], 126
gauze 紗/纱 *shā* [Ch], *sya, usuginu* [J], 126
get 得 *dé* [Ch], 112–13, 117, 140–41
ghost 𦨞 *fang*ᶻ [Z], 165
go out 出 *chū* [Ch], *de-, izu* [J], 169, 222n2
great, large 太 *tài* [Ch], *futo-* [J], 137
greed, corruption 貪/贪 *tān* [Ch], *tham* [V], 153

hall 堂 *táng* [Ch], 20–21, 25, 87–89, 91, 143. *See also* **dining hall**
have 眉 *mi*ᶻ [Z], 159, 166. *See also* **eyebrow**
heart 心 *xīn* [Ch], *shin, kokoro* [J], 123, 170, 187
heaven, sky 霄 *mbwn* [V], 160. *See also* **sky**
heavenly stem. *See* **second of the ten heavenly stems**
hemp 麻 *má* [Ch], 162. *See also* **what**₃
hold 持 *chí* [Ch], *chi, mot-* [J], 126

horizon 地平線/地平线 *dìpíngxiàn* [Ch], 190. *See also* **earth**₂; **flat; line**
horse 馬/马 *mǎ* [Ch], 44, 54–55, 59, 162, 170, 187, 222n26. *See also* **what**₁; **what**₂
house 房 *fáng* [Ch], 165
housing site 垈 *dae* [K], 135
hungry 餓/饿 *è* [Ch], 93–94
husked rice 屵 *san* [Z], 165

icicle 冰柱 *bīngzhù* [Ch], 氷柱 *tsurara, hyōchū* [J], 174
if 其 *qí* [Ch], 46, 52. *See also* **winnowing basket**
inform. *See* **tell**

journey 辶 *chuò* [Ch], 170, 187
joy 樂/乐 *lè* [Ch], 93–94. *See also* **music**

Keio University₁ 慶應 *Keiō* [J], 188
Keio University₂ 庆応 *Keiō* [J], 188
Keio University₃ 応 *Keiō* [J], 188
knife 刀 *dāo* [Ch]. *Combining form* 刂, 170, 187

large. *See* **great**
letter, message 信 *xìn* [Ch], 213n30. *See also* **text message**
line 線/线 *xiàn* [Ch], 190. *See also* **horizon**
literature. *See* **culture**
lofty 堯/尧 *yáo* [Ch], *nhiêu* [V], 155–56
long 長/长 *cháng* [Ch], 170, 187, 222n3
long time 久 *jiǔ* [Ch], *ku, hisa-* [J], 125, 129–30

many₁ 夥 *nhiêu* [V], 155–56
many₂ 多 *duō* [Ch], *đa* [V], 155–56
message. *See* **text message; letter**
milk; breast 乳 *rǔ* [Ch], *nyū, ti* [J], 126, 127

moon₁ 月 *yuè* [Ch], *jyut⁶* [C], *tsuki* [J], *wol, dal* [K], *ndwen* [Z], 14, 27, 109–13, 116, 128, 140–41, 143, 153, 159–60, 170, 187, 189, 194

moon₂ 朤 *moon* [E], 143–44, 155

moon₃ 胖 *ndwen* [Z], 159–60

mother 母 *mǔ* [Ch], *mo, haha* [J], 126

mountain 山 *shān* [Ch], *san, yama* [J], 123, 135–36, 165, 169, 218n24, 222n2

mountain pass 峠 *tōge* [J], 135

music 音樂/音乐 *yīnyuè* [Ch], 音楽 *ongaku* [J], *eumak* [K], *âm nhạc* [V], 105, 131

must 須/须 *xū* [Ch], *su, subekaraku* [J], 126

net 羅/罗 *luó* [Ch], *ra* [K], 179

new, recent 買 *mới* [V], 154–55. See also buy

newspaper 新聞/新闻 *xīnwén* [Ch], *shinbun* [J], *sinmun* [K], 105, 131

night 夜 *yè* [Ch], *ya, bam* [K], *haemʰ* [Z], 118, 159

none 冎 *ndwi* [Z], 166

nun. See Buddhist nun

obtain. See get

older brother 昆 *kūn* [Ch], *gon, mat* [K], 109, 119

overflow 濫/滥 *làn* [Ch], *lạm* [V], 221n19

pass. See mountain pass

period of time 期 *qī* [Ch], *gi* [K], 116–18, 133

person₁ 人 *rén* [Ch], *hito* [J], *vunᶻ* [Z], 20, 59, 87–88, 91, 159–60, 168–69. *Combining form* 亻, 53, 160

person₂ 文 *vunᶻ* [Z], 159–60. See also culture, literature

rain 雨 *yǔ* [Ch], 160

recent. See new

recognize 認/认 *rèn* [Ch], 59, 211n16

resemble 像 *xiàng* [Ch], 47, 52, 53. See also elephant

rice. See husked rice

rice field 畓 *dap* [K], 135

road 路 *lù* [Ch], 63–64

rock. See stone

root₁ 根 *gēn* [Ch], *kon, ne* [J], 126–27

root₂ 本 *běn* [Ch], *bổn* [V], 156

run. See walk

same 同 *tóng* [Ch], 64

say, speak₁ 說/说 *shuō* [Ch], 26, 47, 211n16

say, speak₂ 講/讲 *jiǎng* [Ch], 26, 211n16

say₃ 云 *yún* [Ch], 47, 53, 59. See also cloud

seat 座 *zuò* [Ch], *suwa-* [J], 167–68

second of the ten heavenly stems 乙 *yǐ* [Ch], *eul* [K], *ất* [V], 118, 156

see 見/见 *jiàn* [Ch], *gyeon, bo-* [K], 109, 119

shine 照 *zhào* [Ch], 112–13

short, brief 短 *duǎn* [Ch], 213n30. See also text message

sit. See seat

site. See housing site

skin 皮 *pí* [Ch], 162. See also year₄

sky 天 *tiān* [Ch], *ten, ama* [J], 112–13, 129, 130–31. See also heaven

slope 坡 *pō* [Ch], 23

snow 雪 *xuě* [Ch], 135

speak. See say

special 特 *tè* [Ch], 93–94

speech 言 *yán* [Ch], 59–60, 170, 187, 211n16

square 方 *fāng* [Ch], 53, 64, 165

stone 石 *shí* [Ch], 62–63, 88

sugar 糖 *táng* [Ch], 20–21, 25, 47. *See also* **edible sugar**

table 几 *jǐ* [Ch], 162. *See also* **what₂**

table 几 *jǐ* [Ch], 162. *See also* what$_2$
tell 告訴/告诉 *gàosu* [Ch], *kō, nor-* [J], 26, 126, 211n16
ten 十 *shí* [Ch], *sap^6* [C], *jū* [J], *sip, yeol* [K], *thập* [V], 20, 69–71, 81, 87–88, 91, 109
tennessine 础 *tián* [Ch], 63, 171, 187
text message 短信 *duǎnxìn* [Ch], 213n30. *See also* **short, brief; letter, message**
think 思 *sī* [Ch], *si, omo-* [J], 125
this$_1$ 女 *nei^x* [Z], 162. *See also* **female**
this$_2$ 尼 *nei^x* [Z], 162. *See also* **Buddhist nun**
this$_3$ 呢 *nei^x* [Z], 162
three$_1$ 呸 *ba* [V], 140, 221n18
three$_2$ 三 *sān* [Ch], *tam* [V], 153–54, 165–66. *See also* **brothers**
time. *See* **period of time; long time**
tiny 幺 *yāo* [Ch], 170, 187
tolerate 忍 *rěn* [Ch], 59
tongue$_1$ 舌 *shé* [Ch], 89, 143
tongue$_2$ 脷 *tongue* [E], 143, 155

visit 訪/访 *fǎng* [Ch], 64, 211n16

walk, run 走 *zǒu* [Ch], 26
water 水 *shuǐ* [Ch], 135
wave 波 *bō* [Ch], 23
weather. *See* **rain**
what$_1$ 鸡马 *gi^{j}ma^z* [Z], 162. *See also* **chicken; horse**
what$_2$ 几馬/几马 *gi^{j}ma^z* [Z], 162. *See also* **table; horse**
what$_3$ 鸡麻 *gi^{j}ma^z* [Z], 162. *See also* **chicken; hemp**
winnowing basket 箕 *jī* [Ch], 46, 52. *See also* **if**
work 工 *gōng* [Ch], 91

year$_1$ 比 *bi* [Z], 159, 162. *See also* **compare**
year$_2$ 毕 *bi* [Z], 159, 162
year$_3$ 年 *nián* [Ch], *bi* [Z], 159, 162
year$_4$ 皮 *bi* [Z], 162. *See also* **skin**
you$_1$ 明 *mwng^z* [Z], 159–160. *See also* **bright**
you$_2$ 伖 *mwng^z* [Z], 160

General Index

abbreviation, 101, 157, 188, 221n18; cursivization and part-selection, 129, 142; in Japanese *kana*, 129–30, 131, 137; in premodern Korean writing, 178–80. See also *hiragana*; *katakana*; simplified characters

abjad scripts, 86

adaptation, 8, 89–96, 102, 150, 198–99; of Chinese characters for Japanese, 121–29, 178; of Chinese characters for Korean, 110–11, 113, 115–21, 218n22; cultural diffusion and linguistic structure in, 158, 221n21; direct, 120–21, 151, 153, 179, 180; of Latin alphabet to English, 90–91; linear and composite, 136–37, 138, 163–64; manipulation to form new characters, 166; in Vietnamese writing, 138, 139–40, 152–57; in Zhuang writing, 138. See also disambiguation; phonetic adaptation; semantic adaptation

Adlam script, 215n5

alphabets, 6, 21–22, 86, 209n20; alphabetical ordering, 223n14; misuse of term, 209n18; relationship to spoken language, 15–16, 17; superiority myth, 172, 186–87; use to represent Chinese, 58, 211n19; Vietnamese, 182, 223n9; Zhuang, 183. See also Hangeul; Hanyu Pinyin; Latin alphabet; romanization

ambiguity: and context, 32, 130, 154; and conventionalization, 140–41; and emergence of *kana*, 130, 174; in English spelling, 90, 174; in Japanese names, 128; in rebus usage, 46; simplification and, 59. See also disambiguation

Analects (Lunyu) of Confucius, 2, 3*fig.*; in Classical Chinese with Japanese *kanbun kundoku* markings, 101*fig.*

ancient Chinese, pronunciation of, 210n10

Arabic script, 85; used for Uyghur language, 85, 215n1

arbitrariness, 19–20, 171, 209n20

articles, 68, 215n4; English *the*, 102, 141, 220n3

Babylonian, 8

Bacon, Francis, 2–3, 13–14, 190, 196

Baekje kingdom, 99, 108, 122

Barry brothers, 215n5

biángbiáng noodles, 169; *biáng* character, 169–71, 170*fig.*, 187–88, 222n3

Bouyei ethnic group, 146–47
Buddhism, 77, 99
Buddhist texts, 77, 100, 180, 214n10
Burmese, 103

Cantonese: compared with Classical Chinese, 69, 70; compared with Mandarin, Japanese, Korean, and Vietnamese, 151; *McDull* cartoon, 75–76, 75*fig.*, 214n7; used to pronounce Classical Chinese, 71, 81; written form of, 57, 72–75, 75*fig.*
case-marking particles, 142, 148, 154–55, 158, 180, 194
character encoding, 187, 223n12. *See also* Unicode standard
chemical elements, 62–63, 171, 187, 213n31
Cherokee syllabary, 91, 207n5
Chess Master (Qí Wáng by A Cheng), 60, 212n23; word boundaries in, 72
China National Committee for Terminology in Science and Technology, 213n31
Chinese, spoken: features of, 103; Old and Modern, 67; regional varieties, 7, 56–57, 73; tonal system, 107. *See also* Chinese languages and varieties
Chinese characters: adaptability of, 7–8, 27; basic principles of, 54; creation of new characters, 134–35, 143–44, 155, 167–71, 188, 224n16; cultural value of, 181–82; dissemination of, 1–2, 7, 65, 77–80, 89, 97–100, 138, 144–47; distinguished from Classical Chinese, 7; 'dragon', 4; education in, 83–84, 163; elimination of, 180–81, 186; fake, 139–40; future and legacy of, 187, 198–200; invention of, 5, 29, 40–41, 53–54; as mor-

phographic, 20, 25–27, 65; myths and misunderstandings about, 2–4, 25–26, 190–91; number of, 61; as open set, 62–63; playful manipulation of, 167–71, 218n23; as representations of things or ideas, 2–3, 13–14, 25–27, 65, 66, 189, 190–91, 195, 198; simplification of, 58–60; sound and meaning, 95, 109, 111, 116, 123, 199; stylization, reduction, and conventionalization of, 54–56, 141; technology and, 185–88, 200; traditional and simplified, 58–61, 211n13, 212n22, 212n24; as universal writing, 2, 4, 65, 79, 80, 189, 194–95, 196–97; use in headlines and signage, 181; used to write English, 84, 86–89, 91, 91–94, 111–13, 140–41, 143, 194, 199. *See also* adaptation; Chinese writing; Classical Chinese; phonetic-semantic compounds; Standard Written Chinese
Chinese cultural influence, 6–7, 76–77, 80, 181–82
Chinese dialects, 7, 73, 76; contrasted with Chinese languages, 56
Chinese languages and varieties, 6, 7, 20, 56–57, 73, 76, 103, 199. *See also* Cantonese; Hokkien; Mandarin; Middle Chinese; Old Chinese; Shanghainese; Taiwanese
Chinese linguistics, 190
Chinese writing: based on Mandarin, 72; for Cantonese, 57, 72–75; codification and standardization of, 54, 55–56; direction, 72; in the modern era, 185, 187; for non-Mandarin Chinese languages, 56–57; origins of, 5, 29, 40–41, 53–54; punctuation use in, 72; twentieth-century

reforms of, 57–58, 211n17; word boundaries and, 72. *See also* Chinese characters; Classical Chinese; oracle bone inscriptions; Standard Written Chinese

Chosun Ilbo (The Chosun daily), 181

Chŭ Nôm. *See* Nôm writing

Classical Chinese, 7, 66–67; *Analects* of Confucius, 2, 3*fig.*, 101*fig.*; compared with Mandarin and Cantonese, 69, 70; as dead language, 76; and dissemination of Chinese culture, 6–7, 80; distinguished from Chinese characters, 7; literacy in, 196–97; in the modern era, 188–89; pronunciation of, 70–71, 80–82; replaced by vernacular, 57, 171; and speakers of different Chinese languages, 56–57, 73, 76, 196; use for cultural communication beyond China, 76, 79–80, 144, 199. *See also* Japanese adoption of Chinese writing; Korea: Classical Chinese in

Committee on Script Reform, 58–59

complex characters, 58, 60. *See also* traditional and simplified characters

composite adaptation, 163–64

compound characters, 50–53, 55, 143–44, 164, 165. *See also* phonetic-semantic compounds

computerization, 185–86, 187, 223n12. *See also* Unicode standard

Confucian classics: *Analects*, 2, 3*fig.*; in Japan and Korea, 101*fig.*, 108

consonant clusters, 22–23

consonantary scripts, 86

conventionalization, 54, 55, 141–42, 163, 220–21n10

Coptic, 8

cuneiform, 5–6, 8, 186–87, 198

cursivization, 129, 137. *See also hiragana*

Cyrillic script, 15, 85; used for Uyghur language, 86, 215n1

Demotic, 8

dictionaries: English-language, 212–13n28; number of characters included in, 61–63, 212nn26–28; ordering and finding characters in, 223n14; Zhuang–Chinese, 162

digital fonts, 56, 187, 223n12

direct adaptation, 120–21, 151, 153, 179, 180

disambiguation, 96, 102, 138; compound graphs, 47–54, 143; conventionalization and, 141–42; dependence on structural features of spoken language, 164, 199; in Japanese writing, 130, 132–34, 137–38, 174; in Korean *hyangchal*, 117–18, 132; in linear vs. composite systems, 163–65; use of Chinese characters for, in modern Korean, 181; use of phonetic determinatives, 117–18, 132–34, 136, 138; in Vietnamese, 154–55. *See also* ambiguity

Dragon Ball manga, 177*fig.*

Dream of the Red Chamber (Hóng lóu mèng by Cao Xueqin), 57, 211n18

Du Ponceau, Peter S., 209n23

Egyptian writing, 5–6, 8, 29–32, 31*fig.*, 186–87, 198

Elamite, 8

elephant, 22, 196; English word in Chinese characters, 93–94, 141, 194; as pictograph, 34–35, 43, 44*fig.*, 47, 52; rebus use, 47, 52–53

emoji, 14, 208n14

encryption schemes, 87

'horizon' character, 190
hun (gloss), 109, 116, 217n12
Hundred Yue, 144
Hunmin Jeongeum. See Hangeul
hyangchal, 113, 121, 179; compared with
    Japanese and Vietnamese adapta-
    tion, 125, 126, 153; disambiguation,
    117–18, 132; phonetic and semantic
    adaptation, 116–18, 120. See also
    Korean writing; Old Korean
hyangga (country songs), 114. See also
    "Song of Cheoyong"

ideographs, 25–26, 65, 209n23, 224n2
idu, 179
Indic scripts, 77
Inoue, Hisashi, Nihongo nikki, 173fig.,
    174, 175
input systems, 224n15
invention of writing, 5–6; transfor-
    mation of pictures, 29–38. See also
    pictographs
Iriy, Panel of, 29–31, 30fig., 210n3
Italian, 68–69, 70, 82

Japanese adoption of Chinese writ-
    ing, 77–78, 80, 100, 216n4; kanbun
    kundoku, 101–2, 101fig., 130, 214n10;
    pronunciation of Classical Chinese,
    80–81, 214n10. See also Japanese
    writing system; Sino-Japanese
Japanese language: compared with
    Mandarin, 149; grammatical
    structure, 103–6, 122, 125, 216n8;
    number of basic syllables in, 107,
    217n11; particles and suffixes, 104–5,
    106, 132, 142, 163–64; poetry, 122,
    218n23; pronunciation of, 107;
    relationship to Korean, 216n8; tonal
    contrasts and pitch accent, 107. See

also Japanese writing system; Sino-
    Japanese
Japanese writing system: absence of
    word spacing, 132; adaptation of
    Chinese characters for, 95–96, 102,
    121–29, 137, 142, 178; creation of new
    characters, 134–36; disambiguation
    in, 130, 132–34, 137–38, 142, 172–74;
    furigana, 174, 175; kungana, 127; as
    mixed-script, 121, 129, 130–33, 164,
    172–78, 219n35, 222n5; in the modern
    era, 137, 171–78, 185, 187; on and kun,
    123, 218n24; reduction in standard
    kanji, 223n11; romanization in, 172,
    194; treatment of names, 128. See
    also hiragana; kana; kanji; katakana
Japonic language family, 103
Jeju Island, language of, 216n5
Jesuits. See Ricci, Matteo
Jing (Gin/Kinh) ethnic minority, 220n9
Ju Sigyeong, 223n6

kana, 121, 130–32, 142, 219n35, 219n37;
    katakana and hiragana, 174–75,
    222n4; as moraic, 131; used for
    disambiguation, 132–34, 137. See also
    hiragana; katakana
kanbun kundoku, 101–2, 101fig., 130,
    214n10
kanji: adaptation and cursivization of,
    137; Chinese characters as, 6, 96; ef-
    ficiencies vs. effort to learn, 177–78,
    222n5; in Japanese mixed writing,
    121, 130–32, 172, 219n35; as morpho-
    graphs, 121, 130–31, 132, 137; newly
    created, 135–36; Original Kanji
    Contest, 167–69, 168fig.; phonetic
    disambiguation of, 132–33; playful
    manipulation of, 167–69, 168fig.,
    188; proposal to replace with

Lu Xun, "Diary of a Madman," 214n5
Luwian, 8

Macau, 58
Malaysia, 58–59
Manchu language, 215–16n1
Mandarin: adaptation of Classical
    Chinese writing for, 57; as basis for
    written standard, 72–73; compared
    with Classical Chinese, 69, 70;
    compared with Middle Chinese,
    Sino-Japanese, and Sino-Korean,
    105*table*; compared with Vietnam-
    ese, Japanese, and Korean, 149; fea-
    tures and grammar, 22–24, 103; four
    tones, 23–24; popular writing in, 7,
    57, 71, 72; transcription of pronunci-
    ations, 209n21; use of term, 20; used
    to pronounce Classical Chinese, 71,
    81; word order, 24. *See also* Standard
    Written Chinese
manipulation of characters, 166; play-
    ful, 167–71, 218n23
Man'yōshū (Collection of ten thousand
    leaves), 122, 123–27, 219n30; pho-
    netic adaptation in, 129, 178; playful
    usage in, 169
Matisoff, James A., 190
Mayan writing, 207n4
McDonald, Edward, 209n23
McDull (cartoon), in Cantonese, 75–76,
    75*fig.*, 214n7
Melancolia I (Albrecht Dürer), 9–10, 10*fig.*
Mesoamerican writing, 5–6, 198, 207n4
Middle Chinese, 103, 216n6; borrowed
    as Sino-Japanese and Sino-Korean,
    106, 108, 123, 151; vocabulary
    compared with Sino-Japanese and
    Sino-Korean, 105*table*
mismatch, structural, 102

Modern Standard Chinese, 7, 103. *See
    also* Mandarin
Modern Standard Japanese. *See* Jap-
    anese language; Japanese writing
    system
Mon-Khmer language family, 103
Mongolian, 183
moon character: in Chinese, Japanese,
    and Korean, 27, 109*table*, 110–111,
    115–16, 189; as component in *biáng*
    character, 170; crescent moon emoji,
    14, 208n14; semantic adaptation of,
    110–11, 116, 128, 140–41, 153, 159–60,
    194; spoken pronunciations of,
    14; used to write English, 111–13,
    140–41, 143, 155; as visual represen-
    tation, 14; in Zhuang, 159*table*, 160
moras, 131
morphemes, 19, 20–21; English exam-
    ples, 20–21, 35, 37; Japanese and
    Korean, 106; newly introduced,
    62, 213n30; single-syllable, 22, 65;
    speech-related, 211n16. *See also* mor-
    phographic scripts
morphographic scripts, 15, 18–21; Chi-
    nese as, 65; contrasted with ideo-
    graphs, 25–27; English represented
    as, 18–19, 87, 88, 88*table*, 91, 113, 118;
    introduction of new morphemes,
    62; Japanese *kanji*, 121, 130–31, 132,
    137; nonarbitrariness in, 19–20;
    semantic and phonetic adaptation
    of, 38, 95, 111. *See also* adaptation;
    Standard Written Chinese
morphographs, 21, 26, 111, 113, 118. *See
    also* syllabographs
Mullaney, Thomas, 186
music, related words from ancient
    Chinese source, 105*table*, 130–31,
    148–49, 151

Nam Việt kingdom, 144–46, 145*map*
names, adapted into Chinese characters, 128
Neuromancer (Gibson), Japanese translation, 175, 176*fig.*
newspapers, 180–81
Nguyễn Du, "The Tale of Kieu," 147
Nguyễn Trãi, 147; "Poem 47," 152–53,
155–56, 156*table*, 221n14
Nihon shoki (Historical records of
Japan), 219n31
No Smoking symbol, 10, 11*fig.*, 12–13,
14, 25
Nôm writing: and the ascendance of
romanized script, 182–83, 223n9;
disambiguation in, 154–55; innovations in, 182; literature in, 182; new
graphs created for, 155–57, 221n18;
poetry, 147. *See also* Vietnamese
writing
nonglottographic writing, 208n11
Norman French, 106, 150–51, 217n10
North Korea, elimination of Chinese
characters, 180
Nùng ethnic minority, 220n9
nǔshū (women's writing), 22

Ō no Yasumaro, preface to *Kojiki*, 128
Okinawan, 103
Old Chinese, 67, 216n6; pronuncia-
tion of, 71, 80–81, 213n2; and the
Sino-Tibetan language family, 103.
See also Classical Chinese; Middle
Chinese
Old English, 150
Old French, 150–51
Old Japanese, 103, 122, 124–25, 134. See
also *Man'yōshū*
Old Korean, 103, 115–16, 122, 129, 134,

152–53, 178; phonetic determinatives, 133*table*. *See also* "Song of
Cheoyong"
oracle bone inscriptions, 41, 198;
archeological expeditions and
deciphering, 41–42; characters as
pictographs, 43–45, 44*fig.*; disambiguation of graphs, 52; of divination
on turtle plastron, 42–43, 42*fig.*,
45; phonetic extension in, 45; ten
heavenly stems in, 217n20
Original Kanji Contest, 167–69, 168*fig.*
Ötkür, Abdurehim, *Iz* (Trace), 85
Oxford English Dictionary, 212n28

Panel of Iriy, 29–31, 30*fig.*, 210n3
Papua New Guinea, 208n10
Phan, John, 147
Phoenician alphabet, 6, 209n20
phonetic adaptation, 94–95, 102, 134,
194, 199; cursivization and part-
selection in, 129; English examples, 140–41; in Japanese writing,
121–22, 125–29, 137, 142–43, 163–64,
178; in Korean, 111, 113, 116–18, 152,
163–64; *kungana*, 127; for particles
and suffixes, 113, 116–19, 122, 126,
130, 132, 137, 163–64; with semantic resonances, 126–27, 219n30;
in Vietnamese writing, 153–55;
by Zhuang-speaking peoples,
220–21n10; in Zhuang writing, 158,
166. *See also* phonetic-semantic
compounds
phonetic components, 55, 63–64, 198; in
composite adaptation, 164; double-
phonetic components, 165–66,
165*table*; transparency of, 64*table*
phonetic determinatives, 132–34,

133*table*, 136, 138; "first" as example, 118, 133*table*, 134

phonetic extension, 37–39; ambiguity in, 46, 47–51; in oracle bone inscriptions, 45, 46–47, 52. *See also* rebus usage

phoneticization, 171, 186

phonetic-semantic compounds, 50–53, 54, 143, 160*table*; for chemical elements, 62–63, 171, 187, 213n31; for colloquial words, 72; for morphemes related to speaking, 59*table*, 211n16; new characters as, 135, 155–56, 156*table*, 159–60, 159*table*, 162, 221n18; prevalence of, 64, 65; and pronunciation change over time, 63–64; simplification of, 59–60. *See also* phonetic components; semantic components

phonology, 39

pictographs, 34–38, 191–92; cloud, 47, 53; creation of compound characters from, 52–53; elephant, 34–35, 43, 47, 52; eye, 44*fig.*; loss of representational quality, 43–44, 44*fig.*, 54–55; in oracle bone inscriptions, 43–45, 44*fig.*; phonetic extension of, 37–39, 45–47, 52; and playful manipulation of Chinese characters, 167; square, 53, 211n14; winnowing basket, 45, 47, 52. *See also* ideographs; pictures and writing

pictures and writing, 29–38, 40

Pinyin transcription system. *See* Hanyu Pinyin

pitch accent, 107

Poe, Edgar Allan, 198; "The Tell-Tale Heart," 192

poetry, 92, 131, 210n10; Japanese, 122,

218n23; Korean, 180; Vietnamese, 147, 152; visual wordplay in, 126–27, 219n30; Zhuang, 147. *See also* *Man'yōshū*; "Song of Cheoyong"

Poison symbol, 11, 11*fig.*

pottery, writing on, 40–41, 41*fig.*

prefixes, 31, 36, 192; Japanese, 125, 219n36

Qín dynasty, 77, 97; military control in Vietnam, 144

Quốc Ngữ, 223n9. *See also* Vietnamese writing

radicals, 211n12. *See also* semantic components

rebus usage, 37–39, 40, 95, 198; basket used for 'if', 45–46, 47; bypassing of, by creating compounds, 52–53; for Classical Chinese characters used for spoken language, 72; cloud used for 'to say', 47, 192–93; elephant used for 'resemble', 47, 52–53; English examples, 38, 39*fig.*, 46, 47, 48, 49–53; language dependence of, 47, 192–93, 210n11; in Vietnamese, 155. *See also* phonetic extension

reduction, 54, 55

Ricci, Matteo, 1–2; on Chinese characters as universal writing, 194, 196–97; on dissemination of Chinese writing, 1–2, 7; on representation of "things," 2–3, 13–14, 27, 65, 66, 189

ritual texts, 183–85; Zhuang religious manuscript in Old Zhuang script, 184*fig.*

rōmaji, 172

Roman alphabet. *See* Latin alphabet

Romance languages, 67–70, 82, 103, 213n4

romanization, 58, 172, 185, 194, 211n21. *See also* Hanyu Pinyin

Romanization Association (Japan), 194

rubi (*ruby*) text, 174, 175

Sankei Shimbun (newspaper), 167

scribes, 95; in English examples, 92–93, 111–12; Japanese and Korean, 101, 108, 110, 111, 122, 138; Korean, in Japan, 100

scripts: adaptation of, 89–95, 92, 150; creation of, 207n5; defined, 15; distinguished from spoken language, 84–85; invented from scratch for a language, 89, 215n5; relationship to spoken language, 15–17, 21; three basic types, 21–22. *See also* alphabets; morphographic scripts; syllabic writing; writing systems

Sejong, King, 178–79, 207n5. *See also* Hangeul

semantic adaptation, 94–95, 199; accompanied by abbreviation, 157; combined with phonetic adaptation, 94, 95, 113, 116–19, 138, 143, 194; and creation of new characters, 134; English examples, 138, 140–41; in Japanese writing, 121, 122, 123–25, 126, 127, 129, 142; in Korean writing, 111, 113, 116–19; moon character, 110–11, 116, 128, 140–41, 153, 159–60, 194; and near-equivalent words, 224n3; in Vietnamese, 156–57; for word roots, 116, 119, 123, 130, 135, 142, 155, 157, 163; in Zhuang writing, 158, 159*table*, 162. *See also* direct adaptation; phonetic-semantic compounds

semantic components, 50–53, 54, 59*table*, 60, 63, 143, 211n12; in composite adaptation, 164; in oracle

bone inscriptions, 52–53; for speech, 211n16; stabilization of, 55. *See also* phonetic-semantic compounds

Sequoyah, Chief, invention of Cherokee syllabary, 207n5

Shanghainese, 57

Shirakawa Shizuka Institute of East Asian Characters and Culture (Ritsumeikan University), 167

Shuōwén jiězì, 212n26

sign language, 208n9; written representation of, 208n9, 208n13

Sign Writing, 208n9

Silla kingdom, 99–100, 114–15

simplified characters, 58, 223n11; *biáng* character, 222n3; ease of use, 60, 212n22; in Singapore and Malaysia, 58–59; techniques for simplification, 59–60. *See also* traditional and simplified characters

Singapore, 58–59

singular and plural nouns, 23, 24, 88, 94, 102

Sinographic cosmopolis, 208n7

Sino-Japanese, 105*table*, 106, 151; pronunciations of, 123, 125, 129, 218n24

Sino-Korean, 105*table*, 106, 108–10, 119, 151; direct adaptation in the writing of, 120–21, 180; instruction in, 181; pronunciations of Chinese characters, 109–11, 109*table*, 116; written in *idu*, 179–80

Sino-Tibetan language family, 103

Sino-Vietnamese, 147, 150, 151, 153

Sino-Zhuang, 147, 150

Smallpox Demon, 115

smartphones, 186, 224n15

social distancing, 168–69

"Song of Cheoyong" (Cheoyongga), 114–20, 152–53, 178, 179, 217n17; direct adaptation in, 120; embedded in Classical Chinese narrative, 114*fig.*

sound and meaning, 95, 109, 111, 116, 123, 199, 217n12, 218n24

South Korea, use of Chinese characters, 180–81

Southeast Asia, 77. *See also* Vietnam

Southern Zhuang, 220n9

Spanish, 68–69, 70, 82, 213–14n4, 220n4

spoken languages: acquisition of, 208n9; relationship to writing, 7–8, 13–14, 15–16, 84–85, 192, 194, 197–98; without written form, 9, 208n10

Standard Chinese. *See* Mandarin

Standard Written Chinese: characters in use, 61–64; in Hong Kong, 74; as morphographic script, 20–21, 25–26; used by speakers of non-Mandarin Chinese languages, 72–74. *See also* Chinese characters

steles: defined, 209n2; Egyptian, 29–31, 30*fig.*

structural mismatch, 102

stylization, 54–55

suffixes, 104–5, 113, 154–55, 158, 163–64; phonetic representation of, 116–17, 119, 122, 126, 130, 132, 133*table*, 137, 142

Sumerian writing, invention of, 5. *See also* cuneiform

Sutton, Valerie, 208n9

Swahili, 39

syllabic writing, 15, 21–22; English represented in, 16–17, 89, 91, 92–93; Japanese, 17, 130, 219n35; practicality of, 17. See also *hiragana*; *kana*; *katakana*; syllabographs

syllables, 21*table*, 22, 39–40

syllabographs, 21*table*, 93, 113; Japanese, 127, 129; Korean, 111, 179. See also *kana*

symbols and diagrams, 25; emoji, 14, 208n14; No Smoking and Poison symbols, 10–11, 11*fig.*, 12–13, 14, 25

Tai-Kadai language family, 103

Taiwan: Taiwanese, 57; use of traditional characters, 58, 60

Tales of the Three Kingdoms (Samguk yusa), 119–20, 119*fig.*

Tày ethnic minority, 220n9

Taylor, Insup, 222n5

terminology, 27–28

Thai, 103, 146

Tibetan, 103, 183

tonal systems, 24, 107; Modern Standard Chinese, 23–24; Zhuang and Vietnamese, 148

traditional and simplified characters, 58–60, 211n13; comparison of, 59*table*, 60; ease of use, 212n22; similarity of, 61, 212n24. *See also* simplified characters

Unicode standard, 56, 186; computer systems before, 223n12; encoding of emoji, 208n14; encoding of new characters, 187–88; representation of unencoded Chinese characters, 187, 224n16

universal languages, 197, 224n2

universal writing, 191–97, 224n2

Uyghur language, scripts used for, 85–86, 215n1

verb tense, 23, 36, 104, 105*table*, 106, 137, 149, 217n9

vernacular writing, 7, 71–72, 171; Japanese poetry, 122; Lu Xun as advocate, 69n5

Vietnam: adoption of Chinese writing,